T for Texas

T for Texas
A State Full of Folklore

Edited by

Francis Edward Abernethy

Publications of The Texas Folklore Society Number XLIV

University of North Texas Press
Denton, Texas

Copyright © 1982 by The Texas Folklore Society
E-Heart Press, Dallas

Printed in the United States of America

Permissions:
University of North Texas Press
P. O. Box 311336
Denton, Texas 76203
(940) 565-2142 FAX (940) 565-4590

ISBN 1-57441-103-9

Contents

Preface   *by Francis Edward Abernethy*   vii

Goin' Home with the Dasypus Novemcinctus the Mystique of
    the Armadillo   *by Hermes Nye*   3

The Home Place   *by Sid Cox*   15

A Place Against the Sky   *by Martha Emmons*   23

My Favorite Texan and Folklore
    by Mrs. John Q. Anderson   31

Love Among the Elephant Ears & Other True Stories
    by Al Lowman   43

Bill Warren of the Big Thicket   *by Campbell &*
    Lynn Loughmiller   57

A Tale of Not So Long Ago   *by June R. Welch*   69

Night Horse Nightmare   *by Paul Patterson*   77

Texas Country Schoolteachers: Living Proof of a Legend
    by Lou Rodenberger   85

Legal Lore from the Courthouse
    by William N. Stokes, Jr.   95

Persimmon Beer   *by R. L. Cowser, Jr.*   105

A Letter from the Long Circle   *by Wayne Echols*   111

"The Glamor of the Gay Night Life" The Classic Honky Tonk
    by James Ward Lee   117

How to Have, to Hold, or Free Oneself of a Lover
    by Dolores L. Latorre   127

Pecos Bill: His Genesis and Creators   *by James M. Day*   135

The Vampire in an Age of Technology
    by Leslie M. Thompson   149

Pull Rings, Kidney Machines, and the Oral Tradition
    by Lawrence Clayton   161

Folklorish Remnants of Peyote Ceremonialism
    by Ernestine P. Sewell & Charles E. Linck   167

Animal Metaphors & Verbal Abuse Social Relations & Values
    Among German Speaking Farmers on Cypress Creek,
    Kerr County   *by Glen E. Lich*   177

Within the Walls Texas Prison Folklore
    by Martha Anne Turner   195

Oil Field Jokes from the Llano Estacado   *by Jim Harris*   211

Happy Jack and the Booger Man   *by Roy W. Lawson as told to
    his daughter Mrs. Patt Roach*   219

When You Call Me That, Smile! or Folklore, Ethology, &
    Communication   *by Francis Edward Abernethy*   225

Folk Stories from the Elmdale Community
    by Nancy Patrick/Student Contest Winner   233

Piecing Patches and Quilting Up a Storm
    by Gail Y. Litton/Student Contest Winner   241

Chronological & Bibliographical Listings of Texas Folklore
    Society Publications   *by Herbert C. Arbuckle, III*   251

Contributors   275

Preface/*Francis Edward Abernethy*

The editor and the Society's secretary,
Mrs. Martha Dickson

Preface   In which the editor celebrates his tenth anniversary

I've had this job ten years now and I'm still impressed with it. I've hunted some big bucks, caught some fine fish, and played some great gigs, but nothing in my professional life has been as important to me as the Texas Folklore Society and the welfare of its members. Of course, the main task of running the business has been done by the Society's secretary, Martha Dickson, who filed everything when we first set up shop in the summer of '71 and has been maintaining order ever since. This gives me time to lean back, prop my feet on the desk, and meditate—and look wise and philosophize. That's what this preface is: some meditation on the spirit and history of the Texas Folklore Society and its role in preserving folklore and presenting it for public consideration. It behooves us periodically to pause and look back down the road from whence we came and to venerate our elders, the old builders who laid the bed on which we now travel.

Core members of the Society are a motley group but they share a strong feeling of kinship. Probably sixty percent are school teachers, the rest a hodge-podge of professionals, radicals and conservatives, long hair and short. But they are bound together by an umbilicus that ties them all to the same mother soil, by a feeling for a specific piece of land, and for that land's primal culture, its folklore. Their roots run deep into this Texas earth, and they are folklorists by birth and their land's bond, rather than by academic credentials. They are also romantic and sentimental and they adjourn their annual meetings with parting's sorrow and sometimes tears.

The Texas Folklore Society has been preserving and presenting folklore in Texas for seventy-two years. In its time the Society has published forty-four annual hardback volumes, eleven special supplementary volumes, numerous monographs and newsletters, and has promoted the publication of sixteen more books on folklore. It has brought to Texas—and sent out from Texas—the finest scholars and lecturers in the field of folklore. It has sponsored programs displaying folk arts from Texas and the world. And it has had sixty-six annual meetings, most of them alone but some in concert with the Texas State Historical Society, the Texas Academy of Science, folklore societies from other states, and with the American Folklore Society.

Most Society regulars would not blink an eye if they were told that the Society was conceived of the Holy Spirit and born of the Virgin Mary. However, as a philosophical deist I see these matters figuratively rather than literally. On the other hand, the Society's conception was the result of a seed planted by that Holy Spirit of Harvard, George Lyman Kittredge—and I am *not* trying to make an analogy in which John Lomax becomes the Virgin Mary. Lomax took with him to Harvard in 1906 the cowboy songs that he had been learning and collecting since his boyhood days in Bosque County. Kittredge and others were delighted with them and sent him home to Texas with the great commission to establish a branch of the American Folklore Society for the further collecting of Texas folklore.

Lomax returned to Texas and began teaching at Texas A&M and began an association with another folklorist, the linguist Leonidas Warren Payne of The University of Texas. In 1909 Kittredge's suggestion became an accomplishment. Lomax and Payne met after the Thanksgiving Texas-A&M football game and resolved to found the Texas Folklore Society as a branch of the American Folklore Society. The Society was officially chartered at the Texas State Teachers Association meeting in Dallas on December 29, 1909. Charter Membership closed with ninety-two members, the initiation fee was fifty cents, and the annual dues were a dollar.

The founders were very significant because of the differences that existed between the personalities of the men and between their attitudes about the collection and presentation of Texas folklore, and because of the fact that they remained the closest of friends in spite of these differences. Payne was an academician, a linguist, and a comparative folklorist with an eye to the international. In his first 1910 circular to the members, Payne presented a philosophy and wrote a list of suggestions to workers that would satisfy the most scientific of modern folklorists.

Lomax was the other side of the coin. He loved the romance of the cowboy and the old west. And he loved the sound of the songs the cowboy sang. His collecting was invaluable. His promotion of the Texas western image and the circulation of the songs in *Cowboy Songs and Other Frontier Ballads* spread one brand of Texas folklore throughout the world. His work was popular. He meant it to be, and when a song needed alteration for art's sake, he borrowed lines from variants and straightened it out.

Payne and Lomax worked together, and the tolerant and liberal philosophy established by the founders of the Society made it a comfortable bed ground for all kinds and colors of Texas folklorists.

The activities of the Texas Folklore Society were pretty well established during its first decade, when members began their annual meetings where they read papers and discussed a wide variety of folklore and brought in national and international folklorists as guest lecturers. Texas folklorists who were to lay the philosophical groundwork as the officers and leaders were Walter Prescott Webb, Stith Thompson, Dorothy Scarborough, Herbert Bolton, Lomax, and Payne. And in 1916 the Society issued its first major publication, now called *Round the Levee,* which was edited by Stith Thompson.

The first phase of the Texas Folklore Society ended with the San Marcos meeting in 1917 and the problems of World War I and its aftermath.

The next chapter in the preservation and presentation of folklore in Texas began with J. Frank Dobie. After his discharge from the army Dobie returned to The University in 1919 as an English instructor. He lasted one year before he became disillusioned with the teaching profession. He resigned in 1920 and took a job managing his uncle Jim Dobie's ranch. If there is one point that can be counted as the exciting force in Dobie's life as the director of the Society and the state's leading folklorist, it is a night he sat around the campfire and listened to a vaquero tell tales of buried treasure in the Brasada. He later said of that time: "During the year I spent on Los Olmos Ranch while Santos talked, while Uncle Jim Dobie and other cowmen talked or stayed silent, while the coyotes sang their songs, and the sandhill cranes honked their lonely music, I seemed to be seeing a great painting of something I'd known all of my life. I seemed to be listening to a great epic of something that had been commonplace in my youth but now took on new meanings." Dobie discovered the depth of his roots through his discovery of Texas folklore.

Dobie returned to The University in 1921 and with Leonidas Payne awoke the Society from its four years' sleep. He was elected the Secretary-Treasurer and took upon himself the duties of editor of the second PTFS, which came out in 1923. Except for two years during World War II the Society has met annually and has not missed a year without at least one publication, either of its own editing or by sponsorship.

Dobie was inspired by Lomax's work and Lomax's approach to his subject, and his aim, like Lomax's, was to get the general public involved in folklore. Dobie didn't begin as a popularizer. His first instructions to collectors of folklore, published in *Coffee in the Gourd* in 1923, were in line with Payne: " . . . no legend should be adorned, 'doctored,' or changed from its usual form. It should be written as it is usually told." He had earlier sent out under his own name Payne's 1910 Pamphlet with its solidly academic instructions to collectors.

Dobie soon shed the academic approach and renounced utterly the Society's connection with the American Folklore Society. By 1930 he and the Texas Folklore Society had achieved statewide attention, and in *Man, Bird and Beast,* the Society's publication of that year, Dobie presented his philosophy of folklore as a balance to one of the articles written by Leonidas Payne. Payne, still the scholar, had written an article on research in folk music, and his central question—and it was a very responsible and logical question—was what to do with all the folklore the Society had collected. Dobie replied, "He seems to be saying that the collections should lead to monographic disquisitions on the historical and ethnographic evolution of each particular song with particular attention to its borrowing from other songs." After further attack on the academic methods, Dobie continued with his own criteria which he was to adhere to throughout his career; "I look for two things in folklore . . . flavor and vitality . . . and a revelation of the folk who nourished the lore. . . . Folklore that is interesting—whether it be accompanied by footnotes or not—is good to print and preserve."

There was plenty of room for academically oriented folklorists during Dobie's twenty-year tenure, and the Society and the state went through phases that included interests in Indians, archaeology, history, and natural science. The Society was affiliated for a while with the Texas Academy of Science. It led the successful fight to preserve the Texas Longhorn. And it flung itself wholeheartedly into the chauvinism of the Texas Centennial years. The Society's emphasis throughout Dobie's editorship remained on field collecting and popular presentation, and he recruited many collectors, especially among Mexicans and Blacks, who didn't even know what folklore was until he told them. Books, magazines, and newspapers throughout the United States carried his folklore articles. Dobie defined folklore for a lot of us, and his influence is still a strong force inside the Texas folklore scene.

Forty years of the Society's life was under the guidance of two men, Frank Dobie from 1923 to 1943 and Mody C. Boatright from 1943 to 1963. There was no immediate change when Mody officially took over, but the center of Texas folklore soon became an institution rather than an individual. It was to become the Texas Folklore Society at The University of Texas, and those of us who came into the Society during the Boatright and later the Wilson Hudson years were to view the association as immutable.

Under Mody's leadership the Society became more academically centered than it had been, and he re-established its association with the American Folklore Society. The national society since then has met twice on the University campus and once in conjunction with the TFS annual meeting. Under Mody the papers read at meetings and published in annuals remained about the same in content, probably with a movement toward more analytical papers. Like Dobie, Mody kept no hard and fast boundaries and definitions of folklore. He was a social historian and his own studies of the cowboy, the oil fields, and the American frontier were soundly grounded in an understanding of society and history. The leadership he gave to the studies of folklore in the English department was the beginning of the strong folklore center which is now a permanent part of the University. Mody promoted the collection and study of oral history and of folklore in a modern industrial society. One of his main contributions to the study of folklore in Texas was through the Society's annual student paper contests, which involved students from colleges and universities throughout the state in preserving and presenting folklore. Mody's time as Secretary-Editor was also coincident with the increase of a national academic interest in folklore and the institution of folklore courses throughout the state. Because most of the state's teachers of folklore were trained as English teachers, much of their guidance and inspiration came from the Society and the folklorists at The University of Texas.

Mody was a beautiful, gentle, and wise man. His leadership was not as flamboyant as Dobie's, but in some ways it was more productive. His encouragement of the academic investigation of collected folklore and his own social analyses of folklore were conclusive steps in the study of field materials, necessary for a full understanding of the subject. His encouragement of scholars and scholarship spread his and the Society's work far beyond his own time.

Wilson Hudson, the Society's editor from 1963 to 1971, became associated with the Society when he began teaching at The University of Texas in 1946. His continuing and growing interest in work in folklore soon made him an integral part of the Society, and when Mody left the campus for a year in 1950 Wilson was put in charge of the next Society publication, which was to be *The Healer of Los Olmos* (PTFS XXV, 1951). In *The Healer* Wilson made a significant addition. For the first time, tale-types and motif numbers were included, a practice which Wilson was to continue after 1951, during his time as Associate Editor and after 1963 as Editor. Wilson's finest contribution to the Society and to folklore generally was his inspiration and direction of James Bratcher's *Analytical Index to Publications of the Texas Folklore Society,* which the Society brought out in 1973. Mr. Bratcher indexed thirty-six volumes of the Society's publications according to tale type, motif number, ballad number, tale synopsis, and finally alphabetically. In balance to his academic bent, Wilson published five books of popular field folklore in his Paisano Series of the Society's supplementary books.

Folklore as a popular phenomenon was on the rise in Texas during the 'sixties. This was the time of the beginning of a lot of area and ethnic folk festivals, of such restoration projects as those at Winedale and Nacogdoches, and later at Lubbock, of Stan Alexander's folk music club at North Texas State University which spawned such moderns as Steve Fromholz and Michael Murphy, of John Lomax, Jr. and Mack McCormack's Houston Folk Music Club, and to move up into another league, of the Institute of Texan Cultures. One of the most popular and enduring of the folk studies associations was the annual Folklore Symposium founded by Jim Byrd of the English Department of East Texas State University in 1962 and still going strong.

I became the Secretary-Editor of the Society in 1971, and the

Headquarters were moved to Stephen F. Austin State University. It was a sad day in August when we loaded all those Austin years into a station wagon and rolled them 250 miles east. But even though a geographical tradition was broken, the business and the purpose were to remain the same. If I have made any identifiable differences in the Society it has probably been because of my interest in East Texas folklore, in ethnic studies, and in editing the Society's annuals around one theme.

Which brings me to conclusions reached after viewing seventy-two years of Texas folkloring as a Texan, a folklorist, and a Society member.

The major work of preserving and presenting folklore in Texas has from its beginning centered in the Texas Folklore Society. The development of departments, divisions, and centers in universities has not significantly changed this because the academic approach, even though it has preserved, has not been successful in its presenting. As I look back over the Society's history I find that the period of time when folklore received its greatest attention and had the greatest effect in making people conscious of the infinite variety and richness of their culture was the time when it was least associated with academicians, during the 'twenties and 'thirties of J. Frank Dobie. Academicians, of which I consider myself one, are the brightest lights which a civilization shines, but they are prone to dabble in esoterica and pedantry, and to dwell in a rarified atmosphere that relates but poorly to the general public. So, professional folklorists may cuss the Dobies and Botkins and *Foxfires* and picture books by *Life* and *National Geographic* for their sometimes creative approach to their subject, but these are the forces that have focused the public eye on folklore, and these are the forces that have made the public conscious through folklore of the beauty and richness of their culture.

I conclude with an examination, or more accurately, a statement of the Texas Folklore Society's direction as I see it.

I believe that the Society's main purpose is to search for ways to preserve folklore without embalming it and to present a fairly well-educated public with the treasures of their culture's folk life. I do *not* believe that our purpose is to proliferate esoterica and pedantry among a small, specially educated clique. I further believe that the Texas Folklore Society's purpose is to preserve and present the folklore of Texas. This does *not* mean that our purpose is to be chauvinistic or provincial, both of which are brought about by states of mind rather than geographical locations. It means, as Kittredge said so many years ago, that Texas really is the folklorist's happy hunting ground, that we have all the fields we can ever plow, and that the work and the room to work is as wide as its borders and as inexhaustible as the winds that blow across the Staked Plains. And this work should be done by those who know the land and love it and understand it. And finally, I believe that the purpose of the Texas

Folklore Society is *not* to hide the light of the lore under a bushel of academic guidelines and definitions and scholarly verbiage but to let that light so shine among men that all the world—but, Lord, most especially Texans—may see the richness of the land and its people and its history and its continuity. In this land and its people and its history Texans must realize the place of their belonging, a mother land to moisten with their sweat, and finally to nourish with their bones.

I shall now get my feet off the desk and address myself to the matters at hand.

This miscellany, *T For Texas*, is a pretty good representative of the people in the Society and the kinds of folklore they are presently interested in. I was especially pleased to get papers on family reminiscences. Mody Boatright's study of the family anecdote as folklore made us realize what a wealth of material most of us have at hand. And these recollections of family tales and traditions are just as much folklore as records of the Trobriand Islanders.

The Texas Folklore Society thanks the family anecdotalists, Herb Arbuckle for the TFS bibliography, and this book's writers for their generous contributions. The Society could not operate without the moral and material support of William R. Johnson, president of Stephen F. Austin State University, and Roy E. Cain, head of the Department of English, and we thank them sincerely.

And since this is my anniversary edition I want to mention my family, all of whom have been supportive and involved in the Folklore Society since my beginnings in 1959. Hazel has done a lot of proofreading over these past ten years, and I thank her for that and for being the rock on which my life is built. And I thank my children, who grew up acting silly but who now pay their dues regularly: Luanna Cherry (Cole), Robert Morris, Sarah Elizabeth (Whitbeck), Margaret Leslie (Duffin), and Benjamin Talbot.

Most of all, I wish to thank the members of the Texas Folklore Society for many years of treasured friendship. You are dear and generous hearts and I hold you warmly.

And as he rides off into the sunset, you can hear him singing, guitar strumming . . .

T for Texas, T for Tennessee,
T for Texas, T for Tennessee,
T for Thelma, the gal that made a wreck out of me.

Francis Edward Abernethy
Stephen F. Austin State University
Nacogdoches, Texas

T for Texas

Goin' Home with the Dasypus Novemcinctus/the Mystique of the Armadillo/*Hermes Nye*

Hermes Nye (1908–1980)

Goin' Home
with the Dasypus
Novemcinctus
the Mystique
of the Armadillo

Hermes Nye   1908-1981

The Texas Folklore Society thanks Hermes for the thirty years of pleasure he gave us as he enlightened us with the lore of hippies and hot rods and hanging ten—for "Lasca" impassioned and interminable and the pecadillos of Aimee Semple MacPherson—for his sound advice and legal services, no charge—for his stentorian tones and the thespian flourish of his hand as he read the meetings' resolutions, written Victorianly and elaborately hung with purple ornaments—and for the ceremonial mastering of many a sweet night's hoot. We thank you, Hermes. The Texas Folklore Society is a close and loving group, bound together by long affections, and we adjourn our meetings with the tears of sadness, parting. We are diminished by your going, but we thank you for the love and time you gave us.

One of the last things he did was for the Society. I called him on his last Thursday to jack him up about his armadillo paper that I was trying to get ready for this publication. He swore a great oath that he would have it in on time, in good form, and properly documented. He finished it Friday night, mailed it Saturday, and I got it the next week after I had heard that he had died. With it was an explanatory note, with numbered items for attention, signed, "Peace and love, little brother."

So Hermes, dear boy, you blithest of spirits, I thank you for twenty years of friendship. You were a hearth by which we warmed our souls.

Editor

We have all seen him, perhaps in what has been callously referred to as his natural habitat, that is, "dead by the side of the road"; or perhaps, in a happier hour, as he scurries about in the brush, searching for grubs on a sunny winter afternoon. Yes, it is the little armored one, the armadillo, so named by the early Spanish explorers.

He is about the size of a large tom-cat, but hump-backed and heavier, with a ridiculous bottle-shaped head which terminates in a long snout, and with a wide mouth from which flicks an eight-inch sticky tongue. His rigid, tapering tail, about as long as his body, is covered with bony rings, and all four feet are armed with powerful yellow claws. His pointed mule-ears are of thick pebbled leather, and like a knight of old, he is armored from arse to appetite—and beyond —his head, shoulders and rump protected by scutes, or bony shields of ossified skin, and his middle by nine moveable belts of the same. His coloring is a sporty, mottled yellowish white and brown; he grunts softly to himself as he pokes nervously about; and if you disturb him, he will loosen up his anal scent glands and remind you of a burning garbage dump in August.

He was classified more than two centuries ago by the great Linnaeus, who dubbed him *Dasypus novemcinctus,* the rough-shod nine-banded one, and also classified by the folk of various New World countries as *peba,* pig tank, *tatus de folha,* gravedigger, 'dillo, poverty pig, Hoover hog, and hard-shelled 'possum.

He is a mammal, and although he has teeth, his zoological order is Edentata, or toothless. His sub-order is Xenarthra, which we are not surprised to learn, means "strangely formed." Two infra-orders branch out from Xenarthra, each one of them, you might say, more bizarre-looking than the other—the pilosa, or hairy edentates, where we find the sloths and the true anteaters; and the cingulata, or armored edentates, where we find all the armadillos.

We should speak softly of the armadillos, since they pre-date us mere hominids by about twenty million years. True, the big boys indeed are gone with all their roses—the glyptodont, or turtle armadillo, with his huge club-shaped tail studded with bony knobs, and about the size of a rhinoceros, and with him *Dasypus bellus,* resembling but three times the size of, our Texas armadillo, who roamed these parts more than ten thousand years ago.

There are less than twenty species of modern armadillos, ranging in size and heft from *Priodontes giganteus,* or giant armadillo, which is five feet long and weighs in at about one hundred pounds, to the pink fairy armadillo of Western Argentina, which is heavily furred and only about six inches in length.

Well, "Once you've seen an armadillo, you're ready to believe anything," so runs the saying; and we are not surprised to find folklore clustering about our subject like flies around a boarding-house syrup pitcher. Burmeister's armadillo, for instance, is said to utter a cry like that of a human baby. Another species, the *pichis* of Patagonia, in spite of his lack of body fat, is alleged to be able to hibernate. When he gets meat-hungry, *Chaetophractus villosus,* the eighteen-banded one, is said to kill small snakes by throwing itself upon its victims and cutting them with the sharp edges of its shell. As an encore, this species is reputed to form a hole in the ground by putting its snout into the soil and then turning its body, after the fashion of the three Aggies with the step-ladder installing the light globe, "so that a conical hole is formed without any digging."[1] Then, too, folklore to the contrary, the only armadillo which can roll up into a complete ball is *Tolypeutes tricinctus,* the three-banded 'dillo of Brazil, which resembles in this position, nothing so much as a large ripe cantaloupe.

Our own *Dasypus novemcinctus,* whom we shall call *the* armadillo from now on, seems to have sprung up first in South America, but like any striving wetback, to have gradually worked his way northward.[2] He had reached the vincinity of modern Vera Cruz about two thousand years ago, and by the sixteenth century found himself fitting easily into the Howling Wilderness concept of post-Columbian explorers. Soon after the year 1500, Europe was being edified by engravings and woodcuts which depicted the armadillo, variously, as being possessed of wings, as capable of being ridden like a horse, as sitting on a nest of eggs, as having vicious teeth and a kinky tail that was armed with a deadly sting.

His debut into polite scientific society in Texas came when he was sighted by Audubon in the Rio Grande Valley in the 1850s. In the past century or so, as man advanced, killing off our little beast's predators, so he came along also, swarming up into Texas, Oklahoma, and Louisiana, and being, as one account insists upon phrasing it, *successfully* introduced into Florida.

Warming now to our subject, we come with feigned reluctance to the matter of the armadillo's sex life. Jim Franklin of Austin, the Michelangelo of armadillo art, has depicted the male as mounting the female from the rear. E. P. Walker's *Mammals of the World,* however, states flatly that "Breeding takes place in July and August, the female then lying on her back."[3] Whether this missionary position is due to the anatomy of the animal or whether it is merely behavioral mimicry picked up by the 'dillo while looking for insects at X-rated drive-in movies, is matter that merits further study.

Susan Block, Dallas antique dealer and a dedicated field observer of the creature, writes as follows:

It has unmentionable breeding (never 'mating' as that is considered obscene), habits. All 'eye witnesses' flatly declare (1) that the pair stands on its hind legs with the tail for stability and faces each other while breeding; (2) that the pair performs the amazing feat of rolling into a double ball (this version is usually followed with the explanation that armadillos are endowed with the human virtue of discretion in their most intimate moments); (3) that they breed mouth-to-mouth, only in the confines of their deep in the ground and of course out of sight.[4]

We may note here, the folk believe that 'possums breed mouth-to-mouth, that porcupines lie side by side, and that elephants, out of modesty, take up a back-to-back position.

We come now to the more prosaic matter of the armadillo's

method of crossing bodies of water.[5] *Dallas Morning News* columnist Frank Tolbert reported in his article for August 22nd, 1974, as follows:

. . . I saw a pair of armadillos crossing a narrow creek about two feet deep, in Somervell County. One armadillo apparently 'inflated' his body by taking a very long gulp of air while floating across the creek. The other one exhaled or 'deflated' and then calmly walked under water to the other shore.

Ms. Block confirms this quasi-messianic feat of walking if not *on* the water, then at least *underneath* it, and a current Disney documentary exhibits an armadillo eluding a panther by taking to the water.

In addition to its amazing aquatic skills, the armadillo's home-making, dietary, and foraging habits have been the object of intense concern.

Few other creatures seem to require as many homes, or burrows. Some of these shelters are for sleeping, others, more commodious, for the aforementioned breeding; still others are used as shallow food traps for insects. These burrows, sometimes four feet deep and three times as long, make our creature both hated and feared by the farmer and the stockman.[6]

In his omnivorous quest for food, the 'dillo diggeth where he listeth, and is even said to gnaw away at buried corpses and at the roots of pecan trees. Once he has brought the tree down, our little horn-plated Paul Bunyan proceeds to crack and feed upon the nuts, just with what is not specified, but certainly not with those rudimentary peg-like molars which serve him as a sorry excuse for teeth.

Methods of extermination are as few as they are ineffective. The ranch owner mounts a .22 in the rear window of his pickup, but the 'dillo is a tricky target, jerky in his movements and like a second-story man, at his best after dark.

Joyce Roach of Keller, Texas, reports an incident in September, 1974:

I happened to be visiting my nearest neighbor, and noticed a bunch of holes in her yard. "Mrs. Medlin," says I, "what are all those holes from?" She says, "It's them ole armadillers again," and with that, she drew up her blunderbuss and fired away. When the smoke cleared, there was another big hole in the yard. I asked her how she could tell the armadiller holes from the ones she made with her gun. "Well," she says, "I never thought about that. I reckon me or them armadillers one is sure making a mess out of my yard."

Some folks just try to run the rascals down, but this, like high-diving, is easy until you try it. For one thing, the creature is said to have a poisonous bite. For another, he is alleged to be likely to rise up on his hind legs and attack you. And for still another, he is a superb broken-field runner, and his armor allows him to scamper through the tightest of the tight-eye thickets.

If there is any soft terrain near him, and there usually is, he can dig in within a matter of minutes, and once he gets those novemcincti covered, you have had it. No use to grab his tail. Some folks say that it will merely come off in your hand, and most certainly he will hunch his back and expand those moveable belts, to produce an effect like that of a Chinese finger-ring, so that the harder you pull, the harder he sticks.

There is lore to the effect that armadillo hounds can be trained to roll the animal over and attack his softer underparts. Mrs. Leila La Grone of Carthage, Texas, suggests the use of moth-balls. "For generations," she writes, "East Texas country folks have been using moth balls to keep armadillos from destroying flower beds." In the far-away Matto Grosso of Brazil, Indians trap the armadillo by setting barrels into the ground, covering the tops with grass, and then sprinkling corn over the grass, a method which would seem equally hazardous to both man and beast.

In spite of all these deterrents, and in part because of his virtual immunity to parasites, the armadillo continues to enjoy his own private population explosion. He does have a quirky and oftentimes fatal habit of jumping straight up when frightened,[7] and this makes him an easy prey to *Homo sapiens automobilis,* just as his inflexible bodily make-up sentences him to death from floods, drought, and cold weather.[8]

As to his diet, it has long been thought that high on the list of 'dillo *hors d'ouevres* are chicken and bird eggs, and especially those of the bob white, or quail. Back in the thirties, one researcher over a period of seven odiferous and exhausting years analyzed the contents of dozens of armadillo stomachs. When the tallies were in, most contents were shown to be 95% the remains of insects, beetles, termites, flies and spiders and the like. Miscellaneous vertebrates, amphibians, and reptiles made up most of the rest.[9] No egg shells.

Well, then, is the armadillo villain or hero? E. R. Kalmbach of the U. S. Fish and Wildlife Service reviewed the available evidence in a lengthy article some years ago, and summed up for the defense as follows:

Excessive use of range and cover by livestock has resulted in a decrease of upland grass, and when this occurs in the presence of an abundant armadillo population, the latter often is held responsible. . . . it may be stated that the armadillo, through the character and volume of its insect food, has an influence for good. Its misdeeds, including attacks on ground nesting birds, and on certain crops . . . detract somewhat from its generally commendable habits.[10]

Had he been writing in the seventies, Kalmbach might have added that, due in part to the armadillo's low 90-degree body temperature, it is the only animal known to science which can be inoculated with, and thus used in the prognosis and treatment of, leprosy.

Well, the debate will probably rage on and on, and raging right along with it, will always be choice tidbits of armadillo folklore. For centuries now, the belief persists that the beast is really a reptile, that, since he sometimes shares his burrow with rattlesnakes, no such reptile, out of pure crotalian *noblesse oblige,* will ever bite him, that he has no hair, and that, once rolled up into a ball, only placing him near a fire will ever straighten him out. This lastmentioned trait is true or nearly so, of the creature's second cousin once removed, the pangolin, or scaly anteater.

It is true enough, that the female always bears a litter of four, and that they are always of the same sex,[11] a fact which embryologists, DNA people and the like seem to find fascinating, not to say alarming. As to our subject's senses of hearing, sight, and smell, they are thought to be only fair,[12] but there is a general suspicion that, with all that armor going for him, he, like the farmer's old mule, just don't give a damn.

It is alleged that the 'dillo makes an excellent pet. The glittering, fabulous Neiman Marcus *Christmas Catalogue* for the year 1968 advertised a real, be-ribboned armadillo for sale, with the very chi-chi caption:

Armadillo, anyone? Imagine him burrowing quietly under the Christmas tree or at your side for afternoon walks. Shipped live with United States Armadillo Breeders Association registration papers, membership card and bumper sticker.

The breeders' association referred to was a put-on which was dreamed up by some unsung Dallas wag several years ago, and Neiman's is silent as to whether any sales were rung up during the yuletide of '68.

Fred Armstrong, armadillo race promoter of Victoria, Texas, claims that the beast makes an ideal home companion, and in 1974, *Texas Monthly* magazine listed the animal as being the favorite pet of what is dubbed the pseudo-rednecks. All of this calls to mind Hilaire Belloc's observations on the frog:

No animal will more repay
   A treatment kind and fair;
At least so lonely people say
Who keep a frog (and, by the way,
   They are extremely rare).

One predicts that the armadillo as pet has a dim future, and the same can be said for his prospects as a staple item on our menus. His meat is gamey and greasy,[13] on the order of 'possum, but certain folk, most of them just real hungry, find him palatable, and there are many recipes, ranging from the burlesque to the dead-pan serious.

The late Hondo Crouch, court jester and quondam part owner of Luckenbach, Texas, once favored Frank Tolbert with a recipe to be used at Frank's annual Chili Cook-Off at Terlingua: "Armadillo chili: One medium armadillo. Other stuff. Save the shell. Serves four."

In 1974, J. R. Compton of Dallas brought out a single-issue pulp magazine, *Armadilla,* which contained half a dozen 'dillo recipes. Italian Barbecued Armadillo—which requisitions such items as garlic, parsley, tomatoes, bay leaf, and oregano, not to mention four young armadillos halved—sounds like a real winner.

Well, so much for some of the factual and the legendary aspects of the armadillo. In conclusion, we might dwell for a moment upon the armadillo as a fetish, totem or cult-symbol of the counter-culture. One feels that this could have happened only in the permissive, happy-hippie, Scholz-Beergarten, *Texas-Observer* ambience of Austin, Texas. It was there, in the Legislature, that the late "Jumbo" Atwell, representative from Dallas, strove mightily but in vain to replace the Texas steer with the armadillo as the official state animal, his efforts meeting with no more success than those devoted to replacing the mockingbird with the road runner as the official state bird.

It was in Austin also, at the University in 1961, that one David Dean, without saying poodle-dee-do to anyone, just flat declared that a certain seven-day period was National Armadillo Week. Four years and several hundred gallons of Shiner later, in 1965, the campus humor magazine *Ranger* carried armadillos on its masthead, and continued to feature line drawings of the creature either as fillers or as full-page spreads, such as Gilbert Whitehead's famous Dance of the Armadillos. Jim Franklin, whom we have met before in this article, caught the spirit of the thing, and in 1968, to promote a local love-in, produced a smashing realistic portrait of a 'dillo smoking a joint. Next year, Franklin's 36-page *Armadillo Cartoons* was being hawked up and down the Drag. This magazine contained, among other raunchy items, 'dillos being squeezed out of paint tubes, being eaten in slices like watermelon, being used as a landing pad for spacecraft, and in a final burst of artistic fervor, as having intercourse with the State Capitol Building.

A couple of years later, Eddie Wilson strode onto the scene. Burly, black-bearded Eddie, former P. R. man for Lone Star beer, found a for-rent-cheap armory at 6th and Guadalupe. Here he soon established the Armadillo World Headquarters, a sanctuary for the progressive country music which is now known as The Austin Sound. Here, too, Franklin soon had a studio and began working on armadillo murals for his landlord. The lofty walls of the AWH now constitute a Sistine Chapel of armadillo art. Here one may view heroic-sized 'dillos, one of them fantasied as a projectile being shot through the heart of a steel-guitar player, and another, as an underground listening post. Sometimes Franklin, during those years, would appear on stage in what he dubbed his God suit, flaunting an armadillo-shell helmet, black cape and dark glasses, and mumbling out a stream-of-consciousness intro to some famous band.

During this period, prior to the demise of AWH in the early eighties, Eddie booked high on the hog, and such stars of the firmament as B. W. Stevenson, Willie Nelson, Jerry Jeff Walker, and the East Texas String Ensemble were frequently seen and heard. Here, at the AWH, the redneck lion could lie down with the hippie lamb, as both sides swigged Lone Star longnecks and bawled out the refrain to Gary Nunn's *London Homesick Blues:*

Going' home with the armadillo,
To country music from Amarillo
An' Abi-leen.

Franklin's album cover for another frequent and robustious visitor, Commander Cody with his Lost Planet Airmen, depicts armadillos swarming over an outdoor sound stage, clambering over each other and even taking off into space. More recently, Franklin began a series of posters for Lone Star beer, in which the beast is portrayed as of gigantic size and as browsing amidst towering, brown, long neck bottles. Then, too, Franklin's cover for the 20th Anniversary Issue of *The Texas Observer* showed a cautious armadillo emerging from a cactus thicket to view a Dali-esque scene of twenty tall white candles set in a fairy-ring around a wide, blue, open human eye.

For our final point, we may refer briefly to the bestiaries of another day. In these moralistic tales of the Middle Ages, one learned noble self-sacrifice from the pelican, which pierced its breast so that its starving young might feed upon its blood, and spiritual renaissance from the phoenix, which burned itself only to be born again.

By the same token, we of a later century may perhaps read a lesson from this little essay on our *Dasypus novemcinctus.* Said Jim Franklin, in an interview for *Sports Illustrated* magazine:

Armadillos are paranoid little beasts who prefer to mind their own business. They love to sleep all day, then roam and eat all night. They are gentle, keep their noses in the grass and share their homes with others. Perhaps most significant, they are weird-looking, unfairly maligned and often picked upon, and have developed a hard shell and a distinctive aroma. They do far more good than harm, and yet the usual social reaction toward an armadillo is to attempt to destroy it.

"And," adds Eddie Wilson in another context, "they survive like a sonuvabitch."[14]

Notes

1. Ernest P. Walker, *Mammals of the World.* 2nd Ed., Vol. 1 (Baltimore: The Johns Hopkins Press, 1968), pp. 492-503.

2. William B. Davis, *Mammals of Texas* (Austin, Texas: Texas Parks and Wildlife Dept., 1960, Rev. 1974), pp. 267-270.

3. Davis, *op. cit.* Tom Sands, attorney and rancher of Dallas County, Texas, in conversation, *circ.* 1973, Dallas, Texas: "I've seen 'em at it time and again, dog-fashion every time, believe me."

4. In conversation, *circ.* 1970, Dallas, Texas.

5. Davis, *op. cit.*, p. 237. Maurice Burton, *Systematic Dictionary of Mammals of the World* (New York: Thos. Y. Crowell Co., 1962), pp. 86-87. George W. Lowery, Jr., *The Mammals of Louisiana and Its Adjacent Waters* (Baton Rouge, Louisiana: Louisiana Wild Life and Fisheries Commission, Louisiana State University Press, 1974), pp. 148-154.

6. Walker, *op. cit.*, p. 497; Davis, *op. cit.*, p. 238; Burton, *op. cit.*, p. 87. (P. 5, article; quotation from Joyce is NOT in a published article).

7. Lowery, *op. cit.*, p. 152.

8. Davis, *op. cit.*, p. 497; Lowery, *op. cit.*, p. 150. Desmond Morris, *The Mammals, A Guide to the Living Species* (New York: Harper and Row, 1965), pp. 171-173.

9. Davis, *op. cit.*, p. 269.

10. Quoted by Davis, *op. cit.*, p. 270.

11. Davis, *op. cit.*, p. 269; Walker, *op. cit.*, p. 492. Robert K. Orr, *Mammals of North America* (New York: Doubleday and Co., Inc., 1974), pp. 41-42.

12. Walker, *supra,* states that the sight is "relatively good," and that the sense of hearing and smell are excellent; generally, the edentata are credited with the ability to hear insects moving about just below the surface of the ground and thus to zero in upon its prey.

13. Davis, *op. cit.*, p. 268; Walker, *op. cit.*, p. 495.

14. Hermes presented this armadillo paper at the Houston meeting in 1975. It also appeared in *Texas Parade* in August, 1975.

The Home Place/*Sid Cox*

Sid Cox (1910–1980)
credit Ouida Dean

The Home Place

Sid Cox   *1910-1980*

We buried our friend Sid Cox beneath a great oak tree on his Home Place near Blanco Monday afternoon, October 13.

Sid died instantly while shopping in College Station on Saturday, October 11, 1980. Only the day before he had been working with his sons Jim and Dow at building the new stone house near the old homestead, which he, Dawn, and their family had looked forward to occupying.

Following Sid's earlier expressed wishes, Jim and Dow turned to and constructed a casket from beautiful old planks which had been on the Cox family farm for more than a century. Monday afternoon, following brief services in Blanco, led by Baptist preacher David Murrah, a crowd of relatives and friends followed the hearse out to the Cox ranch and gathered around the grave beneath that oak tree within sight of the house. On every hand were the rock fences built by Sid's ancestors.

At Dawn's request, I had the great privilege of reading, beside that simple casket, the splendid essay, "The Home Place," into which Sid Cox had poured so much of himself.

You folk in the Folklore Society can witness to Sid's contributions to Texas lore. Friends and associates in Chimney Valley, Driscoll, Sabinal, Robstown, at U.T. and at A&M can testify to his unique brand of teaching, his impact upon the lives of thousands of young people.

I claim an earlier association. Sid came down from Blanco High School to the Teachers College at San Marcos in 1928 and became an instant personality. We studied English together under Gates Thomas, Deacon Wright, and Sue Taylor. Sid was editor of the *College Star* in 1931-32; I followed him.

I first got acquainted with the Cox farm and Sid's family about 1931, when he led a handful of aspiring scientists into nearby limestone caves, where we found the elusive blind salamander, *typhlo-*

molgi rathbuni. In 1932 I hiked with him for three days up the Blanco River to its headwaters. About 1935-36 he spent many a night writing copy for me when I was going flat broke trying to publish the *Blanco County News* in the old courthouse building on the square. He would have scorned any idea of pay, and I couldn't have paid him anyhow, but after Anna Jane's breakfast, I'd drive him back down to Chimney Valley so he could teach his school on time.

Sid lived in our home when he taught at Robstown; over the years my wife and I have spent many of our happiest days on The Home Place. Sid and I have mercilessly criticized each other's writings, but he had a great deal more reason to criticize than I did.

Sid was the best woodsman I ever followed down a trail. He not only believed in but practiced preservation of the land in its natural state.

No man ever had a better friend.
Roy L. Swift   Floresville

Being at the Home Place sensitizes me physically and mentally. My senses become more alert; memories come out of hiding; emotions stand at attention; imagination goes on a binge. So I spent last night at the Home Place, partly because I like to be there, but mainly because I wanted the feel of it just before I read this paper. It's not far from here [Wimberley, Texas]—just over the horizon to the west, barely out of sight. When you go out of this building, look, if you will, just a little to the south of west. Then in your imagination strip away all the sights and sounds about you, lift off all but the largest vegetation, and lay upon the land a sea of waist-high grass rolling steadily westward wave upon wave. If your imagination is in good condition—and I hope it is, you will see what Great-grandfather Cox and his family saw as they bumped along the vertebrae of the Devil's backbone nearly a century and a quarter ago heading west.

Great-grandfather—his name was Josiah—had come from Crawford County, Arkansas, one of my family's stops on its way from God-knows-where to the place I left this morning to come here. Nobody ever told me why he stopped where he did, but his strong strain of Indian blood may have guided him, for the spot he chose was near a spring that had watered a series of Indian civilizations for thousands of years before he arrived.

When Great-grandfather got there, it had not been long since the last Indian of the last Indian civilization had left—packed up, vamoosed, bow, string and arrow. For thousands of years he and his ancestors had fitted so snugly into their ecological niche that when they left, the only signs above the turf were some old lodge poles scattered around fire rings not yet grown over by grass. And when he left, those were all he left to show his millennia of residence. With him went the name of the pleasant little creek beside which he camped; with him went the name of the round-topped hill at whose base the creek arose; with him went the name of the shallow canyon into which it poured its waters. For the first time in ten thousand years the tall bluffs that stand up between the river and the plateau to the east were without a name.

When the Indian camped beside the creek, the place from which I came this morning was *his* home place. The creek had a name; the hill had a name; the canyon had a name. Everything within his sight was identifiable by name, by memories attached to it, by legend about it and history of it. As I feel this morning, he felt; as I remember this morning, he remembered; as I speak this morning, he spoke, for the natural repository of the history of a land is the people who live on it, and the natural preservative of that history is oral tradition. As the Indian was the last repository of the oral tradition of his old home place, I am the last repository of the oral tradition of mine.

An oral tradition grows best in the generations that are too busy to waste time on writing. It grows fastest when man is most actively in conflict with his environment. And it is preserved best when the family produces in its middle generations a story teller such as my father to bring together the history of the land and the stories of the people who have lived on it.

By the time Papa was born in 1872, Great-grandfather was dead and the land on which he had built his cabin and planted his first crop was called The Old Place. Today the distinguishing feature of The Old Place is the Cox Graveyard, an institution dedicated by the interment of Great-grandfather's body two years after his arrival. Other than the graveyard, Great-grandfather's legacy to family oral tradition was that which he had received from his parents—the vocabulary and speech patterns accumulated in the Middle South. As I stood this morning on the gallery at the Home Place and looked across at the graveyard waiting on me, I was reminded of some of the hand-me-downs from that legacy. The little creek had become The Branch. It arose at the foot of Round Mountain, swept down between the Old Place and the Home Place, and poured into the Cove.

These place names and others like them were left to a widow, three daughters, and two sons who tutored the next generation in the family idiom; and I, in turn got my basic vocabulary from that generation—got it so well that the language I am using this morning is sprinkled with words passed down through old Josiah. Nor would my sons head for E. Bagby Atwood's *Regional Vocabulary of Texas* to find out what was wrong if I told them the backstick was on antigodlin. Even though they were born in the flowback from the frontier, they know that milk that is blinkey one day may be clabbered the next. They know that the cow that gave the milk will stand still if I say "Saw" in a commanding tone, that she may bawl or low from where she grazes in draw, swag, or flat, and that she may bed down in a mott to chew her cud. And they know that if a woods colt were to come through the mott while she was there, it would have two legs, not four.

The heart of the Home Place is the house. Grandpa built it

ninety-five years ago on the exact spot where the old house had been
burned to the ground by an unidentified but well-suspected arsonist
during the troubles that followed the Civil War. It is a two-storey
frame house of virgin pine and cypress held together by square nails
and wooden pegs and braced east and west by finely cut stone chim-
neys. A long gallery, once bannistered, faces south into a mott of
liveoaks that go back to Indian times, and a dog run divides the
ground floor into two rooms warmed by fireplaces in the winter and
cooled in summer by the prevailing south wind.

The site of the house is a lesson in topographical discrimination.
Laid out by sighting the North Star on a clear night and squared with
a hair rope, the house sits so exactly on the divide of a seemingly
level glade that the rain which falls on the north side of the house
drains toward the Blanco and that which falls on the south side drains
toward The Branch. The grove of oak trees catches the south wind in
its leaves and turns it downward toward the perpetual shade beneath,
cooling the air before it is sucked across the porch and into the
house by the dog run.

To the east of the house were corn cribs, and to the north of
them were the hog pens, the cow pen and horse lot. These normal
adjuncts to the frontier farming and ranching enterprise were built to
the north of the natural divide so that drainage from them would be
toward the Blanco half a mile away rather than toward The Branch,
the source of the domestic water supply.

The Home Place has legal metes and bounds described by words
that strike the ear pleasantly, words such as, for instance, *varas* and
meanders. Its history can be read in the deed records at the courthouse at Johnson City. The federal government has made an aerial
map of it to show its boundaries and subdivisions, a cold topographical map which reduces the Home Place to outlines and robs the land
of its personality. Lines represent the miles of rock fences, mute
stone autobiographies, laid so well by Grandpa and his sons that they
have clung together in mutual support, waiting on the generations to
come. Quarried from exposed limestone ledges or torn from the earth
by crowbar, these rocks, once white, have turned lichen gray.

But the Home Place is more than a house, more than a piece of
ground on which cattle graze and taxes are paid. It is the place where
the oral tradition of my family developed, where it was brought
together by my father, where it was passed on to me. From this place
Grandpa and his brother, Judge, anti-slavery Southerns but admirers
of Lincoln, went off to the Civil War, were shot honorably, and returned with stories for generations to come. From this place, Buck
and Bax Taylor, nephews to my grandmother, went off to join Buffalo
Bill Cody's Wild West Show and earn a share of fame and fortune. To
this place at the age of sixteen came Jess Kennedy, my mother's
cousin, a neighbor boy who had killed Ben Cage in self-defense; and
here he stayed until the dark of the moon when Uncle Sam slipped
him through the fingers of the law, carried him to Bastrop horseback,

and put him on a train to California. To this place came an old and wrinkled Mexican in search of Spanish treasure. And at this place Papa turned basic plots such as these into stories that never lost their appeal. By the time I could remember, Papa was nearly blind. I suppose he never saw much better than James Thurber; and he saw a good deal like him and talked a good deal as Thurber wrote.

Papa was more than a teller of stories on their way into family tradition. Often he was the unconscious hero of them, the center of a story about to enter the family oral tradition. Many of these stories center around his blindness. One, for example, is the story of Papa and Old Lee, our big polled Durham bull. One day in cotton season, Papa got back from the gin too late to unload the cotton seed. So he stopped his team under a liveoak tree beside the cottonseed house, unhitched and fed them, and came on to the house for supper. Just as he finished eating, he remembered that he had left a ten-pound sack of sugar in the wagon. The night was black as a crow's wing, but out he went, saying he could see about as well in the dark as in the daylight. And so could Old Lee, the bull. He had bedded down under the tree just about the end of the wagon tongue and gone to sleep to dream, perhaps, of fresh cottonseed and heifers. The first thing Papa knew of Lee and Lee knew of him was when Papa stumbled over Lee's rump and fell spread-eagle with his legs straddling something and his arms around Lee's neck. Lee awoke with a start, jumped to his feet with a frightened snort, and before Papa could say "God damn" went crashing off through a cedar thicket across the road from the seedhouse. Papa left, roughly, in a 90-degree angle from Lee's line of flight, his feet struck the lower limbs of the tree under which the wagon stood, and when he came down his shoulders hit the wagon tongue.

My memories of the Home Place are almost unlimited. It is the place where Grandma took her ouija board off the mantel each morning at ten o'clock and talked with her brother John or Red Fox, the Indian chief whose ectoplasm hung around somewhere out of sight but was always present at ten. It was the place where the Booger Man lived in the old bigmouthed well until my Uncle Sam filled it with rocks and drove him out to some other unknown but dangerous abode. It is where the Christmas tree caught on fire in the west downstairs room and caused loud excitement amongst the women and children. It is where Grandpa waged relentless war against the red ants, decimating colony after colony an ant at a time by hitting them with a clawhammer as they came or went. It is the place I came to in young manhood to milk and feed for Grandpa on cold winter evenings. It was the place of cackling hens and white eggs. It was the place where Papa was born and the place he came back to to live thirty years to the day from the time he married my mother and moved into the log house where I was born. And it is where I heard him die, where his rasping breath went out and faded into silence and another never came in, where I waited until I knew it wouldn't and then looked at the old Seth Thomas clock on the mantel and saw that it was ten past five and growing dark outside.

That's the way he went, from pain to peace. He had no fear of death so far as I could tell; loved the earth; was quite content to become part of it again.

That's Papa and the Home Place. Now I'll turn to myself. The Generation into which I was born was at the turning point between the old and new, and I turned with it, sandwiched between the two. Perhaps you'll gain perspective if I say I remember how hoeing cotton was. The first part of the row, I'd look back to see how far I'd come; the last to see how far I had to go. When the crabgrass had got ahead of the hoe or the tie-vines had bound the seedling plants to the balk, I moved as slow as necessity demanded, but when the row was clean, I set my pace in tune with my thoughts and hardly knew time passed until something roused me from my reverie and I looked back from where I'd come and thought how pleasantly time had passed.

That's what's happening now—the looking back, I mean, toward where I started from too long ago. Looking back, I see how far I've come; and looking forward I see there's not much left to hoe. That's not a morbid thought. Not many men have hoed a more pleasant row, and, as for what's left, I look out on eternity as Papa did without fear of becoming part of it.[1]

In the past dozen minutes and paragraphs I have tried to demonstrate through the example of my own Home Place and my memories of it a thesis that will apply to most Home Places as you and I have known them. That is, I have tried to show that a Home Place is an agriculturally based institution that grows out of a few acres settled under frontier conditions by a vigorous semi-literate family that has moved westward by stages, bringing with it the vocabulary and speech patterns accumulated by its ancestors, that at about the halfway point between the advance on the frontier and the retreat to suburbia this family proliferates into a special cluster dominated by a benevolent patriarch, that in this middle generation some member with a love for story-telling will pull together the oral tradition of the family and tell it in the vernacular, and, finally, that the oral tradition will dissipate and the Home Place will become a symbol in the generation that has retreated to suburbia.

Notes

1. Roy Swift concluded his eulogy by reading the preceding three paragraphs.

A Place Against the Sky/*Martha Emmons*

Martha Emmons

A Place Against the Sky

Martha Emmons

Often the passing of one who stood tall in his day reminds us of Edwin Markham's lines concerning the "lordly cedar" that "goes down upon the hills, and leaves a lonesome place against the sky." It is of such tall cedars that I speak today, of some of our predecessors in the Texas Folklore Society. In no sense would I disparage the fresh new blood we have now. But surely it is in order to list a few of those in our Society *qui ante nos fuerunt.* I doubt that I can tell you anything new. The story of the Texas Folklore Society is published history. You already know it, or, as in Thurber's story, "you can look it up." You are aware of our proud heritage. Organized in 1909 by Dr. L. W. Payne and Professor Lomax, then of A & M, it was first named the Folk-Lore Society of Texas. From the first it had the blessing of George Lyman Kittredge, of Harvard. He suggested the idea to Mr. Lomax, he was among the first life members, he attended the 1913 meeting, and he wrote the preface to *Publication* Number I, in 1916. In it he declared Texas to be the "happy hunting-ground for the folklorist." The avowed purpose of the Society was to gather and preserve folklore of the area. First president was Dr. Payne; first secretary, Professor Lomax. From the beginning the Society was off and running. In an article in the first numbered *Publication,* Dr. Robert Adger Law wrote, "Within a month or two its membership numbered about one hundred." First regular meeting was April 8, 1911. But there was no numbered *Publication* until 1916. It was edited by Stith Thompson, and is available now under title *Round the Levee.* As you know from your study of history, the long-seething unrest in Europe boiled into World War I, in 1914, and took first place in every man's thinking. It discouraged further publications and even caused suspension of annual meetings of 1918-1921. Then in the early '20's with the return of the native J. Frank Dobie from his sojourn in Stillwater, Oklahoma, came a new head of Texas Folklore Society, another *Publication* in 1923, called *Coffee in the Gourd;* and in 1924 came *Publication*

Number III, called *Legends of Texas.* It was widely publicized and widely read. That is when I joined the Society, received my copy of *Legends*—and found I had been a folklorist all my life.

Already my American history students and I, in Taylor High School, were going up and down the land like the Father of all Evil, seeking whom and what we might devour in local history. The line between history and legend is thin at best, and in local history still thinner. So before we knew it we were neck deep in both history and legend: tales of good men and of bad men, legends of the San Gabriel River, and of places now haunted by spirits of those who had gone before.

A class of mine received a letter from Mr. Dobie. He mentioned having seen some published reference to our work in local history and folklore, and suggested that "some member or members of your class, or your teacher" come to the meeting of the Texas Folklore Society, in April, and report some of our findings. We talked about it in class, and legends began to pour forth. Eddie Johnson, in his deep, sepulchral voice, advised, "I'll tell you what you do. We'll bring you the dope, and you go over there and tell 'em." Bring me the dope they did; and on the appointed day I did "go over there [Austin] and tell 'em." I told 'em all they would ever need to know about so-called "bad men" of the area, especially about Sam Bass. Certainly that paper had all the documentation that even the most exacting scholar could ask. Every day some one or ones of us met another person each of whom was "the only one in the room when Sam Bass died." Their name was legion.—You can't look that one up.—I gave names and places of some whose descendants were still around. I had no desire to start anything with them.

Arriving only in time for the afternoon program I spoke before an audience all new to me. I had never seen a one of them. Including J. Frank Dobie. Today I call to your attention three persons at that meeting who stand out in my mind, limned against the sky.

On my left sat—but I always remember him as standing—Dr. L. W. Payne. I remember his eager, smiling face, his tall, slim figure, his long-tailed coat, and certain of his mannerisms: rolling his palms together, and rocking back and forth on his feet. I also recall that in subsequent papers when I included songs, I could always count on Dr. Payne to be on his feet, rolling his palms, and rocking in rhythm, and really getting with it.

On my right and on the front row—all this in that old YMCA building, second floor, across from main campus—on front row and to my right sat Mr. Dobie. If ever there was a potent, inspiring listener, J. Frank Dobie was that. He sat forward much of the time, often agape, eager, credulous, and in any case responsive to every syllable. Somewhat scared at first, I soon felt easy, and I thought, "Anybody could talk before this crowd."

Farther back and to my left was one whose changing counte-nance attracted my attention. I had no idea who he was but guessed him off as a professor. I have never seen another person whose facial expressions run such a register, from serious to smiling or to outright laughter. I knew him for a long time after that. Habitually he looked sober. So sober that he appeared half-angry; and when he laughed, which he did easily, literally the day broke across his face, and sunlight flashed. When I sat down, he turned around and with that all-over smile said, "Webb is my name. I too am a devotee of Sam Bass." Walter Prescott Webb, then in the process of writing *The Great Plains.* In *Legends of Texas* I had read his story about Sam Bass. From that hour the soul of Jonathan was knit to that of W. P. Webb.

So much for the Big Three of that, my first meeting of Texas Folklore Society.

In one of those first meetings I remember Mr. Dobie's saying words to this effect: "This is the only organization that you join and attend just because you want to. You expect no professional advancement from it; you have no political axe to grind. You are not pressured to become a member or to read a paper. You belong because you want to. That is the very nature of the Society, one thing that distinguishes it from any other."

On the program in one of those early years was one I had glimpsed the summer before, on the campus of what was then Southwest Texas State Teachers' College, when I was student life director, or something, there. He was pointed out to me as "the darling of the campus." Many are the anecdotes I heard concerning him. He read a paper before the Society, and I remember it well, especially a song he rendered in his own Gates Thomas style. But instead of trying to rehash that paper I give you one of those anecdotes, and let you draw your own conclusions, likewise your own pictures of Gates Thomas, brother of Professor Will Thomas, one time president of the Texas Folklore Society and author of a collection of Negro folk songs published by the Society even before Number I.

One day President Evans called him into his office and instructed: "Mr. Thomas, I wish you would go to the downtown picture show tonight, see if any of our college students are there; if so, how many; and report to me tomorrow."

"Yes, sir."

The faithful henchman did as he was told. He went early and stayed through the beginning of the second show. Next morning he dutifully reported to his superior.

"Mr. Thomas, did you go to the show last evening?"

"Yes, sir."

"Did you see any of our college students there?"

"Yes, sir."

"How many, Mr. Thomas?"

"I counted twenty, sir."

Reaching for a pad, "And their names, Mr. Thomas?"

"I didn't get their names, sir. You didn't tell me to do that."

"That will be all, Mr. Thomas."

I mentioned that he was considered the "darling of the campus."

From the first I could see that the Texas Folklore Society was a going concern. Persons there seemed to be well acquainted with each other, from attendance at previous meetings. I noticed Mabel Major and Rebecca Smith from TCU, also Newton Gaines. Jovita Gonzales gave some lovely stories of flowers, birds, and of mythical heroes, from the Spanish. Victor J. Smith, from Sul Ross College, once gave a delightful paper, about the markings on big rock surfaces in the Big Bend country. He was well known for his knowledge of the region; and if you have not read that particular paper, you would do well to look that one up. It is in one of the *Publications,* I don't remember which one. But if you do, you will still miss the spice of it, in his own bit of a preface. Standing before us, in all modesty, looking every bit the scholar, he spoke of his interest in such records, admitted that his interpretations were largely tinctured with his own imagination and might be in error. "After all," he said, "I do not know just what may have been in the mind of some prehistoric Indian when he passed that way"; and then, with the most engaging, disarming smile, he said, "But you don't either," and proceeded with complete poise to give what at least he read into or from those pictographs.

At the time I became a member, and maybe from the first, the meetings were set as near April 21 as could conveniently be arranged. Nearly always we met in Austin, in that old YMCA building on the corner. One feature of the meetings was the "four-bit dinner," as Mr. Dobie called it; and I think that was on Saturday evening. I didn't look that one up. I just remember it that way.

I very well remember the year I came from Nacogdoches, to bring some of what, as Mr. Dobie said, I had "picked up over there among the piney woods," largely ghost tales. I thought of the miles and I hesitated. But I did go, and I did read a paper. *Read* it I did. I had on a new hat. I would not have worn a hat but I had noticed Miss Fannie Ratchford at preceding meetings and I thought she looked so nice, with her wide-brimmed hat. Mine was not only wide-brimmed, it was of pink horsehair braid. It had narrow velvet ribbons of assorted colors falling off the base of the crown and cascading down my back. Just not my style. When I heard my name called and I stepped out into the aisle, a breeze came in through the open windows, rippled along those ribbons—and took my speech with it right on down and out through the ends of them. I had such a seizure of stage fright, you bet I read that speech. It was no good in the first place, and it was worse by the time I finished with it.

That meeting had one great compensation. I met her of whom I had heard and read much. Miss Adina de Zavala, who left a lonesome place against the sky in the Texas Folklore Society and in the history of Texas. She read a paper, but I couldn't hear it. I was seeing and hearing her when she took her stance in the chapel of the Alamo, facing the forces of demolition (they had already destroyed all of the mission except the chapel). I could hear her saying, "The stones will fall on the head of the granddaughter of Lorenzo de Zavala." As I looked at her that day, I could easily imagine her heaving one of those stones against one of the wouldbe destroyers if he had given her any back talk. But the records indicate nothing of their giving Miss de Zavala any back talk.

Some time along in there we went to Dallas, at the invitation of John Lee Brooks. At that "four-bit dinner," Mody Boatright was asked for an anecdote. He responded with one about a famous old "cuttin' horse" on some ranch in Texas. One day they missed old Charley, and found him in the big middle of a red ant bed, "cuttin' out the bull ants."

Some year right along in there we met in Waco, at the invitation of Mr. John K. Strecker. Before time for the meeting Mr. Strecker became ill, and never did recover. I had to take charge because there was nobody else. Even Mr. Dobie was in England. I think he had arranged the program. My two recollections of that meeting: I did everything wrong; and J. Mason Brewer read a paper on Negro proverbs. You can look that one up, or ask me. I think I remember it verbatim. But what you can't find in the record is my tearing around that afternoon after the close of the session, trying to find that young Black man and tell him to come to that "four-bit dinner" that night at the Raleigh Hotel. But he was nowhere to be found. He had quietly slid out of sight.

Many of you will remember the year that we met at A & M, when John Q. Anderson was president. Such a hootenanny as we did have, out in the park, on a cool spring evening after heavy rains. John Q. kept the furnace, or barbecue pit, stoked. I seem to remember that Martin Shockley assisted John Q. in that chore. That was my first seeing of John Lomax. Everybody else knew him. But there had been some years when I had not attended regularly. I had known his father and Alan in the earlier years. As John stood there with one foot on that barbecue pit, he led us, in his own way, in a number of songs, including the one about old Long John's escape from prison somewhere in East Texas, maybe Navasota. To elude the officers Long John had devised a pair of shoes. They'uz the funniest shoes/ That ever was seen/ With a heel in front,/ And a heel behind/ You never could tell/ Whichaway he'uz a-gwine./ I'm long gone, etc.

What a lonesome place against the sky all of you will leave behind you!

My Favorite Texan and Folklore/*Mrs. John Q. Anderson*

John Q. Anderson (1916–1975)

My Favorite Texan and Folklore

Mrs. John Q. Anderson

The people who live upon the high plains of Texas can see the lights of night in towns and villages fifty miles away. If they ride in automobiles or on horseback about the country roads and highways beneath the starry skies, they can sense the feeling that Earth and Heaven merge—that they can truly "hitch their wagon to a star"—and that there is a oneness with the universe.

In this environment, however, there is loneliness and monotony. During the growing and harvesting season, the prairies ripple and undulate like the sea inviting dreams of far-away places. A person can see the same scenery so much of the way that a journey of any distance seems a thousand miles long. There is not anything to be done about the harsh weather, the constant winds and the searing summers, except to take things that come persevering in what "seeing forever on a clear day" and "catching a falling star" at night has made a boon.

The Panhandle was basically frontier in its settlement and pleasures when John Quincy Anderson was born there, near Wheeler, May 30, 1916.[1] There were large ranches, a few small ranches, and a few small towns. The population of the county was so scanty that it took all of the residents to make a successful social event. Worship was at a Union Church. Any passing minister, of any denomination, was welcomed and heard. The Anderson family made the music for most of the community activities, which included square dancing, play-party games, box suppers and religious singing. John Q., who was called "Quincy" by everyone, was the fifth child in the family which grew by two more children, though the youngest sister died early in life.[2] His eldest sister, Esther, had been given a parlor organ by her parents shortly before John Quincy was born. When she helped tend him, she sat with him in her lap while she pumped and played. This early contact with music might have been the reason he developed "perfect pitch" and an ability to play all stringed instruments, the piano, and the organ by ear. He later perfected his skill on some of the instruments by some instruction and self-study.

As soon as he was old enough, Quincy joined the family in the music-making outside of the home. As is true in most rural societies, he had spent many nights sleeping on a pallet with diverse other infants and youngsters while the adults danced in another room. He became expert in calling squares and in singing play-party games by the hours. He also joined in the hard and necessary work of farm life and gracefully accepted the basic ethics that are credited with making this nation great. He very early "hitched his wagon to a star" and found every individual and all things worthy of his notice. Without knowing it, he was gathering the material for what became, among his many varied scholarly interests, the pursuit that brought him the most delight.

From the time that his mother died when Quincy was not quite fifteen until June of 1952, when he completed his doctoral degree at the University of North Carolina, his life was filled with setbacks, delays, and, often, undue responsibilities. At the time of Mrs. Anderson's death, the older members of the family were married. Because he was small in size and could more easily be excused from farm work, he took care of the household for his father and two brothers. He cooked the meals, cleaned the house, washed the clothes, ironed the shirts, and even had Sunday dinners for several tables of kin a number of times.[3] In order to see that his youngest brother finished high school, he delayed his going to college an extra year. Then, at age seventeen, he sold his horse (the horse the song "Patonie" reminded him of then and later) for sixty dollars and went to Oklahoma.[4]

He stayed at Choctaw, near Oklahoma City, with his Grandfather and Grandmother Grant until Oklahoma State College opened. He was admitted under the provision that he would make a high grade-point average to stay enrolled, for Kelton High School was not accredited. He earned his way as clerical student-help for various professors, by typing theses and other papers, and by working anywhere he could find a job when he was not in school. Two times during the Great Depression, he dropped out of college to go to full time work to help his Aunt support two little orphan nieces in her care. When he graduated from Oklahoma State, he had determined to study for the higher degrees. He took a job in an Oklahoma City bank to earn money to commence his studies. Meanwhile, the compulsory military service bill was passed by the Congress of the United States. He decided to enlist and to get that year of service behind him so that his education would not be interrupted again. His enlistment was completed prior to the attack on Pearl Harbor, and he was back in service by Christmastime. By the time that he returned from World War II, he had spent six years away from his studies and had served his Country five and one-half years.[5] He embarked upon the pursuit of his higher degrees. He worked for the Agricultural Extension Office on the Louisiana State University campus, while getting his Master's Degree, and as a Teaching-Fellow at the University of Texas and the University of North Carolina.

During all of that time and until about 1955, he had continued lifting his voice in song but did not sing the old or country songs. In college he was a member of a popular dance band trio, the Choral Club, the Glee Club, and the Methodist Church choir. Wherever he went he usually sang with his local church's choir and in the *Messiah* when possible. He also did not play any musical instruments. He enjoyed the cultivated arts—drama, ballet, opera and symphonies.

Then at a meeting of the Texas Folklore Society, in Austin in 1955, when he was elected Vice-President and Program Chairman for the 1956 meeting, he went to the home of Dr. and Mrs. Mody Boatright to visit with some of the long-time members of the organization. The discussion was about folksongs, particularly murder ballads. Recalling the elderly lady who sang "Waco Girl" with tears streaming down her face and with peculiar locution, Dr. Anderson asked if that song belonged to the category they were discussing. He sang the song for them. Afterwards, he had to sing "Waco Girl" at every meeting he attended. He realized what he had been singing the first seventeen years of his life were not just country songs but were folksongs that had been learned in the true-manner—by word of mouth from others.

Later, Dr. Anderson mentioned the fact that he knew many folksongs to Miss Sue Albright, then on the A&M Library staff, and said that he needed an instrument to assist his remembering them. She brought him a one-hundred-year-old C.F. Martin from the attic of her Aunt's home in Cooper, Texas, to use as long as he wished.[6] From that time forward, a day seldom passed that he did not play and sing for his relaxation at home or for preparation for programs and for classroom lectures later, when he successfully introduced folklore studies. The tone of the instrument, which he played without a pick and on which he used steel strings, blended perfectly with his tenor-baritone voice. He eventually remembered and sang several hundred of these Panhandle songs of his youth.[7]

The folklore courses were begun in the following way. In 1956 the Texas Folklore Society meeting was on the campus of Texas A&M University. It was the first meeting at which the Society had staged the newly activated student-paper contest. The three winners were on the program. Hermes Nye, with Dr. Anderson's assistance and with the support of the Council members and officers, championed these contests. It was, also, the first meeting at which the Hootenanny was made a permanent unofficial part of the annual programs. This practice was originated, largely, on Dr. Anderson's part, though the members had been getting together to sing when and where they could—often in small groups—for years. Because of the interest engendered among the students, in the community, and by campus and local newspapers, a delegation of students came to Dr. Anderson begging that he hold a non-credit course in folklore for them.

In the spring of 1957, the entire class enrolled in a two-hour course in American Literature had gone to the English Department Head and asked that Dr. Anderson be allowed to meet an extra class with them each week for additional assignments and lectures. They did not ask for extra credit and it was not possible for the professor's work-load to be reduced. The class was conducted, and the aspiring folklore students knew that.

Consequently, in 1958, the study of folklore was introduced for non-credit for both the teacher and the students. Dr. Anderson used this non-credit course to commence gathering comprehensive materials for a survey of world folklore through the various schools of scholarly approach in the field of American Folklore. He considered contrary ideas and approaches stimulating to enquiry, and so he was never involved in the sometimes bitter rivalry that often occurs among scholars. He cut the stencils, ran off the mimeographed pages, and assembled the more than 200-page books that were eventually to be distributed and taken up at the end of each semester. The course was taught one semester with no credit for anyone; two semesters, with credit for the students only; and, from 1960 until 1966 as part of the official curriculum. Folklore Studies continue to thrive at Texas A&M University.

Originally the folklore courses were limited to thirty-five students and were voluntary, in no way replacing any required courses in English. Because Dr. Anderson considered it important for the students to hear the songs to be able to understand and to study them, he used his newly rediscovered music to illustrate his lectures in classes and elsewhere. The English Department did not have the equipment or the money to furnish that kind of material.

The John Avery Lomax Folklore Society, honoring the late John A. Lomax, Sr., who was teaching at Texas A&M when he collected many of the ballads that later made him internationally famous, was established in 1960 by some of the brightest members of the Cadet Corps.[8] This student group had monthly meetings and those students who played and sang performed. The membership grew rapidly with students from all disciplines on campus and with many interested townspeople. The sponsor's wife was invited to be the co-sponsor and started the practice of having the membership, along with wives or friends, to their home twice a year. The refreshments were planned from menus of those childhood gatherings in the Panhandle when Dr. Anderson was growing up there. Play party games, candy breakings, and, as always, playing and singing were the order of the evening.

The first concert that the John Avery Lomax Folklore Society gave was held in the Memorial Student Center on the A&M campus in 1963. It was announced on short notice but it drew nearly two hundred townspeople and students.[9] At about the same time Dr. Anderson started accepting local invitations to present programs on folklore and folksong so that he could give promising student-singers an opportunity to appear in formal circumstances. These programs won wide appeal, also, and once the group began to have regular concerts on the campus, there was always a large appreciative audience. The concerts that they gave at other colleges won acclaim.

Students aware of the voluntary folklore course mentioned to Dr. Anderson that they were embarrassed at student meetings, especially those attended by undergraduates from Eastern schools, because they did not know anything about philosophy and other esoteric matters. They asked him to conduct a seminar in "Great Ideas," which, again, was a non-credit course for professor and students, though all the requirements for a regular graduate course were demanded. The seminar was conducted from 1961 through 1963.

In writing about Dr. Anderson's ability as a classroom teacher, Dr. Stewart S. Morgan, Head of the A&M English Department, repeatedly stated that he was a superior teacher who had a large following among the students who exerted themselves to get into his classes "in spite of the high standards he upheld and of the almost excessive amount of work he demanded of his classes." He mentioned Dr. Anderson's extensive scholarly publications in the fields of American Literature, American Humor, American Studies, Folklore, and Southern History, noting that he "seemed to value more his victories in teaching than in publication."[10]

When Dr. Anderson was given the Faculty Distinguished Achievement Award for *Teaching* by the Association of Former Students of Texas A&M University in 1961, President Earl Rudder sent a copy of the Selection Committee's statement to him. It read in part: This man's exacting nature makes it necessary for his students to work very hard. Yet his talent as a teacher is such that students maneuver to get into his classes. His students and his associates regard him as a most superior classroom teacher and he is truly outstanding in his skill of generating enthusiasm in his students.[11]

In the Texas Folklore Society, he held the following offices: Vice-President, 1954-1955; President, 1955-1956; Councilor, 1956-1958; Member of the Advisory Board, Paisano Books, 1966 until death; and Representative to the Texas Heritage Foundation, 1956-1958. He presented papers at thirteen meetings of the Society and on programs of thirteen other academic organizations, including the Louisiana Folklore Society, on folklore topics. He was guest lecturer in folklore for the American Studies Seminar at Mississippi College in 1962, 1963, and 1964. In addition he gave fifty-two lectures on folklore topics for other professional and community organizations and on other university campuses. He published one book in folklore, *Texas Folk Medicine* (Encino Press, 1970), but several of his books, particularly those on humor and southwest literature, contain much folk materials.[12] Forty-nine of his published articles are on folklore, and the last article that appeared, after his death, was "Texas and Southwest Medical Lore in the Anderson Collection, University of

Houston" in *American Folk Medicine—A Symposium,* edited with an introduction by Wayland D. Hand.[13] One of his contributions to *Southwestern American Literature: A Bibliography,* of which he was senior editor, is the section on folklore.[14] The book, recently issued, is dedicated to the memory "of R. H. Porter, Mody C. Boatright, John Q. Anderson and other publishers and scholars who believe in the Southwest."[15] In the "Introduction," the co-editors, James W. Lee and Edwin W. Gaston, Jr., dedicated their labors in the final stages of the work to his memory. M. Thomas Inge's *The Frontier Humorists* (Archon Books, 1975) is "Dedicated to John Q. Anderson, 1916-1975, one of the best friends American humor and folklore ever had."

One Saturday evening in 1962 or 1963, Dr. Anderson came into the den after hours of paper-grading and picked up his guitar. He strummed and sang the old songs awhile and, then, picked up a copy of Dr. Everett A. Gillis's book of poems, *Sunrise in Texas,* and set one of the poems to music. To his surprise, in Monday's mail, he found a request from Dr. Gillis for him to set some of the poems to music. From that request came the completed book manuscript *Ballads for Texas Heroes.* The heroes included are Austin, Houston, Bowie, Wallace, Ford and MacDonald (Texas Rangers), Crockett, Parson John, Jim Cooper, and Babe of the Alamo. Heroes went out of style in the 1960's and this lovely little book was never printed.[16]

Dr. Anderson introduced the study of folklore to the University of Houston in 1967 after going there as Professor of American Literature in 1966.

On the morning after the operation had brought the sad news that Dr. Anderson's cancer was terminal, I paid my second visit to him in the intensive care unit of St. Joseph's Hospital in Houston. When my visit was over I stepped into the long, empty corridor and was overcome by a feeling of loneliness and thoughts of the harsh realities of life and of the Panhandle. I sensed an intrusion of my desolation and turned to see the tall, handsome surgeon who had performed the operation.

"Mrs. Anderson," he said, "I just want to tell you that I have performed many, many operations on children, old people, young people and others, but this one has hurt me more than any of the rest."[17]

"Thank you," I said. "He is very special—not just to me—to many others."[18]

"I know," he said.

Notes

1. His birthdays were always sad ones, because his family attended the community cemetery cleaning on Memorial Day. He was the son of Albert Slayton and Emily Eugenia (Grant) Anderson, both of whom were descended from Colonial American families. An ancestral grandfather of his mother's fought in the American Revolution and took part in the Boston Tea Party. The Grants, however, came to America in about 1840 and settled in Michigan.

2. The brothers and sisters are Albert Anderson (Wheeler, Texas), Esther Shinn (Mrs. A. C. Shinn of Albuquerque, New Mexico), Bessie Baird (Mrs. C. C. Baird of Wheeler, Texas), George B. Anderson (deceased in 1975 less than a month after his brother's death), and Leonard Eugene Anderson (Miami, Texas).

3. He used to speak of preparing the lunches for himself and his younger brother and "riding off across a cow pasture to school." His sister-in-law was kind to help him when she could, and his sister Esther was like a second mother.

4. During his senior year in high school and the time he remained at home to see his younger brother through school, he kept a diary in a small blue notebook. In it he expressed his aspirations and his decision to break away from the Panhandle environment. The original journal is with his personal and biographical papers in the Special Collections of the University of Houston's archives. His sister, Mrs. Shinn, and his cousin Tamsey Leitch of Baltimore, Maryland, have typescript copies. He attended Davis School for his elementary education and Kelton High School, Kelton, Texas. An autograph book among his papers shows that most of his friends and teachers expected him to distinguish himself in life.

5. He enlisted in the Headquarters Company of the 96th Infantry Brigade at Fort Sill, Oklahoma, on September 21, 1940, and was discharged on September 21, 1941. He was secretary to a General and the company participated in the Louisiana maneuvers. He was re-enlisted at the Presidio of San Francisco, on January 12, 1942, in the Headquarters Company of the Fourth Army and was discharged at Fort Washington, Maryland, on January 12, 1943. He was commissioned Second Lieutenant, Adjutant Generals Department, on January 13, 1943, and served in administrative capacities at Several stations in the United States (New York, North Carolina, South Carolina) and overseas in England, France and Germany. He was separated from service at Camp Chaffee, Arkansas, as Captain AGD, on April 20, 1946. We were married on August 24, 1946, after having had to postpone the wedding which had been planned for December, 1941.

6. Miss Albright thought the guitar was a mandolin. The instrument was returned to her in 1966 for the use of a descendant of the original owner who had taken it off to college in the nineteenth century.

7. He sang six hundred folksongs from memory, including the Creole Gumbo and Slave and Civil War songs which he learned for special studies. Most of the songs he sang are in his ballad book on deposit in Special Collections, The University of Houston Archives, with his other papers. Tape recordings are on deposit at the Library of Congress, The University of Houston Archives, Texas A&M; and, in single tapes at Indiana University; the University of North Carolina;

Old Courthouse Museum, Vicksburg, Mississippi; Radio House, UT, Austin: and in various individuals' possession.

8. The Charter Members were Kenneth F. Allen, Thomas G. Bredlow, Frank B. Buchanan, III, Weldon K. Curry, Patrick K. Decker, James W. Moore, James A. Moore, Thomas N. Payne, John L. Penrod, Thomas E. Strickland, Thomas L. Sutherland, Jr., Norman H. Stutte, Clark C. Straughan, and Marion M. Walton.

9. Among the singers was Joseph S. Graham, Jr., of Monahans, Texas, who sang a version of "Patonie."

10. Letters from Dr. S. S. Morgan to Dean W. W. Delaplane, March 14, 1957; to Dr. Paul C. Calloway, October 2, 1957; to Dean W. R. Hubert, March 25, 1960, and April 22, 1961.

11. Letter, May 25, 1961, from President Earl Rudder and Dr. Anderson's reply, May 26, 1961.

Part of Dr. Anderson's thank-you for the congratulations stated, "I am pleased to have the full text of the citation to show to Mrs. Anderson without whose inspiration and encouragement my work would not have been possible." I did not see this beautiful compliment until after he died.

This teacher-scholar did as much in each of the many areas claiming his professional interest. Dr. Floyd Stovall, retired Poe Professor at the University of Virginia, directed his doctoral work at the University of North Carolina. He wrote me in April of 1979, "One of the many talents your John Q. had was that of a genuine interest in a variety of things—as Emerson and Folklore!"

Mary Schiflett, writing to Dr. Harvey Johnson of the University of Houston, November 27, 1971, as "one of his many admiring former graduate students," said: "Dr. Anderson is a genial friend who is sincere in his interest in everyone in the Academic community. To him, there is no higher calling than that of a teacher, and he strives all of the time to make the most of his many fine talents in a manner that will give inspiration to his students and lend credit to his university. He is a consummate scholar who prepares each lecture with care, adding information and points of view so that each student will find something of genuine merit in each class session. He is listed as professor of American Literature, but his own knowledge and curiosity does not stop at that border: he ranges wisely, with humor, and with enthusiasm, over world history, world folkways, world literature, the arts, comparative languages, and on and on so that the field of interest is unending."

Though the title of Professor Emeritus of English was bestowed upon Dr. Anderson on May 31, 1974, the presentation was not made until January 28, 1975, just twenty-two days before his death. A delegation from the English Department made up of Dr. Joseph Doggett, Dr. and Mrs. Thomas W. Ford, Dr. and Mrs. Patrick G. Hogan, Dr. Lee Pryor, Dr. Robbie Moses, Dr. Julia Mazow, and Dr. Hunter came to present the certificate, which had just come, to him at our home in Houston. We dressed in the University of Houston colors for the brief

41

ceremony, and Dr. Doggett read the following statement: The Administration of the University of Houston at the request of the faculty of the Department of English confers upon you the title of Professor Emeritus of English with profound gratitude for the signal contribution you have made to the scholarship and advancement of the department's programs during your active years. Your presence, wise counsel, and ready friendliness to both faculty colleagues and students have been through the years, a constant source of inspiration and pleasure. We wish therefore, on this occasion, to express our warm affection for all you have meant to each of us. Your absence from our daily academic activities is sorely felt.

On November 16, 1974, the American Studies Association of Texas met in Houston and approved the following resolution: Whereas, because of his active interest in the founding of the American Studies Association of Texas, his years of tireless service and his valuable contributions to the interdisciplinary studies in American scholarship, Be it Resolved that John Q. Anderson be named the first DISTINGUISHED FELLOW of the American Studies Association of Texas.

Among the members who came to our home that day were Dr. and Mrs. Eugene Jones, Dr. E. Hudson Long, Dr. Melvin Mason, and Professor J. Frank Peirce. It was one of the most pleasant days of our dying-time. It was filled with interesting conversation and much laughter.

12. The books are *Louisiana Swamp Doctor* (LSU Press, 1962), *Tales of Frontier Texas* (SMU Press, 1966), *With the Bark On: Popular Humor of the Old South 1830-1860* (Vanderbilt Press, 1967). He was also on the Editorial Board of the *Mississippi Quarterly* for folklore and was a member of the Bibliography Committee of the Society for the Study of Southern Literature, whose checklist appears in that journal.

13. The 27,049-item collection is on deposit with the Anderson papers in Special Collections at the University of Houston.

14. He was chairman of the organizing committee of the Southwestern American Literature Association and served as Chairman of the Editorial Board from 1970 until his death. The book was issued by Swallow Press in February, 1980, and the royalties will go to the association for use in future publications.

15. The Bibliography was advertised to issue in late 1972 or 1973. As is true with most scholarly publications, a "reasonable length of time" can be up to ten years. The co-editors had to see the final stages of the publication through alone. The extensive bibliographies and other materials which Dr. Anderson used in preparing his contributions are on deposit at the University of Houston.

Many of the most active members of the Texas Folklore Society are on the list of Editorial Advisors and were contributors to the work. The officers and councillors of the Southwestern American Literature Association conferred an Honorary Membership to me at the 1977 meeting of the Texas Folklore Society in El Paso, Texas.

16. Dr. Gillis, a former President of the Texas Folklore Society, composed the music and the poem "Babe of the Alamo" at my request. The music for the other poems is Dr. Anderson's. The dedication page of his *South by West* read: In Memoriam / John Q. Anderson / who carved his name in the Inscription Rock of our affection and admiration

Paso por Aqui

Bells from remoter distances proclaim
The sterling metal of his larger fame;
But to our personal memories—far more dear
His message carved on stone: *"I passed by here."*

17. Dr. Richard Hirshberg. As another evidence of his specialness, the Texas Folklore Society named him to its roster of Distinguished Fellows at the Waco meeting April 14, 1979, and formally presented the award at San Antonio April 4, 1980. The citation read: "Know all men by these present that in recognition of his many years of distinguished service as member, officer, and contributor to the Texas Folklore Society and particularly as a renowned National scholar and author in the field of Folklore and in the Society's sincere appreciation of his leadership John Q. Anderson, 1916-1975, is hereby designated Fellow of the Texas Folklore Society." "My Favorite Texan and Folklore" was on the program of the 64th annual meeting.

Love Among the Elephant Ears & Other True Stories/Al Lowman

*Harmon (1834–1918) and Rebecca
(1835–1916) Lowman*

Love Among
the Elephant Ears
& Other True Stories

Al Lowman

I have tried to reconstruct these stories exactly as I heard them.
Almost exactly. However the original tellers may have embroidered
the fabric, I have followed their course in altering neither names nor
circumstances. I cannot vouch for the authenticity of detail. At times,
simple facts were deemed insufficiently expressive; literal truth was
exchanged for essential truth. Perhaps Andre Maurois had this in
mind when he asserted that "There are certain persons for whom pure
truth is a poison."

These anecdotes have been told, especially at family funerals,
as long as I can remember. The facts are always essentially the same,
but intense competition among the tale spinners means that fresh,
new particulars are constantly being remembered. Contradictions
never bother them. They have always hewed to the Emersonian
philosophy that "a foolish consistency is the hobgoblin of little
minds."

Daddy used to say, "Not all of the good people came from
Staples, but most of the best ones did." He did nothing to discourage
me from believing that this Central Texas settlement was mankind's
first rest-stop on the road from the Garden of Eden. It is a restful
country all right—rolling black land creased with tree-lined streams
and draws. The hub of this little world is a somnolent unincorporated
river village originally named for a country store around which the
community grew. There was never a paved road into the place until
1950. The atmosphere there was perfectly described in the late 1940s
when Daddy's youngest sister attended services in the Methodist
Church. Later she observed that, in tempo, the hymns resembled
funeral dirges. Thus the congregation sang "A Charge to Keep I
Have" as if it were in full-scale retreat.

Despite Daddy's perfect willingness to have his children believe
that Staples was the font of every blessing and worthwhile wisdom, I
caught on soon enough that there was, in fact, life before Staples.

Our family's emigrant ancestors had arrived in South Carolina from southern Germany in 1752. A hundred years later my great-grandfather, Harmon Lowman, married and took his bride to southern Alabama on the eve of the Civil War, then to Staples in 1878.

This great-grandfather was simultaneously a schoolteacher, a sometime minister of the Methodist Church, and a farmer. He must have been remarkably astute to have combined three professions that would offer the least promise of financial gain. Nevertheless he was willing to try to make it on his own. All he wanted from his government was a postage stamp. A letter he wrote to a former neighbor in 1909 shows the old man to have been perfectly "wrathy" about his taxes.

We have a good school at Staples. The Principal is paid $75 & two assistants are employed at $35 Each. I am opposed to this School Community tax. I am taxed for 1908—$8.75—added to State Ad valorem of $10, totaling $18.75 which is quite a Sum for an old Confederate to pay to Educate the Children of those who are abler to work than I. If they would take what they wear in unnecessary dress and spend on Sumptious fare and riotous living, I dare Say we would not have to levy a tax to Educate their Children. I question Seriously any man's religion who favors taking my dollars to pay tuition of his children.

There is an Educational Craze today—Agricultural, Mechanical, etc. —which is costing much, Creating new offices, Officers to fill them at fat Salaries; hence high taxation and high rendition of property.

Crime of Every type is on the Increase. Murder, robery, burglary, petty theft, rape, drunkeness, Suicide, Night riders like in Tennessee, etc. Surely wickedness is waxing worse & worse.

All this was written nearly ten years before adoption of the federal income tax and before numerous other changes that would have pleased him no more.

A year or so before his death his son Joel and grandson Cliett were supposed to haul the old man to a doctor's appointment. As they prepared to leave the house, Uncle Joel discovered that his car had a flat tire. Figuring that this was a slow leak, he grabbed a hand pump and began inflating. Periodically he was spelled by grandson Cliett, then a sturdy fifteen or so. Great grandpa knew all about fixing wagon wheels, but the operating principle of pneumatic tires eluded him. Since pressure gauges were not commonly used, the way to check a tire was by kicking it. As Uncle Joel was pumping away, young Cliett proceeded to give a test kick. Suddenly, and without warning, Grandpa Harmon whacked him across the butt with his cane: "You fool you," he exclaimed irritably, "you kick the air out of that tire faster than your daddy can pump it in."

By all accounts Great-grandpa's children were of far more equable disposition than he. Despite his reserve my grandfather

Quincy was actually buoyant and optimistic—good humored, rather than humorous. Quincy Lowman exuded what Mark Twain had described as "the calm confidence of a Christian with four aces." An enterprising sort of fellow, he and a younger brother formed a partnership in 1889 to buy the local gin and mill. A year later the partners established the community waterworks and later added electric generating service. In 1908 they bought the Staples Mercantile Company.

In 1894 Grandpapa Quincy paused in his upward bounding long enough to wed the Reverend W. A. Scott's eldest daughter, Mellie. The groom was thirty-seven, the bride nineteen. The story goes that, as he brought her home after the ceremony, he turned in the buggy and said: "Make yourself at home, Mellie, I've got to go to the gin awhile." She made herself at home all right, and he must not have stayed too long at the gin, because they had twelve children. She called him "Mr. Quincy" and deferred to him in most ways. On cold winter nights she retired thirty minutes early to warm his side of the bed while he finished reading the *San Antonio Express,* banked the fire and blew out the kerosene lamps. As a commentary on changing times it should be noted that bedwarming procedures have changed drastically in the intervening generations.

There was another personality in that household whose contribution must be noted. Amy Vanderber was already middle-aged when she arrived there in the fall of 1896. She stayed until her death thirty-two years later, fulfilling a dual role as housekeeper and guardian of those youngsters who fell between the cradle and the schoolhouse door. "Miss" Vanderber never, but never, spoke of her past. The most insistent pleadings of the children she loved deeply never loosened her tongue. Not until the 1900 census was published was some of the mystery cleared away. She was from Arkansas, born there in 1844. And she told the census enumerator that she was a widow. Uncle Travis remembers that she received but two pieces of mail in all those years—letters with a South Carolina postmark. Who were they from? What was in them? "That's none of your business," she explained.

Just how limitless her devotion was becomes apparent when it is pointed out that her bedroom behind the kitchen was the night nursery for the pre-schoolers. When a new baby arrived (about every eighteen months) the child that was evicted from the crib was put in Miss Vanderber's bed, a bed that probably never completely dried out for fifteen years. Up for most of the night fetching glasses of water and giving potty training, she slept even less as the youngsters contracted the usual assortment of childhood diseases. Another day started at five in the morning. To steady her nerves, her only resort was to a surreptitious pinch of snuff. One wonders how that could have been enough. When she died in 1928, Miss Vanderber was buried in my grandparent's plot.

Beyond the immediate household there were other relatives and friends whose antics are part of the family's oral tradition. Marvin

Scott, Grandmama's younger brother, was a large man with a large manner and a large appetite. He fit the description of a man-about-town. Staples actually had a surplus of that kind. Some old business directories list him as a druggist, but he never passed the examination for a license.

Scott was acting postmaster at Staples from 1924 to 1927, but he never passed that examination either, so they gave the job to his wife Myrtle who presumably achieved the requisite score. But like Ma and Pa Ferguson in the governor's chair, it was a case of two office-holders for the price of one. Marvin's real occupation, however, was checker player. His game never stopped. The board was spread out on a counter top because only in that position could he keep an eye on his house. If Myrtle headed his way, the checkers were hastily cached.

More than he loved checkers, Marvin Scott loved to eat. He was in a class with William Jennings Bryan, although he lacked the latter's media coverage. If gluttony had been an art form, Scott would have played the young Raphael to Bryan's Michelangelo. Marvin worked at it. Thirty minutes before a feast, he would plop an aspirin in his mouth on the novel theory that "It whets the appetite!" And so, when the last gargantuan meal had been consumed, the problem was not so much to account for his death as to explain how he had lived so long. But no one ever doubted that Marvin Scott loved every breath of life he drew.

His good friend was Rufus Holmes. Like Scott, Holmes loved to eat. He also suffered chronic indigestion, thus he carried with him a quantity of baking soda which he dipped as some people dip snuff, the purpose being to secure relief by inducing eructation. And where did Rufe Holmes carry his soda? At the start of each day he simply poured a supply of it loosely into his trousers cuff, and then resorted to it as needed. Holmes had a son named Arnold, thin as a rail, whose inevitable nickname was "Skinny." Holmes explained this phenomenon saying "That boy eats so much it makes him pore to tote it." When I was a teenager I wasn't much better filled out than "Skinny" Holmes, and Daddy was convinced that it was for the same reason.

During the pre-World War I years the Methodist preacher in Staples was the Reverend W. L. Hightower, a wonderfully volatile character who thought that living in charity with one's neighbors was OK in principle if not carried to extreme in practice. For years he drove a Model T which, like its owner, had a mind of its own. One morning the reverend had enough. He set about to hand crank the machine and, try as he might, it simply would not respond. Finally he removed the crank handle and straightened to his full height. At that moment of confrontation he looked like John Steuart Curry's version of John Brown at Potawatamie. His face was masked in divine fury. With a secure grip on the crank handle, he purposefully and methodically used it to demolish the radiator.

Daddy used to say that the Lowman children didn't exactly grow up in that household; they were "jerked up." The game was survival with at least tattered remnants of one's emotional health. When she was about seven Aunt Evie managed to get herself locked in an upstairs closet. No one could remember that it ever had a door key. It was naturally a frightening experience for a child, but comfort arrived quickly with the appearance of brothers Quince and Fred, themselves thirteen and ten respectively. From outside the closet they began addressing themselves in loud conversation to Evie's predicament on the inside.

"Well there ain't no key, so it'll be quite awhile before we can get 'er open. Better breathe real slow now, Evie, so you don't use up all your air," suggested Quince. Helpfully, of course.

Picking up the cue, Fred chimed in: "Yeah, that's a mighty little closet. You gonna have to make that air last an awful long time."

Now brother Terry, a year older than Evie, dropped by to offer sympathy and concern. Echoing the others he worriedly proclaimed, "I just hope and pray that the house don't all of a sudden catch fire and burn to the ground. Evie'd suffocate for sure."

From inside came the sound of muffled sobbing. "Don't cry, Evie, that makes you breathe faster, and when the air's all gone you'll be out like a light. How long you reckon it'll be 'fore she passes out, Quince?"

"Oh I 'spect she'll be unconscious in about twenty minutes 'less we can get this door open, but there don't seem much prospect of that. I imagine Papa's gonna hafta use an axe to knock it down."

"Well in that case you better move to the back of the closet, Evie, 'cause that axe could come a-bustin' right through that door panel and cleave your head plumb in two."

"Fred's right, Evie. Get back just as far as you can and breathe real slow. Everything's gonna be O.K. Maybe."

After awhile Papa came up the stairs, routed the tormentors, and rescued Evie. She survived this traumatic experience with little more than raging claustrophobia and other minor quirks that need not be detailed.

About 1920 Aunt Ila was sitting on the front porch swing with her date of the evening, Joe Francis. It was ten o'clock and overhead some of the younger boys were getting ready to turn in. Uncle Travis, then twelve or thirteen, had the urge but lacked the desire to traipse to the outhouse past the orchard. Unaware that anyone was sitting below, he walked to the edge of the sleeping porch, hiked his night shirt and watered the elephant ears behind the swing.

Ila heard, and knew immediately, what was going on. Joe Francis was a little slow. "What's that?" he exclaimed. "An armadillo, I suppose." Ila was proud of her quick thinking, but pride turned into panic when Joe jumped up hollering "Let's catch him." I must have been awfully young when I first heard that story because I was curious enough to ask, "What happened next, Daddy, did he get drenched?"

but Daddy never answered. I was too young and literal minded to recognize the tale was appropriately ended. If you grew up on this b---s--- like I did, you don't need to be told that the armadillo sequence was a later invention anyway.

Hunting, whether of armadillos or other small game, was a favorite sport among the lads of Staples, and a .22-calibre rifle was the *sine qua non* that marked the passage from childhood to adolescence. On the way to the river bottom a boy and his new possession would pass Marvin Scott's drugstore where the village "elders"—like Lowman Howard, Johnny Vinyard and others—held forth. The conversation would proceed thus:

"Whatcha got there, son?" (As if it weren't perfectly obvious).

"Got me a new rifle." (Proudly).

"Izzat so. Whatcha gonna do with it?" (As if that, too, weren't obvious).

"Fixin' to go squirrel huntin'." (Confidently).

"Whoa now. You got it broke in yet?" (Just the right note of concern).

"Whadya mean?" (Mystified).

"Well you can't expect to shoot a squirrel from the top of a big pecan tree unless you got that rifle broke in." (Emphatically).

"How come?" (Thoroughly mystified).

"It'll ruin the rifle. You'll strain the bore and it won't ever shoot right again. You gotta work it in gradually." (With the assured manner of one who knows).

"Howdya go 'bout breakin' in a rifle?" (Still puzzled, but wanting to do everything right).

"Oh that's easy enough. You hafta be careful to avoid long shots. Don't try to hit a squirrel when he's in the top of an eighty-foot tree. If you'll just be patient he'll hafta come down to the lower branches where you can get a better aim at 'im anyway." (Makes sense).

"But what if he stays in the top of the tree?" (Who the hell knows how to read a squirrel's mind?)

"Son, there ain't no squirrel that can stay more'n five minutes in the top of one of them big trees. The air up there is too rarified. He's gotta come down to a lower elevation to get oxygen. That's when you shoot him." (Sounds reasonable).

"Well how long does it take to get a rifle broke in?" (Go ahead, gimme the bad news).

"Give it three weeks to a month, dependin' of course on how much huntin' you're gonna do. I know that sounds like an awful long time, but it shore would be a shame to ruin a purty rifle like that, one that yore pa paid good money for." (Overweening concern).

"Lord no, I waited forever to get this thing."

The same old palaver worked time after time after time on each lad who proudly displayed his first squirrel rifle.

Even when the world appears to stand still, as it does in Staples, things have a way of moving on. Faces change. Grandpapa Quincy fell victim to stomach cancer in 1920. Times had been tough for farmers and those whose livelihood depended upon them. Friends and neighbors had been unable to pay their bills at the store and the gin. Grandpapa was not the foreclosing sort and was himself virtually bankrupt from buying and holding cotton in a declining market.

Grandmama and Miss Vanderber still had a houseful of young ones to raise and educate. Daddy was one of two in his family who declined a college education. He never wanted to be anything but a farmer. Grandpapa's youngest brother, Uncle Lewey Lowman, felt the same way. He was the kind who made a crop when no one else could. In 1914 he moved off to Nueces County just as the range was being divided into farms. His glowing reports of that country inspired others to emigrate. My grandfather bought property down there in 1916 and sent Daddy and his brother Quincy to take charge.

Uncle Lewey was also the black sheep of that staunch prohibitionist family. At age ninety-one Cousin Charlie Howard once told me in a sorrowful whisper that "Poor Lewey was drinking when the family came to Texas." And how old was Lewey at the time? "Fifteen." But something is wrong here because Uncle Lewey was born, according to the family Bible, in 1876. The family left Alabama in 1878, according to Goodspeed's *Memorial and Genealogical Record of Southwest Texas*. This would mean that Lewey had started his drinking a good dozen years earlier—at the age of two! According to Cousin Charlie and others, it was his drinking that finally got him. When he was seventy-one.

Daddy was still tending that Nueces County farm about 1924 when he accepted an invitation from Uncle Lewey to accompany him and his twin sons on a quick trip to Staples. Daddy visited his folks, then prepared to return South. The twins were to alternate driving while Daddy sat with Uncle Lewey on the back seat. When they reached the first wet precinct of Guadalupe County, Uncle Lewey signaled a stop to buy whiskey. If the bottles he cast from car windows had taken root on Texas roadsides, his planting efforts would have dwarfed those of Johnny Appleseed.

The trip in those days was arduous enough, as the gravel road wound through a frustrating maze of property lines. North of Beeville the terrain becomes quite hilly. At this point of the journey, Uncle Lewey was in a congenial stupor, the pauses in his conversation lasting twenty minutes or longer. The twins always despised his drunkenness, and Daddy made no effort to communicate other than to respond as briefly as politeness required.

Suddenly Uncle Lewey lurched in Daddy's direction and delivered an astonishing judgment. County commissioners, he intoned, were spendthrifts by habit and fools by heredity. Singly and collectively they could waste more tax money than any mortals on earth. How so? Daddy inquired innocently. "Well," said Uncle Lewey with a malevolent gleam, "the dumb bastards gravel these roads to the top of the hill, then spread more gravel on the reverse slope." Daddy could find no flaw in the procedure and said so. "Son," explained Uncle Lewey in triumphant disgust, "no damn fool is gonna get stuck going downhill!"

I spent years trying to find a message in that pronouncement. There isn't any. He was wrong.

As years went by, more and more members of the family followed that road to Nueces County. Within the next decade Grandmama and five of her children lived there. The two youngest taught in a rural school and lived in the adjacent teacherage. Daddy farmed nearby and two more brothers lived and worked in Corpus Christi.

Around 1933 or '34 family members gathered one Sunday for dinner at the teacherage. Uncle Quince had been feeling poorly; his problem was diagnosed as constipation. Grandmama recommended that he try her laxative, a patent variety called Fleets. He finally took a dose about mid-morning. At noon the folks converged upon the table, the blessing was offered and the meal began. Uncle Quince took a sip of tea that was brim full of finely crushed ice. Suddenly he jumped from his chair and raced to the bathroom. In a few minutes he was back to help his plate and sip a little more tea and ice. Again he had to beat a hasty exit. Returning a second time, he ate a few bites of food, took another drink and left once more. Now when he came back Grandmama said, "I declare, Quince, that Fleets seems to be doing you a world of good." "It's powerful stuff, all right," he agreed, "That time I heard ice tinkling in the commode."

At the time of this episode Uncle Travis was still a bachelor, but that status eventually changed. He was almost thirty when he got married. I vaguely remember his courtship on the eve of World War II. Daddy and Uncle Quince knew the moment they met Clera that their younger brother had done something indisputably right. The surgical removal of a carbuncle from the index finger of her right hand had resulted in the nail growing downward over the tip. Her explanation for this phenomenon, however, was a work of imagination that delighted the cognoscente. It was the result, she explained, of having spent her formative years poking holes in hot biscuits in order to fill them with Blue Ribbon syrup. Aunt Clera's ability to improvise a first-class lie was probably the most important item in her dowry. It conferred instant status within the family, something other spouses earned more painstakingly.

Hot biscuits never lost an argument in a Lowman household, where food was a matter of consummate interest. The ice cream season, also, was unusually long. The passion for custard, frozen or unfrozen, is best illustrated by a tale told on Uncle Harmon when, in the 1940s he was president of the college at Huntsville. At the time he stood about five-ten and weighed about two fifty. He was . . . rotund. His weight was a formidable challenge to Aunt Marguerite's perseverance, itself a thing of awesome dimension. She left the house one afternoon with strict instructions for Uncle Harmon to stay out of the kitchen. Her instructions, by the way, were always strict. She was a Hightower and it is common knowledge that Hightowers never waver.

Uncle Harmon woke from his nap ravenously hungry. Like Oscar Wilde he decided that the only way to deal with temptation was to yield to it. He made a beeline for the refrigerator, opened the door and surveyed the contents. His attention was arrested by a half gallon pitcher on the top shelf. The contents had the color and consistency of boiled custard. Hot damn! Simultaneous with this incredibly fortuitous discovery came the fateful crunch of tires on gravel—Marguerite back from her meeting. Uncle Harmon seized the pitcher in both hands, turned it to his lips and chug-a-lugged half the mixture before pausing to catch his breath and savor the delectable taste of . . . waffle batter.

Food was never consumed in the Lowman household without a blessing that has been in use by at least some part of each generation since Great-grandpa's time. His version went like this: "Our gracious Father. Make us humbly and truly thankful for each and all our blessings. Pardon and forgive our sins. Save us in heaven. For Christ's sake, Amen." Daddy used much the same blessing, turning it into a fast mumble which more closely resembled a witch doctor's chant than a petition to the Almighty. I was out of high school before I knew what "F' cry secka men" was.

Daddy was not the archetypical Lowman; there was no such animal. Nonetheless, certain family characteristics seemed somehow magnified in his personality, perhaps because his formal education ended at high school and he remained a farmer like his forebears. His mercurial temperament alternated between an easy laugh and a hair trigger temper. As a farmer his outlook was a compound of hope and desperation in equal measure. Never much interested in innovation, he relished the tried and true: old times, old friends and old values such as integrity, loyalty and a full day's work.

He wasn't afraid of his children. He never worried about his household popularity rating. One knew where he stood. There were few options and no begging, pleading, beseeching or cajoling. Once, in his early teens, my brother Ted was sent to perform a particular task according to Daddy's specific direction. Alas, Ted had a vision all his own, and when Daddy came to inspect progress, there were explanations to be given. "But Daddy, I thought. . . . " "You can stop right there," interrupted Daddy. "Now I know what went wrong."

My fondest boyhood memories are of Daddy and his two older brothers spinning the most hilarious stories around the most trivial events. There was nothing economical in their style of telling. The emphasis was on levity, not brevity, and the imagination, skill and plausibility with which one applied the embellishment. Storytelling was interrupted as one or another of them would interject a particular that seemed to fit. When the trialogue was finished, one could all but see them mentally stepping back to survey their creation before exploding in laughter that soon turned to coughing and choking. When the commotion subsided Uncle Quince—whether the tale was his or someone else's—would reassure the skeptics by saying, "And that's a true story."

I can vouch for this next tale because I was there. In 1946 Daddy was an honorary pallbearer at his aunt's funeral. About ten days later, on a Sunday afternoon, Aunt Nunnie's daughter, Orena Cliver and her invalid husband, drove up for a visit. I had witnessed their arrival from my front bedroom window and told Daddy of his cousin's appearance. He met her halfway down the sidewalk with a hug and a kiss.

At this point, he spotted Mr. Cliver sitting in the car, and remembered that a stroke had left the man either unable to walk or unable to talk. Oh my God, which was it? If the man were unable to talk, he still must be invited in, but if he were unable to walk, it would be tactless to do so. There was an awkward pause as Daddy frantically searched his memory.

The pause lengthened. Time died. The world was consumed in deafening silence. Suddenly Daddy heard a strange voice—unrecognizable, although it came from his own mouth. With dazzling savoir faire the voice inquired: "Orena, how's your Mama?" She looked at him as if he were absolutely crazy. "Why, Fred, we just buried Mama ten days ago."

Daddy could hardly wait for company to leave so he could tell that one on himself. So what was Mr. Cliver's disability, could he not walk or not talk? I swear before Almighty God I cannot remember.

Without a doubt Uncle Quince had more presence of mind than Daddy did. He also had an Irish Setter named Ranger whose utter brainlessness and complete worthlessness was redeemed by total loyalty. While Quince recovered from a heart attack in 1948, the dog seldom moved from the foot of his bed. The year before, Daddy and his brother had bought the old Petty farm on the river between Martindale and Staples. After two or three years Daddy sold his interest to Quince who became sole owner. It was his weekend retreat and Ranger's. Around 1953 an unexpected rain interrupted the great drought of 1947-57. Uncle Quince and Ranger were out surveying the effects.

The morning calm was broken by the approach of a car—Uncle Harmon and Aunt Marguerite en route from Staples where they had stayed overnight. They were dressed fit to kill because Harmon had an important appointment later that morning in Austin. Spotting brother Quince they pulled to the edge of the road to chat a minute, but neither got out of the car. Ranger, older but never wiser, was chasing butterflies from one mudhole to the next. In a moment Aunt Marguerite, in the driver's seat, opened the door for some reason now forgotten. To Ranger an open door meant one thing: get in and go. He barreled through the biggest puddle in sight and plopped himself, panting and drooling, across Aunt Marguerite's lap, his muddy forepaws extending to Uncle Harmon's right trouser leg. His tail wagged happily in the narrow crevice between the steering wheel and Aunt Marguerite's bosom. His lustrous eyes gleamed with affection as his tongue traced the contours of Uncle Harmon's face.

The ordinary pet owner would have been aghast, mortified, filled with apology. But Quince knew an apology would be like turning a garden hose on the Chicago fire. Instantly he quipped, "Marguerite, I know where you can get another one just like him." Within a year Ranger had mysteriously disappeared. Uncle Quince maintained, and Daddy agreed, that their sister-in-law had stolen him for her very own.

In the fall of 1952 I entered Southwest Texas College at San Marcos, while continuing to live at home. I had been enrolled for several semesters when Daddy summoned me one Saturday morning to drive the pickup as we toured the 600-acre pasture. All went well until I noticed a small cedar post, scarcely larger in diameter than a stave, lying across the road. Obviously it had fallen from a cedar cutter's truck. I could have driven around it, but it posed no obstacle, and I saw no harm in driving over it. I couldn't have been more wrong. "Why in hell did you run over that cedar post?"

"But Daddy," I protested, "I only hit it with three wheels." "Well, now that's mighty God-damned fine," he boomed. "There's not one in a million who knows how to hit a post with three wheels. Would you mind telling me where you learned that trick? What course would I have to sign up for? I didn't know this college recruited faculty that could teach such crap."

His outburst had been a thing of beauty and has remained a joy to this day. The diatribe had continued at such length and with such passion that his voice betrayed unmistakable pride in his ability to sustain the rhetoric. He waited for a response. Suddenly I felt it might be safe to goad him a little. With mock gravity I calmly remarked, "I didn't learn that in school. That's natural born talent. Just goes to show how a college education brings out innate ability in people."

By this time he could hardly keep a straight face. His last word on the subject was a fervent "Damn!" Irritated at first by my indifference to his peevishness, he was now secretly delighted to have a new anecdote for his repertoire, an anecdote to be repeated again and again in the short time left to him. Even today, when a family member needs to minimize disaster of his own making, the response is predictable: "But I only hit it with three wheels"—as if it could have been worse. Occasionally an individual will presume to take satisfaction in a job that is less than well done—like the kid who comes home from school pretending to be pleased as punch at having made sixty on a freshman biology quiz when the highest grade in class was only 95. Then the response becomes an accusation, *i.e.*, "Sounds to me like you hit it with three wheels."

Those who did not understand Daddy might have detected a virulent strain of anti-intellectualism in his outburst. Not so. Indeed some of his best friends were college professors. By way of explanation—not defense, mind you—he seemed to reason this way: any person of average intelligence and honest intention had little alternative, when confronted with a choice, but to identify with the Democratic Party. Only those who were mentally deficient or mean in spirit would conclude otherwise. In those days most of the college faculty at San Marcos had, in his view, made the proper affiliation. Ergo they were persons of character, sound judgment and unassailable integrity.

This is not to say that Daddy lacked Republican friends. Man cannot survive by bread alone; he must have argument. Consequently these Republicans likely had more than their share of invitations to supper. Perhaps there was a streak of masochism buried in their psyche. Had Daddy not relied on the same rote table grace used in previous generations, he might have been inspired to improvise a prayer for their salvation before breaking bread. Make no mistake, though. He regarded his Republican associates fondly, much like the good shepherd whose lamb has strayed, like a family member unable to resist the baneful influence of alcohol. There was no one Daddy esteemed more than his Uncle Lewey Lowman, whose very existence was fueled by whiskey. Fortunately he did not carry the added burden of Republicanism. One such affliction, in Daddy's view, was enough. Well. Daddy was right about some things.

If a good story could be made from the circumstances, death itself would not spare an old Staples boy from being the butt of a joke. In 1954 Bill Sherrill dropped dead of a heart attack late one afternoon as he stood with his foot on the running board of his pickup. The day after the funeral Daddy stopped for coffee at the Swing Inn Cafe on the circle in San Marcos. The manager was Butch Carlyle from Staples, of course. With the coffee poured, something was said about Bill Sherrill's fatal heart attack. Butch appeared to be greatly agitated. "It was all my fault," he said remorsefully. "What do you mean?" Daddy asked. Feigning to grope for words Butch stammered, "I feel like . . . if I'd been there . . . I could have talked old Bill out of it."

Like his father before him, Daddy's death from pancreatic cancer in 1956 came at the low ebb of his fortunes. Drouth had nearly wiped him out. In my admittedly prejudiced view, both of these men fit a description supplied once by W. H. Hutchinson. "They were individuals with individual responsibility for their own actions, and if in the end the hand life dealt them was a busted flush, they did their damndest to make it stand up against all odds." And, as I've pointed out to my children, that's not a bad heritage to look back on.

The times I have described are gone; those who lived them are about all gone, too. The other evening I phoned Cecil Howard at Pleasant Ridge to verify some dates in this material. He answered on the seventh ring: " . . . LO?" (Cuz never puts the hell in hello, and the last syllable is always a question.). I identified myself and asked him what he was doing. "Settin' out in the backyard. But I'm telling you, son, you gotta let this phone ring way longer than you once did."

Ain't it so.

Bill Warren of the Big Thicket/*Campbell & Lynn Loughmiller*

Big Sandy Creek in the Big Thicket
credit F. E. Abernethy

Bill Warren
of the Big Thicket

Campbell & Lynn Loughmiller

During the 'sixties Campbell and Lynn Loughmiller roamed the Big
Thicket. They learned the land and they learned the people, and their
contribution to the cultural history of the area was published in a
book called *Big Thicket Legacy* (Austin: University of Texas Press,
1977). The book is a collection of taped interviews of Thicket old
timers who tell about their own times and their families' times living
in and off that particular piece of Texas wilderness. The following interview with Bill Warren consists of stories left out of *Big Thicket
Legacy*. It is personal narrative and family saga told with the true
sound of the Big Thicket.
Editor

Introduction to W. A. (Bill) Warren   August 1892-April 1974

Bill Warren spent his life in the Thicket. As a young boy he helped
his daddy literally cut and hack their way into high ground on a little
ridge between Black Creek and Pine Island Bayou.

No one told a story better than Bill Warren. It was effortless and
natural, his timing and emphasis superb. He spoke with boyish enthusiasm for his stories centered around his boyhood experiences—
ordinary events from the fabric of daily living. It was almost like
being with him in the woods as he told of hunting turkeys, chasing
bobcats, or stumbling on to a bear's den—experiences he enjoyed between chores on the farm.

The fourth generation still lives on this little ridge, essentially un-
changed since the first clearing made way for the original homestead,
with a few cultivated acres of corn, peanuts, sweet potatoes and ribbon cane. The Warrens maintained an attractive homesite, surrounded by a five foot fence that had good gates and giant pecan
trees growing just outside. In the beginning it was with great physical
exertion that the Warrens hacked their way into this remote area, but

its appeal to each generation makes it even more difficult to leave.

W. A. (Bill) Warren

My mother was a little girl when they come to Liberty County from Tennessee, somewhere over there, I think. Whittington was my mother's name. The Malinda Whittington tract of land over there in Liberty County, at Devers, was the land they got when they first come to this country. They give 'em a league and a labor. The Hollands was kin on her side. I don't have no kin on my daddy's side. There was three boys, but two of 'em died.

We come here from Devers, and that was over fifty years ago. That house over there is where my daddy and mother lived.

We have four boys and two girls. We been awful lucky—our whole family livin', livin' right 'round us here.

My daddy got me to buy the first ten acres I got out here. I said, "I ain't got no use for no land," boy-like, ya'know. Papa said, "Well, ya'better go buy it. You'll see the day ya'will." So I went over there and bought the first ten acres for one hundred dollars. That was over sixty-five years ago. The other twenty cost a little bit more. But land's just got away from us. A fella asked me the other day what I'd take for it. I said, "I wouldn't price it 'tall. You can't go out and pick ya'a place now like ya' used to. You used to pick the place ya'wanted and might near pay your own price. We picked the highest, best land.

Folks here have always hunted. We'd bring in what we killed, skin it—women folks jump in and help us. We'd cut it up and put it on the roof there, or build a scaffold and put a smoke under it, cook it slow with a little fire and smoke. We smoked lots of meat and it's awful good, too. Dry it and make hash out of it. Cut it across the grain to make it tender. Oh, it was good.

Now I've been huntin' all my life and always lived where there was plenty to hunt. When I was a boy, my daddy butchered four of them old big hawgs one evenin' and hung them over to cool. The next mornin' he got up about four o'clock, and he was goin' to work on his hawgs. I was just a boy, ya'know, just a small boy, big enough to shoot, and I said, "Papa, let's go cat huntin'." He said, "Aw, the devil, boy, I've got to cut up my hawgs; I ain't got time to fool with you." I said, "Oh, yeah, but it won't take but a while; let's go." He loved to hunt, and he said, "Well, I might go a little while with ya', but I've got to come back and go to cuttin' up my hawgs."

We walked down a ole road, and there was palmettos in there that was ten feet high, grow a big body like a palm, but not as tall. Few of them would be three feet around. That was in Liberty County. We walked down the old road, didn't strike a trail, and he said, "I got to get back and go to cuttin' up my hawgs." I said, "I'll circle these palmettos and if I don't strike, I'll be up ta'help ya'." He said, "All right."

So I went in there, and I had about four dogs, and they was pretty vicious. I thought they'd catch anything. One of those old dogs commenced barkin', and I said, "My word, I didn't think them dogs was afraid of anything." They was scared; they run to me. And I had a big spotted dog I thought would catch anything I told him to catch. He understood ya' just like a man; we called him Talker. I said, "Catch'im Talker." And he run under those palmetto fans and squatted down on the ground like a cat or somethin', and he wheeled back, and he come back by me so fast—he didn't even stop when he got to me. I said, "My goodness, Old Talker seen a bugger in there." I had a little old single-barrel gun, ya'know, and I got down on my belly and I crawled toward where that dog turned back, and I was layin' there lookin' and I made out three biiig animals bedded up, just about fifteen feet from me. I looked at'em, at the nose and hair and everything, ya'know, tryin' to see what they was. I'd never seen a bear, but I said, "Them must be bear." My daddy had hunted bear a lot, but I was just a boy—had never been bear huntin'. "Well," I said, "I'll just shoot'em." I was layin' flat, wasn't on my hunkers. I was layin' flat, lookin' under them palmettos, ya'know, and I just slid the gun out in front of me and set it agin' the top of my shoulder, layin' flat, pushed it agin' my shoulder and shot right in the middle of'em. And boy, they took out of there and I commenced to whoopin' to the dogs. I had one little bitty dog. He was the first one taken off. He went to screamin' and away they went.

Well I jumped up, didn't have anything but fine shot then. I'd done shot my buckshot, the only buckshot I had, and I taken after them dogs with that fine shot. The dogs run off and directly I heard them comin' right straight back, and I heard that thing hittin' them palmettos goin' through, but I couldn't see'im, and they passed by me and went back towards home. Well I was after'em just as hard as I could go. They passed between the house and the field, through the palmetto swamp, and my oldest brother was out there. He said, "Wait a minute, them dogs is comin' back with that cat." I said, "Cat your foot, that's the biggest bear you ever seen in your life." He said, "A bear!" I said, "Shore, I done shot'im."

And here they went after every gun and every horse. They jumped on the horses and my daddy, he was a little late, and he didn't get nare gun, taken off on his horse after them bear dogs without a gun. We had a pile of old rails, what we made fence out of, split rails. This old bear went right up on them rails and looked at my daddy, and he said, "Look out there, Cap, you can't go that-away." The bear jumped down and the way he went, them dogs after'im, ya'know, and run over my brother, one of my little brothers. He was about the same size as me; we was just like twins. He had a shotgun and he killed that one.

My daddy said, "Well, where's your'n?" I said, "That's him." He said, "No that ain't the one you shot; that's the young bear." I said, "Whoooeee, they ever get bigger'n that?" "Oh yes," he said, "that's not a big bear. You shot the big'un, just like ya' said. We're goin'ta take the dogs and go back."

Well, we taken that one in and taken the dogs and went back and the dogs went to bayin', and we all went up there like a army with our guns all ready, ya'know. And when we walked up there, there was a bear a layin' there as big as a shetland pony, and I'd killed that thing! With one little old shot! I hit her in the soft part in the flank, and it went anglin' through. It didn't hit any bones or anything, and it killed her. I never will forget when I crawled in there and first saw her, and that thing looked at me, and me layin' there on the ground not fifteen feet away. I don't know why she didn't jump on me. Papa said, "It's a wonder she didn't eat you up." They say when you shoot a bear's cub and the cub bellers, the old bear will kill anything she can get to. My daddy said if I'd shot one of the cubs, and he bellered, the old bear woulda killed me, shore.

We sold that old big bear and the hides; sold the old bear to a lumber company store. They wanted to sell it out to their customers, the meat, ya'know. We divided the young one up with the people that never had eat no bear meat. That bear meat is good. It's the only meat that won't make you sick, no matter; you can eat all of it you want, and it won't make you sick, and you can drink a cupful of bear grease and it won't make you sick.

My daddy mostly hunted deer and bear and he loved to run cat, always did. Daddy said one time he was comin' in from huntin' by hisself, and he had two dogs and the dogs had run deer until they were plumb burnt out. They wouldn't even run a deer if they saw one. They were just tired out. He was goin' down the old trail home, and all at once them dogs just busted ahead of'im just like they was fresh dogs, and just taken off arunnin'. He taken after the dogs, knew it wasn't a deer, and they treed. There was a big bunch of briars around a old leanin' tree, ya'know, and one of the dogs was barkin' there at the briars where the thing went up the tree. He had a eight gauge, double barrel that fired forty-two buck shot to the barrel. My daddy looked up there, and there was a young bear a settin' up there in the tree. Well he just raised up that old gun and fired on'im and he tumbled out and rared up, and daddy was afraid he'd kill a dog, and he just give'im the other barrel.

Well, just then he heard somethin' behind him. He looked 'round, and the old mama bear was on her hind feet, just like a nigger, just as close as you are, comin' on her hind feet, with her front feet drawed back and her ears layin' back on'er head, and just a comin' for my daddy. He said he just taken that old big gun and hit her across the head just as hard as he could with it, and about the time he hit her, the young dog grabbed the bear by the heel, and she wheeled on the dog. My daddy grabbed his old gun and broke and run, and the bear run back there and muttered over that cub a little and she taken off. Well he reloaded and taken after her. Directly daddy heard'em comin' back through one of them palmetto sloughs and he got ready. As she came by he shot her with one barrel, and she turned a somerset and jumped up and he shot her again, and she still kept goin'. They're pretty hard to kill, a big bear is, ya'know. And he taken after'em, and directly he heard'em just as far as he could hear'em, they was bayin', and when he got in sight of'em—there was two trees fell together, and the two trees made a awful big clay root, ya'know—one dog was standin' on one log and the other one the other, lookin' between them logs, bayin'. He went 'round behind this big clay root, and there was vines and briars on the clay root, and he taken his old gun and kinda poked it through there, and she was set-tin' up there between them two logs with her feet drawed back, and she'd slap at one dog and he'd jump back, and she'd slap at the other, and he'd jump back, and she was just as bloody as she could be where pa'd shot her. And so he just taken that old gun and parted them vines a little bit and shot that load right in the back a'her head, and she just tumbled over and put that foot up there where that load hit, and just tumbled over on her head.

Ya'know, if a bear gets crippled, there ain't nothin' he won't kill that he can get to, and they're fast. They got such a strong scent, a dog can foller'em and not even foller the trail, just run for all that's in'em, and that bear still stay ahead of'em. A bear goes straight and so fast, he'll outrun a horse in them woods. Sometimes a bear will climb a tree, but most a'the time they just bay in the thicket.

Old man Oscar Middlebrook, over at Livingston, wanted to go with Papa to kill a bear. Oh, he'd just give anything if he could kill a bear. So they went huntin' and the dogs rounded this bear up in a real tight thicket, and went to bayin' it. And Papa said, "Now if you want to kill ya'a bear, well just crawl in there where them dogs is and kill'im." He started off, and he said, "I'm goin' to carry that foot to my wife; this is the first bear I ever killed in my life." Daddy said, "You ain't killed one yet." And he crawled in there a little piece, and directly he come back and said, "Josh," my daddy's name was Josh, "You better go in there; I don't believe I'm goin' in there."

It's risky business, sometimes, you facin' a bear and can't hardly move in that bay-gall thicket, get your gun hung up or your foot tangled in them vines. A lot can happen.

One day we was fixin' to move from our place at Devers. There was a big thicket down through there, and me and my daddy just went up there to camp and cut a road out and get ready to start movin', so we didn't take nothin' up there but one old cur dog. We'd go out there and catch coon at night for fun, ya'know. We was cuttin' that road and that old dog went back in that thicket and went to bayin'. My daddy said, "I wish you'd go out there and knock that coon out for that old dog, stop that fuss." Kinda jokin' with me, ya'know. I went out there and directly I got in sight of that dog, and there was a tree fell, broke off pretty high and fell, and the old log was way up above the brush, ya'know, and that dog was up on that log, lookin' down under it. Well, he had his tail tucked 'tween his hind legs and his hair all turned the wrong way, and I didn't crawl in there. I went out of there just like a quail or somethin'. My daddy said, "Why didn't you knock that coon out and bring the dog back?" I said, "That dog wasn't barkin' at no coon; he was barkin' at a bear." He said, "How do you know it was a bear, did you see it?" I said, "No sir, but I seen that dog, and I seen pictures of dogs barkin' at bear, and that was just like'em. He had his tail tucked 'tween his legs and the hair all turned the wrong way. There's a bear under that log all right." He said, "Well, you walk back home and get my gun, and I'll find out what he's after."

Wasn't nobody lived in that country then, and I was scared until I got that old gun. They used to use eight and ten gauge, and he had an old ten gauge at the time. I went and got that old thing and I put two loads in it. I couldn't hardly hold it up. When I got back this old dog had quit and come back out, and wouldn't go back out there no more.

Well we went on workin'. I was movin' the brush while daddy was cuttin'. We went on out through that thicket, but next day, I guess daddy got to studyin' what I'd said about this dog, and we went back down there to that log in that brush and vines, and he seen a buzzard fly up. He went in there and that old bear was layin' there eatin' on a hawg when he slipped in there and shot him. He'd left part of that hawg there from the day before. We lived at Devers then, and where he shot that bear was between Big Pine Island Bayou and Willard Creek. They used to kill a world of bear in there. It was the biggest sport in the world, bear huntin'. Why they'd come from as far as New York to hunt with Ben Hooks and them fellers, bear huntin'.

I used to get more pleasure out of wild turkey huntin'. We lived in Liberty County, but we had moved in this side of Devers, in where that good huntin' was. Well, there was a bunch of us boys, seven of us when we was all livin', and three girls. My brothers had made me hunt the horses one mornin' while they went turkey huntin'. While I was listenin' for the horse bell—it was in the spring, that's when we hunted them turkey, when they was gobblin'—and I heard one gobble. After I got the horse, I wanted someone to go with me after that turkey, but I didn't want my brothers to know, 'cause they'd made me go after the horses. So I went in and told my daddy, "I'll tell ya'somethin' if you won't tell them other boys." He said, "I won't tell'em; what is it?" I said, "I heard the biggest turkey gobbler this mornin' I ever heard in my life. He must a'been as big as a yearlin' deer." He said, "Well, I won't tell'em. We'll get up at four o'clock in the mornin' and go up there."

Well we went up there and he said, "Now you go right where he gobbled yesterday mornin'." The old pines was real big around. They never had been cut. I went over there before daylight and sat down by that old tree, scared, of course. Woods was full of them bobcats and bear and me imaginin' everything. I listened, and it was just breakin' daylight. My daddy had circled 'round this old turkey, and he heard him walkin', and ya'know that turkey flew and lit in the tree right next to where I was settin'. I jumped and ran to the next tree and kept lookin' up there. I said, "I'm goin' to be sure now, 'cause I got that rascal." And directly I seen him move right in the top of that big old pine. I raised up and shot him out, and that thing was so fat he busted his gobble when he hit the ground. You know that big gobble under his neck, ya'know, where his beard comes out, a long beard just like hair that comes out in front of his breast. It's all fat, must have somethin' to do with that noise he makes. You can hear'em half-a-mile. That turkey weighed twenty-four pounds, just the fattest, finest gobbler you can imagine. Papa said he believed that was the finest turkey he ever saw in his life. They roosted in them old pines there, them old bi-----g pines; they never had cut a one of'em. Lots of times turkeys like to roost in the bottom, and they like to roost over the creeks, in hardwoods. I've got more pleasure out of turkey huntin', I think, than any huntin' I ever done.

We moved our hawgs from Devers up in here and we had to kill them varmits, ya'know, and cat and bear was the worst thing on our hawgs. Wolves was awful bad. I've heard'em howlin', whooooo, seemed like fifteen or twenty in a bunch, all howlin' the same time—big old grey wolves. I know one time me and my daddy come from Devers and he told me to stay on the road and wait for him at the gully, and he'd go through the woods. When I got there I seen two little turkeys run off. I stayed there'till he come, and I told him I seen two turkeys run off there, and he said, "Well, we'll camp right here and in the mornin' I'll get one of'em." It looked like two gobblers, ya'know. So we camped there and next mornin', way before daylight, he told me I could get out there and listen. I was there before daylight and he was gone off up in the woods somewhere, left me there and I tell ya', just a little ways from me it seemed like there was twenty wolves. All the howlin' I ever heard, just a yappin' and howlin', all them wolves, ya'know, and me in there at that camp by myself. And when the wolves would howl, the turkey would gobble, ya'know. While the wolves was a howlin' the turkeys went to gobblin', and I got my old gun and went out there and I got it up side of one of them big old pines. That turkey was off as far as them woods down yonder, but I was scared to try to get in that thicket to 'em, and I just put it up by the tree and aimed it at'em and fired, but he was too far off. If my daddy'd a'been there, he would'a killed'im. But them wolves, whooo, them wolves was in there, my goodness alive! They aren't bad about attacking a person, but they say they been known to do it.

I'd rather hunt cat than anything. A cat might dodge 'round in a circle, run his same track. When me and my brother used to shoot'em, there was a lot of'em in here, lots of'em, and they was bad on pigs. Well, when the dogs jumped a wildcat we'd run as hard as we could and get right where the dogs passed and lie down, 'cause the cat would come back on that same trail. We'd see which one could kill him first. We shot them with fine shot 'cause daddy wouldn't let us use buckshot, might kill one another, it was so thick, ya'know.

One time I heard my brother a yellin' and the dogs a barkin'. The gun went off over there and I never heard such a racket. I jumped up and broke as hard as I could over there, and this old cat had run to where he could see'im, and he stopped and looked at'im. He was on a little knoll, my brother was, lookin' in under that palmetto, and that old cat seen'im. My brother shot'im with that squirrel shot, and that old cat made for'im just as hard as he could. My brother had a single barrel, and he didn't have no more shot, and that cat went after'im, and he throwed his hat at 'im, went to hollerin', and the dogs got there and caught the cat. Those dogs knew what a cat was and they'd run in and catch'im and kill'im. A dog that didn't know what a cat was would probably be afraid of'im. He can take them hind feet and he can rip a dog open, ya'know, and catch'em with their fore feet and bite'em. A cat is a bad fighter. I've seen them cat jump for eight or ten feet and land right on a dog's back. Oh, it's great sport when they get to runnin' in a little circle on, say, one acre of ground, ever' dog a screamin' for all that's in'im, and that old cat just goin' 'round and 'round.

Daddy wanted to kill out them cats 'cause they's so bad to get his pigs. And they eat fawns bad, cats do, and you can't have quail or turkey where they's lots of wildcat. They caught one right over in my pasture the other day. They're bad things, them bobcats is.

Bobcats will attack a man. My daddy was attacked three different times by'em. My daddy and uncle went huntin' up on Willow Creek. They separated and daddy come to some old stoopin' post oaks, round the edge of the swamp, and there was a dozen squirrels in'em and they was all a barkin'. And when you hear squirrels barkin', there's a bugger there; they're barkin' at somethin'. A crow is another thing that will find a bugger and tell ever'body. And you should watch out then, there's somethin' there. And these squirrels was up there just a raisin' a fuss, but he didn't have nothin' in mind but a deer, ya'know. The palmettos in that swamp was so thick you couldn't see, and he kept slippin' up until he got under those old stoopin' post oaks. He had a big rifle and he was lookin' for that deer to come out, 'cause when he come out of that swamp he'd be in the piney woods where you could see'im. He was just standin' there lookin' and listenin' for that deer to come out of the palmetto, and he heard a growl. Now they can growl like a lion, these bobcats can. I've had them growl at me. So he looked up and the thing was about eight feet over his head, layin' up there on that old post oak. That's what the squirrels was barkin' at. He had his hind feet hooked to that tree, like you've seen a squirrel; and his front feet just pressin' against the body of it, and he said his ears was just workin' backwards and forth, right over his head, ready to drop on'im. He just throwed his big rifle up and shot him right in the chest, and the thing fell right at his feet. They're sorta like rattlesnakes, they'll growl before they attack. They've got the most vicious growl I ever heard.

There was a feller come here one time and offered Floyd, that's my son, five hundred dollars a'piece for five of his dogs if he'd let him pick'em, and Floyd said he wouldn't let nobody pick his dogs. It's his only sport, ya'know, and he wouldn't part with his dogs. Oh, my lord, he's got some of the best cat dogs there is.

The best cat dog is redbone-bluetick. They're good varmint dogs. Some of'em is slow, and you don't want a dog that's slow. He needs to get up and run. We don't use many Walker dogs. They're really wolf and fox dogs. Sometimes they don't bark enough for me, and they run awfully fast for deer.

Cat dogs bark more when they're close to the cat. Closer he gets the more he barks. They'll get to where they'll holler just like somethin' caught'em, just squealin' when they're close, like people was beatin'em with sticks.

My daddy caught a deer with his hands once, eight point buck, and he hadn't been shot. There used to be a lot of cypress vines in here; the deer would feed on'em. This deer got a roll of those cypress vines as big as your leg around his horns, and my daddy run up there and grabbed him by the horns. He had another fella with'im. My daddy was a big, tall man, awful stout, and he helt that deer while that fella kept tryin' to get 'round to cut his throat. Finally, daddy told'im. "If you don't hamstring that deer, I'm gonna turn it loose." The deer was fightin' and everythin' else, and my daddy just holdin' him by the horns. This fella run 'round behind him and cut his ham strings, dropped him down behind. Daddy helt that deer so long he couldn't straighten out his arms for half an hour.

People used to hunt deer with a light. A deer won't run from a light. You can walk right up there and shoot it. It won't run from you no more than a cow, with a light. The law is awful strict on that now. I haven't had my light on my head for twenty years. I used to kill'em with a light when I had my whole family here, a bunch of little children, but I don't think people should do that because they kill the does, and kill them away from the fawns, and all that kinda stuff, and that's bad!

I've had lots of cow dogs, some of the best cow dogs I ever saw. We used to handle cattle all the way from here to Honey Island. We gathered those wild cows all out of this thicket. I had two of the best cow dogs I ever saw. We'd gather all them cattle that belonged to our neighbors and us, we'd get them all together—and Arthur Gray was buying for three or four packing houses in Houston. We'd have a date with'im and he'd come out and buy'em. We'd have to get on our horses and go round up all of them cattle, maybe we'd be on our horses two weeks, and drive them to China; that's this side of Beau-mont. We'd go up to China and load them on the train for'im.

A cow dog can be worth more than three or four riders. He ain't goin' to let n'airn cow leave. If they start to leave, they'll catch'em by the nose. They won't all catch'em, but they make that cow think they're goin' to, and she'll go get back in the bunch.

I bought a bunch of cattle—I believe there was fourteen of'em—bought them cattle for four hundred dollars right out in the woods where they stayed. Well I went down there to get'em. Old Lim Jordan was the man that was with me and some more riders. So we went down there and the dogs just went rounded'em up, ya'know. We just rode in there and the cattle just stood there. If one started to run off, they'd make him come back. Before we started Lim said, "I oughta brought my Winchester." I said, "What do you want with your Winchester, Lim?" He says, "To kill that old red beef of mine. That's the worst animal I ever seen in my life." I said, "I don't know." I knew what my dogs would do, ya'know. So we went down there and rounded up them cattle, and was drivin'em along, us ridin' along behind, the dogs up there lopin' round, watchin'em. I had a big old wild cow there; she throwed up her head to run and Lim said, "Good-bye, Joe Baygall." She headed for the thicket to get away, ya'know. I said, "Just let her go"—didn't want nobody take after her. Boy, them dogs caught that old cow, turned her 'round and when she got back in that bunch, I tell you she didn't leave it no more. Lim said, "Well, I've owned dogs, and hunted dogs all my life, and I didn't know what a dog could do." We never had to strike a lope.

We never let nobody use our dogs for rabbits or deer or nothin' like that, because we didn't want to run'em with those dogs. The cur is the best for cattle. He can be trained to do anything.

A Tale of Not So Long Ago/*June R. Welch*

Lucian Thompson Owens (1848–1933)

A Tale of the
Not So Long Ago

June R. Welch

In the olden times, when the 5¢ double dip ice cream cone was the biggest thing going, I used to visit my aunt and uncle each summer in Oklahoma. Auntie was my grandmother's sister; she and Uncle had raised my mother and were of great age. They had no children of their own, and the babies they adopted died young.

Uncle had been a deputy sheriff and one of the high points of my visit was the possibility of seeing the scar on his leg left by a bullet wound. Not long after they married he had come home for lunch one day; being young and foolish and wanting to impress Auntie, he tried to jump the front yard fence. He failed to clear the pickets, and as he fell his .45 went off and shot him through the thigh.

I remember the feeling Uncle had for a Frontier model Colt which he cared for and kept with him. I used to think it was the same revolver involved in the accident, but the one he treasured was a different pistol; it had belonged to Auntie's father, Lucian Owens, the marshal at Decatur.

Auntie was a great talker. In fact, she talked much of the time. (I used to say I could go outside while she was talking and return after playing awhile to find her still holding forth. This was probably an exaggeration.) At the time I believed I was not hearing much of that conversation; fortunately, I was mistaken. I am terribly beholden to her, for she spoke of the days long gone and made me know that the telling of tales was important. (That may be a principal reason for my writing about the past.) And I am grateful, too, that much of Auntie's talk concerned her father, Marshal Owens.

I saw Owens once on a long ago Sunday. My folks had taken me to see him because he was my mother's grandfather and because he had been a Confederate soldier, a Texas Ranger, and a frontier marshal. His daughters idolized him—Auntie and Grandmom and Aunt Cora. My mother talked about him all the way from Gainesville to Decatur, which was a substantial forty-mile trip by gravel road in a black Model A Ford.

As we drove up I saw a big man of great age sitting on his front porch in a rocking chair. He wore a white gunfighter's moustache, black boots, and a wide-brimmed black hat. The old man asked my name and age. He had trouble hearing my answer, provoking a long exchange as one of his daughters leaned over and shouted into his ear explanations of which grandchild had borne me. His expression evidenced dismay that he had caused so much commotion about such an insignificant subject. Finally he seemed to have satisfied whatever small curiosity I had aroused. He never smiled, and that worried me, for I took the expression to reflect dislike.

I explored the storm cellar, pitched rocks into the well that had not been used since Owens tied onto the Decatur water system, and aggravated the chickens. My mother came regularly to the back door to monitor my activities and to caution me about maintaining my appearance.

The occasion was a family gathering of some sort. Cousins previously unmet were present; one older than the rest led several of us around to the front yard and tried to impress the old man with demonstrations of centrifugal force. The cousin ran water into a bucket and swung it in a great circle. We of tender years marvelled that the water remained in place although a portion of the arc was high above his head. It was an inspiring performance.

I was perhaps five years old and unacquainted with centrifugal force. Even that older cousin who used it so well was not aware of its name or properties. He simply explained that the water remained fixed in the bucket because of "the slingin' around."

The old man watched from beneath the damaged brim of the black hat, mildly intrigued, but showing no emotion. My mother—perhaps unaware that she was repeating herself—appeared on the front porch and warned once more against my becoming disheveled. Soon after her departure I was invited to try the water bucket trick.

Everyone backed away. I did as the cousin had done, but with a significant difference; I lacked confidence in centrifugal force. As the bucket neared the top of the circle I hesitated and realized an unfortunate result. I was drenched. Despite warnings from grown people who knew best and had my interests at heart, my appearance was marred.

Now, the immediate lesson was that an unbeliever should not try to employ centrifugal force. Later I would understand that there was a broader principle involved: unless one truly believes in a thing, one is apt to misuse it, and then experiencing a bad result he will probably feel betrayed.

But I did not know all that then, in that sodden moment. I was aware only of my cousins' blinding speed; in an instant they had all disappeared. My mother was grasping my wet sleeve with more pressure than was reasonably necessary. In fact, she was handling me rudely and without sympathy. The only redeeming feature of that dreadful transaction was that as I was dragged past him for repairs, the old man smiled.

Lucian Thompson Owens, born in Kentucky, came to Wise County at a tender age. After service as a sixteen-year-old Confederate soldier he married a girl with Cherokee blood named Tennessee Gift Barnes—the gift they got in Tennessee, I guess. As a member of a ranging company Owens pursued, among others, the war party which massacred the Babbs and carried away their children. In his last years he drew a pension for ranger service in the Indian wars. (On his application, which had been designed for use by veterans of wars with battles which had names, in the space inquiring where he had fought, Owens wrote simply, "wherever the trail led.")

Not long after Quanah Parker took his Quahadi Comanche onto the reservation at Fort Sill—still only a little more than a hundred years ago—Owens became a peace officer in Wise County. He bought a new six-shooter, a .45 caliber Frontier model Colt that became his proudest possession. Trail herds passed through the neighborhood bound for Abilene, Kansas. A fair number of badmen sojourned in and around Decatur, perhaps accounting for that shameful (although traditional) call in a venerable game of chance involving the casting of dice: "Eighter from Decatur." (And the response "County seat of Wise.")

Much effort was required to preserve the civilization recently set down in Wise County, and Owens devoted himself and the pistol to that task. In the meantime his family was increasing, and Tennessee was raising the children alone. His absences from home were frequent and extended as he trailed malefactors and escorted convicted felons by horseback to the penitentiary. (Tennessee's daughters, in their old age, would speak of her beauty and grace and goodness, of how at night when she took her hair down she could sit on the ends of it.) There were troubles. Owens' house burned, and a new one had to be built. A child died.

One day responsible citizens of Sunset, Texas, solicited Owens' help. A gang led by two brothers was harassing their town, which was just across the line in Montague County, outside his jurisdiction. Owens buckled on the six-shooter and rode up to Sunset to meet the gang. (I will call the leaders the Archers, although that was not their name.)

In that classic scene played out a thousand times in movies and television, one afternoon Owens faced the gang on the main—perhaps the only—street. As the Archers tried to ride him down, Owens shot one brother and dragged the other off his horse. Using the man as a shield Owens backed into a corner outside the depot and through the window he shouted for the telegraph operator to wire Dan Waggoner for help. Waggoner, who once had been a partner of Owens, would found one of the great ranching and oil fortunes. (Three buildings dominate the Decatur skyline: the old Decatur Baptist College administration building—which has housed a museum since the school was relocated on Mountain Creek Lake as Dallas Baptist College, the Wise County courthouse, and the Waggoner house.)

Dan Waggoner ordered a flat car hooked onto a locomotive, recruited a couple of dozen well-armed and fun-loving souls, and hurried from Decatur to Sunset to extricate Owens from his perilous situation and bring in his prisoner. Later, Mrs. Archer, perhaps deranged because of the death of one son and the incarceration of another, came to Owens' home one evening. She had a pistol in her purse and intended to kill Owens, but he managed to persuade her otherwise.

Tennessee died in childbirth. The older children cared for the younger ones. They got married, as children will do. Owens did not permit such frivolities to take him away from business and probably he did not attend the wedding of any of his children. And I doubt if any of them were present when he remarried.

Uncle told me about coming down to Decatur from Davis, Indian Territory, to ask Owens' permission to marry his daughter, Rebecca Jane—Jenny. During the trip a couple of drunken louts had made life disagreeable for the other passengers. When the train stopped at Decatur Uncle saw Owens, wearing his star and standing in the door of the depot; he met all the trains. One of the rowdies began a conversation with Owens and the other picked up a rock large enough to require both hands. He hit the marshal in the face with the stone. Uncle said that Owens shuddered for a moment, then he shook his head to clear it. He whacked each of the drunks across the temple with the pistol, and they dropped to the platform. Owens picked up his hat and put it on his bloody head. With one oaf draped across a shoulder, fireman-style, Owens dragged the other off to jail. And Uncle said, "That's the fellow I come to see about marryin' his daughter."

The years passed. The world changed. Owens developed a bad limp from the six-shooter's weight or the cold of the metal on his hip, and his son made a shoulder holster for him. But the time came when he was too old to keep the peace. The frontier had long since closed, and he and the pistol were no longer required to maintain civilization. He had more great-grandchildren than he had grandchildren. Owens sat on his porch and whittled. He went down to the depot to watch the trains come in and go out. The world had filled up with people, and all of them were younger than he was. He read the Bible, pondered Ecclesiastes, noting the Prophet's observations that "A generation passeth away and another cometh, but the earth abideth forever," and "All the rivers run into the sea, yet the sea is not full." Owens considered the phenomena John Kennedy mentioned two generations later, "There is a rhythm to life, and it ebbs and it flows."

He cleaned the six shooter regularly. Put new grips on it. Whenever Mrs. Owens needed a chicken killed he would stand at the back door and decapitate it with a single shot. The pistol linked him with the time when he was useful and there was important work to do. But his eyes were going bad, his hearing was waning, and sometimes his hands were unsteady.

One Sunday company was expected for dinner. Before she trooped off to church Mrs. Owens gave him his instructions. She would need three chickens killed. He sat on the porch for awhile listening to Sunday School children singing in the church across the street, then decided to do his shooting before worship services began —gunshots fit a Decatur Sunday morning badly. Owens took the pistol out of the dresser drawer. From the back step he shot four times before he killed the first chicken. He was so shaken by his poor performance that he gave up on the other two and Mrs. Owens had to wring their necks when she returned from church.

That afternoon the old man gave the six shooter to Uncle, and a few weeks later he died.

Uncle looked upon the pistol much as Owens had. He was of a frontier generation and had been a peace officer too. Uncle kept the gun in the glove compartment of his automobile in case someone attempted to rob him, or trifle with him, or if anybody just needed killing.

When Uncle was full of years he gave the gun to me. It has remained in my safety deposit box ever since, for in my time others have been responsible for maintaining civilization.

Night Horse Nightmare/*Paul Patterson*

Paul Patterson—"some years back"

Night Horse Nightmare

Paul Patterson

Briefly, the scene, setting and stage whereupon is to be enacted a drama of some thirty-six hours duration, not including time out for fretting, fixing flats, and floundering in fogs of frustration.

Cast of Characters: Buster, the leading man—or, rather horse—with Bill Wyatt, Cutter Carpenter, and the horse jingler (me), playing lesser roles in this lop-sided battle of wits, wills, and wiliness.

Opening Scene: Combination kitchen-dining room-den-pantry-bedroom-semi-saddle room and semi-bathroom (i.e., out the window on cold nights) of a typical bachelor's dive on the A. C. Hoover horse ranch lying for some 263 square miles to the south and west of Buena Vista, Texas, west-of-the Pecos.

Time: Around daylight of an April Morning, 1931.

With one exception the entire cast of characters is huddled around the breakfast table, its coffee unsipped, its sowbelly unsampled, and its sorghum syrup unsopped. Though outwardly calm, inwardly pandemonium reigns supreme. Etched deep into each leathery countenance is consternation, not to say dismay. The horse jingler has just bomb-shelled them with the news that the night horse, Buster, has vamoosed, skedaddled (or, if you prefer Bill Wyatt's expression for it, consult the handwriting on the nearest outhouse wall).

As an insight into the gravity of such a situation, never in the annals of horseback history has anybody anywhere heard of an outfit without a night horse corraled and ever at the ready. An outfit without a night horse faced a calamity on the order of a croaton-oiled cat on concrete. Something had to be done—and damned quick! But what? And how? First to mind was an idea to strike stark dread in the staunchest cowboy breast. From Cutter, the boss: "The three of us'll haf to find him and pen him afoot."

But before recounting the first futile foray, let us introduce the protagonist, Buster, lest the sudden shock of meeting him unexpectedly prove too great. Buster, a big, blood-bay with long, anvil head and one little bitty shoe-button eye, was a horse whose lineage was long since lost in the mists and mysteries of time. However, the wide, flat feet and feathered fetlocks hinted of a trace of Clydesdale blood, but for the most part you could say that Buster was cold-blooded. Fact is, every move Buster makes, every step Buster takes will tend to bear this out. One consolation: Buster did not bear the proud Hoover horse brand (a triangle on the left shoulder) which bespoke of noble blood.

Why, then, this common clod, this interloper amongst all this Hoover royalty? Whence had he cometh? (Not to mention whither the hell he had goneth?) Buster had shown up in a horse roundup from that vast no man's land, the alkali flats and salt cedar jungles along the Pecos. A gelding but cut proud, Buster was here snob-nobbing. That is to say, he was here to rub shoulders—and then some—with those blue-blooded Hoover fillies. As a consequence, he wound up in serfdom jingling other but lesser geldings, work we cowboys considered too demeaning for high class Hoover horseflesh.

No noble blood to speak of, no lineage to lay hold of notwithstanding, tucked inside that long, anvil head and behind that one shoe button eye lurked a mind as cunning, as conniving as ever graced the inside of a skull, be it man, beast, bird or bug.

We spotted Buster in the far corner of the north horse-trap, long head hung over the horse-wire fence, looking long and longingly not to say lustfully at old Kempland's *manada* of maidens grazing gracefully across the salt grass flat. Now, one would naturally assume that one eye no bigger than a shoe button would not be as efficient as twice as many human orbs twice as big, let alone six. Even so, with a mere corner of this one, Buster and us spotted each other about the same time and Buster was off in a cloud of clods.

This lop-sided contest of wills, wits, and wiliness lasted until 'way up in the morning, with me being the last to holler 'calf rope.' I would like to say it was because I was set up of sterner stuff, but in truth I had committed the ill-mannered indiscretion of relating and re-relating how I had run the mile down at the State Track Meet in Austin only a couple of summers back. ("Ain't aimin' to brag," as they say we Texans say then go ahead and do, but I brought that entire Memorial Stadium crowd to its collective feet. I deem it only fair to confess, however, that I got so far behind they thought I was ahead. That is, what they didn't know was that the knot of runners behind me was finishing whereas I had another lap to go.) The reason I outlasted Cutter and Bill was because Buster was under my jurisdiction, hence my responsibility. But how was I to know the only way to contain the likes of Buster was to keep him under lock and key with key hidden in the bottom of Cutter's turtle-top trunk and it likewise locked!

Some ingenious fool had whittled out a wooden peg and stuck it into the gate's sliding latch when all Buster had to do was clamp his teeth on it, slide it back and *adios mi chaparito*—in the words of an

Old Mexico song title. But who would have thought a horse would have thought such thoughts? Most especially a total nobody from nowhere when scores of night horses before him, many of them of noble birth, had not solved the riddle.

In a sad state of disrepair we repaired to the shack to rest and/or rant, each according to his own temperament. Bill, the trigger-tempered one was for "grabbin'up the *thirty-thirty* and creasin' the old cold-blooded, owl-headed (reflection on mother)" but Cutter, a cooler head, counseled caution.

"Hit him a fraction low and Lord knows where we would be at."

"Hell, I know where we would be at. Right, igod here. And no more afooter than we, igod, are."

But the boss prevailed.

"What the hell now, then, Cutter?"

"What say you crank up your Dodge *Cuepay* and drive over to headquarters? Get Lon to send Gid Redding over here a-horseback?"

"Not me. I cain't bear to tell ol' Lon a thing like this." (Not that Lon Freeman would have ranted, raved, snorted, and pawed sand. But being the first boss in horseback history to let somebody let a night horse get out would have haunted him, hounded him to his grave.)

"Paul, you then."

"Cutter, you know I don't know nothin' about no machinery." (Which triple-negative thus interpreted means "I would not touch this task with a twenty-foot sucker rod. Be on the order of carrying the message to next-of-kin that the Alamo had fallen or, say, toting those terrible tidings to the widow of General George Armstrong Custer.)

"Then you go, Cutter;" said Bill, "you know him better'n we do."

"Very reason I won't go."

"Which leaves nothin' to do but nothin'," I put in, hopefully.

"By no means;" Bill said, "we're fixin' to give ol' Buster a go in my green Dodge."

"Who ever heard of rustlin' horses in a automobile?" asked Cutter, skeptically, not to mention sarcastically.

"Nobody. But nobody ever heard of a rustlin' horse flyin' the coop neither. This'll make us first both ways."

Cutter said neither yea nor nay but you could tell he was pondering it in his heart. Born with one foot planted firmly on the wild frontier, transition to the machine age was a slow, painful process. To his kind the motor car was too complicated, too cantankerous, hence too susceptible to cold jaw, to cold shoulder, to cold-bloodedness, had maimed, mangled and mauled more of mankind in forty years than the horse had in four thousand. However, if Cutter came up with an objection it would be on religious rather than legal, technical, or sentimental grounds (having 'seen the light' at B. B. Crim's cowboy camp meeting a couple of summers back).

"No, Bill. Best we stick with what the Good Lord provided for sech purposes, the beasts of the field which He give us dominion over."

"Which don't seem to have included that goddam Buster," snapped Bill cynically, not to say profanely, "so I say gettin' dominion over that (aspersion on mother) is gonna take all of them forty-odd horses under that green Dodger's hood—with us throwed in." Perceiving in Cutter a wavering of will, Bill plunged on.

"She's fresh shod, got a good mouth on 'er, shore-footed, and sound in wind and bottom. Not as apt to fall on a man as God's own. . . . " Here Cutter threw both hands up in a give-in, give-up gesture.

If necessity is the mother of invention, extreme necessity is the mother of extreme measures. Bill, the ingenious one, hit upon the idea of Cutter buckling his old kack on the green Dodger's hood—like cowboys had done for years but for transporting purposes only—from job to job. Nobody had thought of buckling them on for business.

Always darkest just before dawn? In our case it was just after. A new day, a new resolve (plus forty-odd horses) notwithstanding, Buster was not allowing us within rifle range much less a lariat's length. However, to err is human. Likewise horse. Yes, even one of Buster's mental magnitude. What he had failed to take into account was (1) Bill's resolve and (2) the total and reckless abandon with which Bill was pressing Green Dodger and her forty horses. Heretofore, Buster had found Bill the most timid of horsemen. That is, Bill was the only one to top him (Buster) off and sweat him out in the corral before venturing outside. Hence a false sense of security-over-confidence on Buster's part. As a consequence the critter commenced playing off, holding something in reserve against a greater need. Or was it the opposite, so as to thumb his tail in defiance at closer range? To further humiliate us with those insultingly insinuating sounds? And cloud our windshield with clods?

But if Buster thought he was obstructing my view he was whistling (literally as well as figuratively) in the wind. I had long since shut my eyes against the wildest ride ever taken by man, bird, beast, or being.

"To hell with Buster," I gritted through gnashed (and chattering) teeth. "Slow this damned thing down!"

"Naw. She ain't apt to step in no dog holes. Nor hub no stumps."

Given the wit, and grit, my reply would have been, "No, but we're jumpin' a hell of a bunch of 'em." Under the circumstances it came out an humble mumble: "Bill, please slow down!"

"You got the door shet. You ain't apt to fall out."

(No. But I was harboring thoughts of jumping.)

Bill's recklessness coupled with perseverance, coupled with desperation along with superior horses was beginning to tell. Buster could no longer out-run or out-dodge the Green Dodger. Fact is, we had pulled within lariat's length of Buster several times, but Cutter was always too busy riding to do any roping. One more stump-jumping, rump-bumping round did it. We coursed Buster into the corral.

"Slam the gate on him!" yelled Cutter, too tangled in his rope to dismount.

"Hell far no," Bill yelled, already in the gate with a salt-cedar stave drawed back. "I'm gonna learn him a lesson he ain't apt to fergit." Be he goof or grammarian, etymologist or ecologist, man is yet to utter a more accurate verb—*learn*—as regards Buster. That horse had learnt it all—now he was teaching.

Meantime Buster had almost completed his corral circle and was now headed straight for Bill, so straight, in fact, that Bill was forced to give ground. But before so doing he fetched Buster a clout atop the skull. The lick, albeit powerful, neither derailed Buster nor his unerring train of thought. The last we saw and heard of him was the haughty figure nine in his tail and the insinuating sounds emanating from thereinunder.

"Well," sighed Cutter philosophically, "at least you parted his forelock."

"Git in, we ain't done with that (expletive excluded) yet." This from Bill. Certainly not from me, or the Green Dodger. That last circle she had matched Buster drop for drop, blast for blast in the emission of gas, water, and steam, all of which she was *still* emitting. This plus seeping sundry oils and various greases. And the way she was giving to that left hind leg it did not take an auto doctor to diagnose it as a hip knocked down. As a consequence we were forced to repair to the shack for repairs, not to mention rest and recuperation.

Quite by accident we eventually brought Buster to book. I say *accident,* actually it was Buster himself that gave us the idea though we were too small of soul to give him the glory. Since it was Cutter who made the discovery, it could have been provident instead of accident. Being the *new* Cutter he was at the window "lifting his eyes unto the hills from whence might cometh his help," (Here I find it apropos to point out that these *hills* were seventy-five miles away.) when through the darkness he caught sight of Buster inside the horse corral sneaking a drink of water. And being the same old Buster he was not sneaking a water-logging bellyful, just enough to keep his speed, as he had been doing all along.

So, sad to say, it was not superior intelligence that brought Buster to book. Nor was it greater fortitude. Seeing as how he thwarted our fair means, we resorted to foul. We wired the gate shut, cut his water off all that day, opened it late that night then slammed it shut on him when he snuck in to water.

Buster, Bill, and Cutter have long since forded that last long river. And it is my fervent hope that they are together. I am sure of one thing. Saint Peter better leave those Pearly Gates locked and leave the keys with a higher authority. Otherwise old Buster will get out. Or in. And whichever the case might be, and wherever old Bill might be he will be "givin' that old pony a powerful good cussin'."

Texas Country Schoolteachers/*Lou Rodenberger*

Mabel Halsell and students at Cedar Bluff ("Last Chance") School in Callahan County in 1938. The author is the girl with the scarf on the back row.

Texas Country Schoolteachers: Living Proof of a Legend

Lou Rodenberger

They stop on Highway 36 to inquire for directions, and when they learn where it is, they come to the old white farmhouse shaded by postoak trees on the eastern edge of West Texas and sit down to reminisce. They are middle age and older, and they relive Sunday afternoon softball games, end-of-school barbeques, basketball championships, singing schools, Sunday school, play parties and Christmas programs, which have been high points in their early lives in places like Friendship, Kokomo, Okra, Lucille, Cottonwood, Last Chance and Pulltight.

These are not unusual activities nor place names for the rural schools of Texas in the first half of this century. What makes these nostalgic conversations unique is that the host and hostess are my parents, who taught in Texas rural schools for more than forty years, and the visitors are their former pupils.

Such get-togethers begin with "remember when" and lead to "remember them"—schoolmates now scattered. Some are successful as farmers, ranchers, oil operators and engineers, but many have chosen service careers as nurses, teachers and preachers. One country high school basketball star, they remember with pride, culminated his career as Chancellor of the University of Nebraska. When these visitors, some almost as old as their hosts, shake hands to leave, they always tell Miss Mabel and Mr. Carl what their former teachers' influence has meant to their lives.

My parents, Carl and Mabel Halsell, are the chief actors in this particular scenario, but traditionally, in American life, successful citizens whose origins are rural, often trace attitudes and actions which have influenced their lives back to schoolteachers who first put them in touch with themselves and the world outside the walls of a one- or two-room country school.

The country schoolteachers in the first half of this century were the intellectual, social and often spiritual leaders in communities where, until the 1940s, there were no books, few newspapers and fewer radios. Diaries and autobiographical accounts, whether the authors taught in Indiana or New Mexico, Kentucky or Texas, reveal that most rural teachers of this era had many experiences in common. There's no monotony in their accounts, however. The human element sees to that.

Similar challenges failures and victories are recorded by Appalachian Mountain teachers Jesse Stuart in *The Thread That Runs So True* and Harriette Simpson Arnow in *Mountain Path.* William A. Owens in *A Season of Weathering* narrates events and describes customs and attitudes at Pin Hook in East Texas that my parents remember as common to their experiences in Central and West Texas.

The first school day, usually late in the fall after crops were harvested, revealed the same challenges in each case—twenty or thirty pupils in one room, four to seven grades to organize, thirty or forty recitations to work into one eight-hour day. Guidance of students during two recesses and one noon playtime on bare school grounds without equipment required ingenuity and energy. There was a bully to subdue, a clown to control and a smart alec to quell. There were bright students to outdistance and slow students to lead. One required diligence; the other, patience.

There is a pattern, too, in events which led these teachers into the schoolhouse in the first place. One of their own early teachers inspired them to love books and knowledge. They began teaching before they were twenty, temporarily certified after passing state exams in almost a dozen basic subjects. To "get a school," which they usually heard about by word of mouth or through inquiry at the county superintendent's office, they had to deal with authoritarian and often contentious trustees.

From that first day they had to be innovators to find creative solutions for discipline problems, lack of equipment and community impoverishment. Soon they learned that not only their pupils looked to them for leadership but so did parents. The teacher became the social focus in life of the community. And so their roles were many.

One other talent many country schoolteachers had in common with my parents. Not only were they born schoolteachers but they were story tellers. I grew up listening to tales which revealed the tellers' sensitivity to human tragedy, tolerance of human weaknesses and belief in the saving grace of wit. Their narratives characterize their multifaceted roles in the rural community and give living proof that the legend of the all-purpose schoolmaster and schoolmarm is more fact than fable.

In our family saga, as Mody Boatright defines family tales, there are stories about how it all began and how my parents' service in the community came to include multiple duties. My father was athletic coach, referee, janitor, bus driver and peacemaker. Early in his adult life he became an ordained Methodist preacher, and he organized union Sunday Schools, preached, led songs and performed wedding ceremonies. He "laid out" the dead and preached their funerals. My mother assisted at home births, made wedding dresses and shrouds and taught Sunday School. She organized play parties, planned birthday parties, baby and bridal showers and holiday programs. She was pianist, counselor and social worker, who once took a motherless newborn to care for until older sisters could take over three months later. Both parents promoted summer singing schools, revival meetings and community plays.

When my father sat down with a yellow legal pad recently and began telling his stories on paper, he entitled one section "Starting My Career." Here's his written version of tales the family has heard often and, although diction is at times that of a writer, not a teller, the intent, order, style and wit of this account is true to the original oral narrative.

This is how it all began for a fledgling teacher in the early twenties:

"When I graduated I liked a few months of being eighteen. At that time, you could get into the teaching profession by state examination. Two of my older sisters had passed these tests and were teaching. The law was you had to be eighteen before taking the test. I decided to fib a little and steal a march on the state. The way I figured it was there were a lot dumber people than I teaching school. I had met a few.

"So as soon as I got out of school I grabbed the old *Seeley's Question and Answer Book* and dug in. At the time I took the exam I was 5' 9" tall, weighed 112 pounds and had just started to shave a little peach fuzz off my upper lip. I went to Anson to take the test. The gentleman conducting the test gave me a cold fishy look when I had finished my application. I knew he had his doubts and I had mine. The test ran for two days. I finished highly pleased. There were about twelve subjects covered and if you fell below 70 on any one, you failed. My papers were sent to Austin. I got my grades in due time. Sixty-nine percent in arithmetic. I knew I hadn't failed arithmetic; I failed to have a beard.

"In July 1917, Dad sold out due to extended drought. We had a small bunch of cattle, but otherwise my dad was a broke man and due to get broker. Anyway, we left Hawley and landed about twenty miles southeast of Baird in Callahan County. Plenty of good grass and water. All I had to do was see after the cattle. I would ride out on my pony with 'Old Seeley' strapped to the saddle, find a likely shade, let my pony graze while me and Old Seeley would go into conference.

"In September, 1917, I was in Baird (Now remember I had passed my eighteenth birthday on August 31.) ready to show 'em how smart I was and how much I had improved in four months. I took it. I got the results in about two weeks. Sixty-nine percent on arithmetic, the rest of the subjects, 85 to 100.

"The place we had leased was sold so we moved again to a small place in Rising Star. The big oil boom hit Ranger in the fall of 1917. Dad sold his cattle, and he and I went to the oil field to work. We worked there until the spring of 1918. Time to move again, this time to Putnam, a village a few miles west of Cisco. I went to work on the Isenhower Ranch. Nothing much but riding pastures and dipping cattle, horses and mules. Two dollars a day was my wages.

"I got the teaching itch again so I approached the rancher with the proposition: 'If I could start early and finish my day's work, could I have the rest of the day to study?' He wanted to know why. I told him I wanted to be a schoolteacher. He said, 'I don't know why in the hell you want to be a teacher. I've never seen one of them that was worth a damn. Why don't you go into the cattle business?'

"I told him that took money and asked him if he would set me up in the business. 'Hell, no,' he answered, 'start like I did with nothing.' Finally he consented to my proposition. I'm not sure he would have if he had known how hard I was going to ride his Morgan horses.

"So me and 'Old Seeley' was hard at it for the next two months with special attention to arithmetic. Those Austin people were stuck on square and cube root. I got the message.

"The first of June, 1918, found me and 'Old Seeley' safely established in a bare little room in the oldest hotel between Fort Worth and El Paso. I was in Baird again ready to give that square and cube root the works.

"I took the exam and not being satisfied with $2 a day, I packed my grip and headed for Ranger where I could get $10 per day as a fry cook. Time passed and in July my brother walked into the kitchen of the McCleskey Hotel where I was working and handed me a long business envelope. I opened it, and glory be! there was my teacher's second-grade four-year certificate. Just look at that big gold state seal. My co-workers wanted to know what it was. I told them and from then until I quit to look for a school, I was known as Professor. O, the devilish people this world has spawned. But, at that, I kinda liked it.

"I quit my job and went home to look for a school. The little school at Admiral in Callahan County was my choice. I borrowed a little red Saxon roadster from a neighbor friend. I had never driven a gear shift car so the first thing I did when I put it in reverse was back completely across the street into a porch. Cars were not made of tissue paper then, so no injury to the car. I made it to Admiral. The trustees were threshing wheat. They were a skeptical smart alec bunch of hooligans. So, I just told them to go to hell and I got in the Saxon 'and rode out of there. I decided to take a short cut home, ran into a sand bed and couldn't get out. Finally, dark came. I was eight miles from home in rattlesnake country. I struck out afoot and made it about daylight. My neighbor and I took a wagon and team and pulled the Saxon to hard ground.

"Automobiles were for the birds. Next try, I went horseback to a little one-teacher school four miles west of Cisco, known as Friendship. It was a big district with three trustees and three one-teacher schools. Each trustee run, and I mean run, his school. The trustee for Friendship was a big, hard-looking, black dutchman by the name of Will Parmer. He owned about half the land in the district and had about $100,000 in a Cisco bank. When I found him, he was plowing barefooted with one mule and a Georgia Stock in some new sandy land. I asked him if he needed a teacher. He implied he could use one. Not knowing any better, maybe, I asked him how much he paid and he said $65 a month. I could leave it or take. He asked me how much I thought I was worth. I had done a little 'hoss tradin' so I told him that I had been making $10 a day. He told me I had better go back to my job. I said 'Mr. Parmer, I'll take the job for $75 a month.' He said 'No!' I offered to split the difference. He said 'No!' Then I told him I would take the job at $65 a month, and he said 'To tell you the truth young man, I think that's all you're worth.'

"I didn't ask him if I was hired. I just pulled out a contract and started filling it out. He said 'You hold on a minute. If I hire you, you will have to board with me and that will be $15 a month.' Afraid he would back out, I told him that was O.K. by me. I handed him the contract, he scribbled his name on it and I mailed it into the County Superintendent's office the next morning. That was the beginning of forty-three years as a teacher in Texas' rural schools."

My mother's preparation to teach was at summer normal school at Howard Payne College the summer after high school graduation. She remembers: "The summer normal course consisted of reviews in all basic grammar school subjects plus a course in school management and one in psychology." She adds, "I greatly wished to start Freshman courses and remain at Howard Payne one year until I finished. This I did not have permission to do."

So she went home to pick cotton to buy clothes and to wait for the day the mail carrier pulled up in his buggy with a white umbrella for shade and called, "Got your sheepskin today, Mabel."

She had a position in a two-teacher school at Romney near Cisco. Principal of the school was my father. They met for the first time the day before school opened in the living room of the home they were to board in.

My mother still remembers that first school day: "Though I had studied my one method book, *How To Teach the Primary Grades,* and I had a long list of songs I had learned by playing them on the piano all fall, I felt the greatest challenge of my life. Those hungry eyes and eager smiles gave me to know I better have something for them.

"An incident the second day created my first problem. Herbert Rich, red-headed, timid and not too clean, came slowly up at recess and said, 'Miss Mabel, I done had that book.' I knew he felt he'd been retained. After searching, I put him in a book I thought was higher. He seemed satisfied."

And it was at that first school that my parents organized a literary society which met twice monthly on Friday afternoons, and soon parents were coming regularly to hear the big room give readings and debate and the little room sing "Have You Seen Polly's Bonnet?," "Merry Brown Thrush," "Bob White," and "Sing a Song of Six Pence."

Through the year, sometimes both parents taught, sometimes only one, depending on a community's needs, whims, and resources. In the worst of Depression years, teachers were paid with script, which could be used to barter for groceries and necessities, providing the holder would take a discount. In 1932, neither parent taught school, and we moved to a farm in Callahan County where my father contracted with a rancher to cut cedar posts on the halves. He also took twelve hours of correspondence courses from Abilene Christian College to extend his teaching certificate. We raised most of our own food. My mother picked cotton. She remembers that they spent the year "doing what opened up to do."

But, in the spring of '33, my father heard that the nearby Cottonwood school needed a principal who could coach basketball. The stories my father tells of that year are family members' favorite tales, and they relish retelling them.

The trustees interviewed applicants in an open meeting in Coffey's general store one spring evening. My father listened to each of the many applicants give a speech on how competent he was. Each would conclude by handing over a pack of recommendations. Dad's turn came finally. He said: "Gentlemen, I can teach school and I can coach basketball and if you hire me I'll do a good job. Anybody can get a recommendation from friends—even a prisoner just out of jail—so I bring none. But I'll be a good teacher. If you want me, mail me a card in the morning out on the route. Thank you, gentlemen." He put on his hat and left. He got the job.

That year, with only five substitutes and a dirt court to work out on, my father coached a winning basketball team. They were bussed to games in Dad's old Chevy and bachelor Tuffy O'Dell's jalopy with 9¢ a gallon gasoline at their own expense. The star player, nicknamed Hump, would get in the car, rare back, prop his brogans up and announce "Well, here come the champeens." One night, Hump was sound asleep with his big feet on the dashboard when a teammate in the back goosed him in the ribs. He jumped and put his brogans through the right windshield. When my father sold his old Chevy, it still had cardboard for a windshield on the passenger's side.

At district playoffs, my father remembers, the big shots scheduled the country kids for three games in one day—at 10, 2 and 8. They won the first game. Then, while the team rested on the floor of the hotel room my father had rented, he went out and got a 30¢ hamburger and a nickel Coke for each player. They won their 2:00 o'clock game. At 8:00, Dad said, "Boys they think we're hicks. Let's show 'em we can still play." They won it! They beat Pete Shotwell's Breckenridge bunch. Shotwell presented the trophy, then stalked off the floor without shaking hands.

At regional tournament in Abilene, Cottonwood made it to the finals. With the score 17 to 17, the referees started fouling the country team's players off. But, with only four players on the floor, Cottonwood still held off the other team. The other team scored the tie breaker only after another country player was benched. They won—but my father says the moral victory was Cottonwood's.

Most memorable for me is the one-teacher school where I learned to read from patient Miss Helen, and where I went again in the seventh grade with my mother as teacher.

Formally named Cedar Bluff, but usually called Last Chance, it was there that my parents established perhaps the first lunchroom in a one-room school. They built shelves into the bookroom, and on an old coal oil stove, students took turns assisting their teacher to make meals out of government surplus foods. What did not show up in the grocery box, my parents furnished out of their pockets. Lunch might be cornbread and beans with a slice of cheese, but it was hot and more appetizing than greasy sausage in a cold biscuit.

The school ground was bare until my mother inspired her students to outline a Texas star flower bed with rocks where they planted canna lillies and flags (iris) bulbs and cacti dug up from surrounding pastures. She provided a ball and bat and when Scrub, Choose Up or One-eyed Cat lost our interest, pupils played Red Rover, Wolf Over the River, Three Deep, Go In and Out the Window and Annie Over (We never called it Ante Over.).

If the day was rainy, both boys and girls spent recess hiding the thimble, playing Cross Questions and Crooked Answers, marching to Victrola music or coloring seasonal pictures run off on the hectograph—a tray of gelatin which reproduced pictures drawn on a master copy with a special purple pencil. The sand table scenes became famous—even the County Superintendent stopped by just to see what new garden scene we had created from mosses and plants we collected on field trips.

We learned to read shaped notes at singing schools in the summer. And the community thespians put on plays called "The Daughter of the Desert" or "Si and I" directed by my parents. School patrons never missed a performance of "Si and I" because of one famous scene when my father as a drunken darky tumbled backward and disappeared into a barrel. There were musicals and play parties at the schoolhouse, too. My father joined the guitar pickers with his fiddle at the musicals, but they played for toe tapping and listening—not dancing, which was frowned on in Central Texas at that time. We sang our accompaniment for dancing—"Old Joe Clark" and "Skip to My Lou"—and called our fun a play party.

The force behind all these community activities was the teachers, whose imagination, energy and compassion reached out to knit a community together into a unit with a spirit long remembered.

The chronicle of my parents' lives appears in outline almost identical to those of other country schoolteachers of their time. It's the stories that make the difference. Their tales and anecdotes have entertained their children and grandchildren at every family gathering. When one of us makes a bed and my mother laughs and asks, "Did you shake the dut off the sheet?" we all remember together her story of the little tongue-tied fourth-grader who began her speech on 'How to Make a Bed' with the instruction, "Well, first you shake the dut off the sheet." The grandchildren think the best story of all is my father's account of giving a recalcitrant fifth-grade boy a promised lick with a paddle, only to startle the class when there was a loud bang and smoke rose from the seat of the boy's pants. His back pocket had a toy pistol cap in it. Hilarity reigned after one student observed, "Mr. Halsell, I heard of knockin' the far outta somebody, but that's the first time I ever seen it happen."

What we all sense when we hear these stories and become aware of the unusual relationship of teacher and pupil and parent revealed by them is what Jesse Stuart concludes in *To Teach, To Love* when he gives this assessment of modern education: "We've lost something we've got to get back. Not the one-room schoolhouse but the spirit of the one-room schoolhouse."

Mrs. Rodenberger's article, delivered at the Society's 1980 meeting, also appeared in the 1980 West Texas Historical Association Year Book.

Legal Lore from the Courthouse/*William N. Stokes, Jr.*

William N. Stokes, Jr. in front of the
Denton County Courthouse.

Legal Lore
from the Courthouse

William N. Stokes, Jr.

The courtrooms and law offices often are the crucibles wherein emotions, passions, concerns, and fears rise spontaneously to the surface.
Here the mettle of men and women is tested, often to the limit; here
the action usually is unrehearsed, unanticipated, and without benefit
of recall. In such an atmosphere, occasional breakouts of humor—in
word, action, and conduct—are inevitable. In earlier days the annual
meetings of lawyers and judges consisted of one part business and
nine parts lobby recitals of these humorous events. Unfortunately
many priceless stories, true, partially true, partially false, or just plain
false have gone over the hill with their narrators. A few have been
preserved, and among these are yarns which I have heard over the
years from my father (lawyer, district and appellate judge of Vernon
and later Amarillo) and from many other attorneys and judges.

We shall require a very minor attention to courtroom and office
practise procedures. We may begin with *the pleading* with which a
lawsuit is initiated. This is a written document wherein the attorney
states his client's version of the case. Here we are concerned only
with one small phase of this process, a paper now long obsolete
called "the general demurrer." This was a device designed to allow a
judge to throw out a frivolous or worthless lawsuit, one which fell on
its face for lack of merit. The pleading as a matter of course and
habit was inserted in every answer filed. It said in essence: "Admit-
ting the truth of everything you say in your lawsuit, you still do not
have a case against me." If the judge sustained the general demurrer,
the case went out of court; if he overruled it, the case was set down
for trial on its merits.

Judge James Brown (not his name) was a trial lawyer in Vernon.
Ma Ferguson appointed him to the district bench. His very first case
involved substantial property. At the bar were two sets of lawyers,
one from Dallas, the other from Wichita Falls. In those early days, ap-
pearances of prestigious lawyers, even from Wichita Falls were not

common and brought a measure of awe to the local bench and bar; lawyers from Dallas were overwhelming!!

In Judge Brown's court, the defendant's attorneys filed the usual general demurrer, but this time the Dallas lawyers urged it seriously. "The plaintiffs just do not state a cause of action at law," they said. And they were persuasive, so much so that at the conclusion of their argument, Judge Brown announced: "You have a good point, and I will sustain the general demurrer." "Just a minute, your honor," the Wichita Falls lawyer almost shouted; "Let us be heard on this." Whereupon he swept into his argument. At its conclusion, Judge Brown said: "Okay, I believe you are right, and now I will overrule the general demurrer." *"Hold it!"* the Dallas lawyer said, leaping to his feet. He then expanded his original argument, whereupon Judge Brown said hesitantly, "Well—I now believe your point is well taken, and I will sustain the general demurrer." Again Wichita Falls came unglued, and at this point, confused and bewildered, Judge Brown rolled his eyes, buried his chin in his palm for a long moment. He turned his head from side to side then announced: "Gentlemen, this is my first case, and I want you to understand clearly that I am not a wishy-washy judge."

My father reported on a case in which he presided as trial judge in Jacksboro. Here again the defense of "general demurrer" was interposed, and the judge perceived quickly that it had much merit. Attorney for the plaintiff was Judge Taylor, a flamboyant Wichita Falls lawyer. Sensing quickly that the court was about to sustain the general demurrer and thus throw him and his client out of court, Judge Taylor launched his argument. His client, of course, was present and listening intently. Judge Taylor's argument was that the judge should not deprive a man of a jury trial. And this brought in the constitutions of Texas and the United States, the British bill of rights and petition of right, the Declaration of Independence, the flag, mother, apple pie, and of course the sanctity of the right of trial by jury. He concluded his argument with a dramatic plea which shook the courthouse windows and took his seat. The court announced promptly that he would sustain the general demurrer. Judge Taylor and his client were out of court.

My father completed his notes on the bench and moved to the district clerk's office. Here he had to hunch over to make way through a steel vault opening. As he passed, he heard one of the clerks ask Judge Taylor: "Judge, what happened to your lawsuit?" Judge Taylor replied sadly: "The court sustained the general demurrer and threw me out of court." Then a long pause, and he added: "And—rightfully so!!"

After the pleadings are filed and the preliminaries completed, a lawsuit eventually arrives at the *trial stage.* In the preliminary skirmishing, motions are made and either approved or rejected by the judge; testimony of witnesses is taken and finally the case submitted to a jury, or if no jury is involved, decided by the court. Following are events related to two widely separated lawyers, Judge Robert W. Hall of Vernon and Amarillo, and Judge John T. Bivens of Pearsall.

Judge Hall was a colorful lawyer, later a chief justice of the Amarillo Court of Civil Appeals. In the early Vernon days, Judge Hall was on the verge of going to trial in a jury case. The jury was seated, but the judge had not yet taken his bench. As always lawyers were shuffling papers, awaiting nervously the opening of the contest. Now Judge Hall had a great sense of humor. In those times should a witness fail to answer to his name he was "called" three times from the courthouse door. A deputy or other person tolled the name loudly. Presumably since the town revolved around the "square," the witness or someone who knew his whereabouts would hear, and he would be brought to the courtroom.

On this occasion a courthouse hanger-on named Flatiron Dempsey did the calling. He had no official status, was really not too bright, but he was good natured and liked. The judge continuing his absence, Judge Hall turned to Flatiron: "Flatiron, I don't see that witness Freely. Please call him, I. P. Freely." Flatiron moved obediently to the door, called the name loudly the three times, reported to Judge Hall: "He ain't here, Judge." Judge Hall, courtroom attendants and loafers all had a good laugh, the judge appeared, and the case went to trial.

The following Sunday my father and a half dozen other young blades were at the home of J. P. McKibbon, the local shoe merchant. Mr. McKibbon had three beautiful young daughters, and several other girls were present. So was Flatiron. To the consternation, dismay, yes even horror of the men who had heard of the prank, Flatiron launched into a summary of Judge Hall's joke. In those times this was unpardonable. But Flatiron moved smoothly, related that he called "I. P. Freely" three times. A stunned silence ensued, whereupon Flatiron explained: "You see, Ol' Judge Hall, he played a trick on me. It was a joke. And the joke was, THERE AIN'T NO SUCH FELLER."

In Pearsall, Texas, lived a famous criminal lawyer, John T. Bivens. He weighed over three hundred pounds, talked with a pronounced lisp. The word was that earlier in life he was shot through the jaw by an irate husband; his mouth being open as usual, the bullet creased his tongue. This handicap, however, was more of an asset than a liability, as it seemed to add to the color of his speech. Indeed, Judge Bivens was one hell of a criminal lawyer, particularly in murder cases.

On an occasion the Judge had filed a motion for "continuance" —a request that the trial of his client be postponed. This was a common form of seeking a delay, thereby allowing witnesses to scatter, forget, die, or perhaps the temper of the public to cool. In order to obtain a continuance a lawyer must produce adequate reasons, a common one of which is that important witnesses are absent. This was Judge Bivens' excuse, only here it was *two* witnesses who were "no shows." The district attorney asked the court to continue the hearing until the following morning. Then he got after the sheriff, who promptly located the two missing witnesses. The following morning, Judge Bivens was assiduously urging his motion for continuance. The judge on the bench interrupted: "Mr. Bivens, I believe your two witnesses are coming into the courtroom now." Bivens replied: "Oh no, I guess not, your honor." Then, turning his great head, he saw the two men on the front seat of the courtroom. Without a moment's hesitation, Bivens turned to the judge and said: "Well, your honor, I will now change my motion and request a continuance on the grounds of SURPRISE." Then, muttering to a bystander he said: "That pair of no good bums promised me faithfully they wouldn't be here."

On another occasion, Bivens was arguing a motion to the court, which the judge promptly overruled. He persisted, and finally the judge lost patience: "Mr. Bivens, I have ruled on this, and I don't wish to hear further argument." "But your honor," Bivens said, "I just want you to read these two appellate court precedents on this issue." "You are overruled, Mr. Bivens," the judge said, "and if you pursue it further, I will have to hold you in contempt of court." Judge Bivens drew himself up, replied: "Oh, if your honor please, I intend no contempt. I was just going to call your honor's attention to the *ignorance* of the Supreme Court of Texas on this proposition."

One of the Judge's lawyer friends in Pearsall was Magus Smith. In those days lawyers journeyed to the town in which a court term was in session and remained for the entire period. Judge Bivens had a fine buggy and a pair of good horses. Usually he picked up Magus Smith and the two travelled to the distant town together. "But he never returned with me," said the Judge. "Invariably something happened in the courthouse that infuriated him, and he sought others to transport him home."

One of these occasions involved a jury argument, with Magus doing the orating. Judge Bivens was attorney on the other side. Magus was at the height of an eloquent address. Someone had tied a jackass to the hitching rack outside the courthouse. As Magus' argument reached its climax the jackass began to bray. Magus continued, but Judge Bivens rose to his feet and interrupted: "If your honor please," he said to the Judge, "let's hear from only one of the gentlemen at a time."

One of Judge Bivens' clients owned a half section of good land near Pearsall. He agreed to convey the tract to the Judge if he were acquitted on a murder charge. At eleven o'clock in the morning, the jury came in with a verdict of "not guility." At one-thirty in the afternoon Judge Bivens filed a deed from his client conveying to him the half section of land. At three-thirty the same day a lawsuit was filed in the district court demanding that the deed be voided, as having been obtained "under duress." At four o'clock, Judge Bivens was waddling down the street. He was accosted by a loafer: "Judge, what about that lawsuit your client filed against you?" "Well," Bivens replied, "I juth don't underthand it. That damn feller agreed that if I got him off that murder charge he would convey me that land. And the jury turned him loothe. And tho I produthed a deed for him, and he didn't look like he wath gonna thign it; and tho I thaid to him, 'Now you thun of a bitch, you'll thign thith deed.' And I put athickthooter up bethide hith head and I thaid, 'Now you thign thith deed or I'll blow your damn head off.' And you know—he thigned that deed juth as freely and voluntarily as anyone ever did ANYthing."

The final phase of a lawsuit's progress is *the appeal.* In Texas we have a system of intermediate appellate courts, which handle cases between the trial phases and the last resort, the Supreme Court. These are called Courts of Civil Appeals, and they are located strategically over the state. The Supreme Court of necessity considers only a limited number of cases, and so in essence, the great bulk of appeals from the trial court is decided by the Court of Civil Appeals.

Now an appellate court differs from a trial court: no jury, few dramatics, all very quiet and dignified. The spectators whisper, judges and lawyers discourse in muffled tones. The only questions at issue are the legal aspects of actions by the trial judge, which are reflected in written records. The appellate court's only function is to decide whether or not the trial court's action was legally correct. If so, the case is "affirmed." If not, it is returned for another go 'round.

Already we have heard of Judge Hall. In later years he became chief justice of the Court of Civil Appeals in Amarillo. He was a stern disciplinarian. He demanded and enforced order, and the proceedings were strictly "no nonsense." In this particular case an old boy appealed from a losing cause in Perryton, 160 miles north of Amarillo. The Amarillo Court promptly ruled against him. But he took advantage of what is known as a "motion for a rehearing," which in essence is a request to the Court to take another look and correct its errors. Generally this motion is in the legal graveyard of lost causes, as it rarely is granted. In this case, however, the Perryton lawyer's motion was strong and persuasive. The Court was impressed, decided they would hear the case argued orally. The Perryton attorney was invited to make his presentation. He turned out a six-foot four-inch hayseed; his clothing did not fit; obviously he was frightened by this his first appearance in an appellate court. He *was* a successful trial lawyer, however, and so in asking the Court to change its ruling on his case he proceeded in the only way he knew—with a jury oration. He opened his address: "If the Court please, I come before you today, preaching like John the Baptist in the wilderness of Judea, crying, Repent Ye! Repent Ye!" Judge Hall always moved quickly to bring such orations to earth, and so he interrupted: "Counsel, do you know what happened to John the Baptist?" The hayseed batted not an eye; his reply was immediate: "Yes, your honor, he was beheaded at the behest of a harlot, but I trust that this court is not operating under such insidious influences."

A phase of law which does not touch the courthouse is in an attorney's office practise. In legal circles many things happen outside the courtrooms. Every lawyer has experiences, tragic, poignant, frustrating, heartbreaking—yes, and comical, which arise in the confines of his own office. So it is with Judge Fires of Childress, Judge Bryant of Haskell and Austin, and so it was *not* with Herman Oberweiss and his will.

In earlier days I delighted in reading to banking and other groups a will purported to have been made by a suspicious and untrusting old German from Anderson County named Herman Oberweiss. It was said to have been filed for probate in Anderson County. Here is Mr. Oberweiss' will:

I am writing of my will mineself, that lawir want he should have to much money to ask to many ansers about the family. First thin I want I don want my brother Oscar get a dam thing I got   he done me out of forty dollars fourteen years since. I want it that hilda my sister she gets the north sixtie akers of where I am homing it now   I bet she dont get that loafer husband of hers to break twenty akers come next plowing. she cant have it if she lets oscar live on it. I should have it bak if she does Tell moma that six hundret dollars she been looking for for ten years is berried from the backhouse behind, about ten feet down. She better let little frederick do the digging and count it when he comes up. pastor Lucknitz can have three hundret dollars if he kisses the book he wont preach no more dumhead talks about politics. He should a roof put on the meetinghouse and the elders should the bills look at. Moma should the rest get but I want it that Adolph should tell her what not she should do so no more slick irishers sell her vakom cleaners. They noise like hell and a broom dont cost so much. I want it that mine brother adolph be my execeter and I want it that the judge should please make adolph plenty bond put up and watch him like hell. I want for sure that oscar dont get nothing. Tell Adolph he can have a hundret dollars if he prove judge oscar dont get nothing. That dam sure fix oscar.

This will amused audiences from all over Texas, in New England, Montana, California, Washington, Oregon, New Mexico, Oklahoma, Kansas, and Nebraska. It is legal in form. It has only one flaw. It's a fake.

Will Sears is an attorney in Houston. He was onetime City Attorney who now engages in a highly profitable and active practise. In the 1930s he was in the legal department of the Federal Land Bank. On a day he apparently had a light work load, and in a session with other lawyers the mistrust of the old-time German pioneers was discussed. At length he took to his desk and drafted this will. Alas, alas that it's not genuine.

A longtime first Assistant Attorney General of Texas was Judge Bruce W. Bryant, originally from Haskell. In 1921 he was requested to rule on a delicate point of law. The A&M College was billed for $20.00, submitted by an irate neighboring farmer, the asserted value of a young bull which died as a result of an operation performed by

103

student assistants in the Department of Dairy Husbandry. The College paid and requested reimbursement from the State of Texas. The question: was this a legal expenditure?

The Judge's reply was an opinion which received wide circulation in its time. Following are excerpts:

The eventful day on which occurred the great tragedy which gave rise to this inquiry, several of the fine heifers owned by the State were in one of the State's pastures. In an adjoining pasture there dwelt an unpretentious bull, just budding into young bullhood. . . . He did not, and could not, boast of an illustrious ancestry. . . . He knew nothing of the ways of the world and had never heard of elite society. (On this particular morning) the air was made fragrant with autumn flowers, cool and invigorating. . . . His bellow was wafted on the perfume laden autumn breeze to the adjoining pasture, where dwelt the well fed, ever groomed, sleek and soft-eyed maidens of aristocracy belonging to the State of Texas. . . . These young bluebloods evidently mistook the innocent effervescence of this young bull as an invitation to start a flirtation. So, from across the way there came an answer, not a deep bass unmelodious roar . . . but a tremulous, sympathetic, soft, even-toned moooooh. This young bull had heard many "moos" before, but none such as this. . . . He answered the call. The flirtation was on. (He advanced to the fence). And there she stood—a young, beautiful, soft-eyed heifer. . . . Evidently she did not ask for his family tree. If she did, she cared not whether he could boast of his progenitors having won blue ribbons at State fairs. She was in love—and so was he. . . . Two hearts beat as one, but one stood still while the other backed off. . . , summoned all his bully strength, and with lowered head made a charge on the fence. . . . (Now) he was in society. . . . The world was his. He was introduced to other young heifers, all members of the exclusive set, and found favor in the eyes of several. . . . He was congratulating himself upon his rapid rise in the world when the unexpected happened. There were shouts, cries and curses. The bull was surrounded by the unfaithful "guards of the princess' chamber." He was kicked and beaten, and before he realized what had happened he found himself a prisoner in one of the State's bastilles, an eight foot corral. Subsequently he was, by employees of the Department of Dairy Husbandry, subjected to great indignities, and by force, threats and fraud compelled to subject himself to a surgical operation, which not only caused him great physical pain, but because of the nature of the operation, which had a tendency to destroy his social standing in the community . . . caused him great mental anguish. . . . That night the stars came out in myriads. The moon shed its mellow rays upon an outraged steer, which had just been deprived of that part of his anatomy which makes a bull a bull. . . . He lay again upon his downy couch, and dewdrops gathered upon the end of his tail, which with the coming of the dawn glistened in the sunlight like so many diamonds. The steer did not arise to greet the dawning sun as the bull had done on the previous morn. His grief was more than he could bear. His sorrow knew no bounds. He refused to be comforted. Partaking of neither food nor drink, his thoughts were only of the humiliation and his sudden downfall. Thus he languished for several hours and then went the way of all the earth.

Citing a precedent from a law book known as *Ruling Case Law,* Judge Bryant held that the State of Texas was not responsible for the acts of its agents; therefore the claim could not be paid.

And finally, in the field of office practise, we have the case of Judge Fires, a district judge in Childress. Prior to his appointment to the bench he was a famed criminal lawyer, particularly in murder cases. He had a client for whom he had done some civil chores; and one day this fellow walked into his office and said: "Judge, I want you to defend me in a criminal case." Judge Fires asked matter-of-factly, "Okay, what's the charge?" "Murder," replied the client. "MURDER???" the Judge replied incredulously: "What's your defense?" "How the hell should I know, Judge; that's why I came to see you. I haven't KILLED the son-of-a-bitch yet."

Persimmon Beer/*R. L. Cowser, Jr.*

R. L. Cowser, Jr.

Persimmon Beer

R. L. Cowser, Jr.

When I was a child during World War II in the 1940s, an annual event occurred around our household each autumn after the first killing frost. Fall is the season during which the wild persimmons get ripe in northeast Texas. The time was usually late October or early November when the first frost came, followed immediately by the picking up of ripe persimmons for the purpose of making persimmon beer, or as it was commonly called, homebrew.

My older brother and I would usually put our 'simmons—the local dialect regularly omitted the first syllable—in a water bucket while our father chose a half-bushel basket for his. We did not have to climb the small trees in order to get the persimmons because the ripest ones fell off naturally. Our job, then, was merely to pick them up from around the trees. "Let the birds and rabbits be the gleaners," my dad would say as he instructed us to leave the damaged persimmons on the ground. These wild persimmons are much smaller than the Japanese persimmon, but they are similar in shape and color. Some people believe the smaller persimmons are sweeter.

To watch my father in the process of converting the persimmons into homebrew was an ever fascinating pastime for me. To make the beer, he would place the persimmons in a crock container, such as a churn, or a keg with one pound of sugar or one pound of sorghum syrup per gallon of persimmons, and then he would add enough water to cover them.

The fermentation process would take from seven to nine days "to work off," depending on the weather; the warmer, the quicker. The concoction needed to be in a dark place where the temperature stayed about the same, as in a cellar. Under no circumstances, should the persimmons freeze. Freezing would arrest the fermentation process.

A teacup of corn meal mixed with water would add flavor to the brew and increase its alcoholic content. To make the brew even stronger, my father would add one pound of baked sweet potatoes for each gallon of persimmons.

After the beer had worked off, aging was not necessary. It could be drunk immediately or stored in air tight bottles. What was crucial to know was when the fermentation process had ceased. The top of the keg actually moved while the fermentation was occurring, and air bubbles would appear and burst all over the surface (like Keats' "beaded bubbles winking at the brim").

If the beer were siphoned off before the process was complete, the beer would have a low alcohol content and would have a sweet, green taste. If it were siphoned off too late, the alcohol would begin to dissipate into the air, and the beer would taste flat and sour, like vinegar.

After the fermentation process had stopped, a hollow tube could be inserted into the crock down to almost the bottom of the juice. However, if the tube were inserted at the beginning it would be a less difficult task to perform because the pulp and the "workings" rise to the top.

Then the beer was siphoned from the container, fairly clear and free of dregs. However, if the clarity was still not satisfactory, another step could be taken which would refine the brew even more. Clean lint cotton was placed in the bottom of a large funnel, and the beer was then strained through the cotton. Or if the brewer had a milk strainer, the pads and strainer for milk could also be used. After either of these techniques had been used, the beer was bright and free of visible impurities.

The beer was capped in air tight bottles immediately after it attained the optimum stage in its fermentation process; otherwise it would turn to something like vinegar. If nothing had been added to the persimmons, the alcohol content would reach 6–7%, a little more than typical commercial beer. If meal or potatoes had been added, the alcohol increased to 8–9%, just under the strength of typical wines.

We never drank the persimmon brew at our home just for its inebriant effects. We reserved it for special occasions such as a holiday or a birthday, or more rarely as a quick energy thirst quencher.

Nevertheless, occasionally some people who were our guests, my mother's bachelor brother in particular, would drink too much. Alcohol is alcohol, and the effects produced on a person from it are the same, regardless of the kind of spirits in which it is contained. My uncle swore, however, that a hangover which resulted from drinking an excessive amount of persimmon beer was the worst hangover a contrite imbiber could have. He insisted the head throbs were stronger, the stomach gripes were queasier, and the thirst more difficult to slake.

This last characteristic posed a further complication. For my uncle also insisted that drinking water after an overindulgence of persimmon home brew merely repeated the effects, to a lesser degree, which the brew produced the first time. Others believed that the greener—"newer"—the brew was, the more devastating its after effects. For these and other reasons, a child was usually given a "snuff glass" full of the beer and no more. I really never learned to like it, but I can remember begging for seconds—knowing I would not get any and not really wanting any—just to be contrary.

My father still has a capper which seals bottles with a manually operated plunger. The caps could be purchased and used with old longneck beer bottles, preferably the dark brown ones, in which regular commercial beer had been sold.

Growing up in a time and place which offered little commercial alcoholic beverages and maturing during the era of prohibition, my father learned from his father how to "make do" with what he had and how to improvise.

Today, when I see ads of the floosier department stores encouraging us to go back to nature with our own wine making kits, I realize how far away from it we have really become—a sordid boon. And I cannot help smirking just a little knowing that I was once a little closer than the typical last-quarter-of-the-twentieth-century American may ever get a chance to be.

A Letter from the Long Circle/*Wayne Echols*

Wayne Echols on Old Paint

A Letter from the Long Circle

Wayne Echols

I admire anybody who sets out to be what he himself wants to be, and Wayne Echols wanted to be a cowboy. I don't know how or why he got through college. He wanted to be in the Rodeo Club, I guess, and wear a cowboy hat pulled down to his ears, and old boots, and Levis with a Copenhagen circle on his hip pocket. And a belt tip that came out of the last loop and flopped down! I never have understood that particular dress custom—probably some phallic symbolism there somewhere.

I remember Wayne well, not so much as a student—he was always more amused than impressed with traditional academia—but as a campus kicker. One episode in our brief association stamped him in my memory.

The SFA Rodeo Club was having a Bull Riding Sunday; I think they called it that. They had borrowed a herd of Brahma bulls and were going to have a hundred rides, or something equally dramatic. I showed up to shoot some pictures, and sure enough, Wayne was one of the riders. I paid special attention when his turn came and watched him buckle down on his bull. He looked over in my direction, kind of winked and grinned, as if to say, "Watch me cool this old daddy."

They opened the chute and this old paint Brahma came roaring out, bell rattling, bawling at every jump, with Wayne hanging tight and looking not much bigger than a popcorn fart. He had nearly made it to the buzzer when old Paint locked one set of wheels and went to spinning like a Victrola record. Wayne started peeling off and when the buzzer sounded he had gone over the side—all but his hand. He'd cheated on his grip loop and now he was tied to that whirlwind of a bull, flopping around like a rag doll.

His buddies ran in and were hollering and yelling and working in close, trying to get the bull straightened out and Wayne untied. The dust was flying and the bull was bellering and hooking and spinning, and it looked like a whole mess of cowboys was being chewed up in a sausage grinder. Finally something came flying out of the middle and it was Wayne.

Once the bull had made his point, he headed on down to the other end of the arena, still dragging his bucking strap and rattling the bell. They lifted Wayne out of the dirt and set him on his feet. He wobbled a bit but he was still able to reach down and pick up his hat without falling over. I saw him behind the pens later on and he was slightly embarrassed, but he didn't let on that his body had been bent in any way. He made it to class Monday morning, attentive and amused, as usual—and still set to be a cowboy.

That was several years back. He went to west Texas after he got out of college and got a job on a ranch, just like he said he would. I still hear from him every two or three years. He found an old OK spur once and sent it to me and he sent me a picture of him on a ranch in Montana, or Wyoming, I forget which.

I got the following letter a couple of winters back and I'm printing it because I think Wayne writes a pretty good picture of the pride, problems, and prejudices of a modern working cowboy. And, Wayne, if you read this, you might drop me a line and let me know you're still alive.
Editor

I've been on the long circle since you last heard from me. As I recall, when I last wrote you was the winter of 77-78 when I was at the mouth of the Mussellshell (on the east side). That was the worst winter in anybody's memory in that country. Even the old fart I worked for, who was born & raised right where we were, couldn't remember a worse one. The main problem was early snows & minor thaws that crusted the snow, then more snow & more little thaw & finally travel outside of the track of a Caterpillar tractor was impossible. Even the 67 year old man I worked for admitted he'd never seen it so bad you couldn't get around ahorseback. And you can imagine how bad it must have been for an old timer to admit something like that to a young feller. As soon as I could, I got the hell out of there & didn't stop until I was in Dickens County, Texas. You may recall Don Karr. He has a small ranch near Dickens & I let my bones thaw out for about two months there.

But I got to missing Montana by May and went back north to work for the Scott Outfit on the Powder River south of Miles City. When that fall came, I ran back to Texas in a panic. That bad winter put the Indian sign on me. But by that October I was back to Sand Springs working for the Brown Ranch, right in the Middle of Montana. I told myself I had 4 easy winters up there and one bad one, which must have been a fluke. (Until the winter of 77-78, the very worst one I ever survived was the winter of 72-73, ten miles east of Channing, Texas.) But I got nailed again. The winter of 78-79 was just as unspeakably awful. The snow didn't crust quite as bad and not near as many cattle died, but the snow was deep and again horseback travel was mostly impossible without benefit of the god-sent, patented Caterpiller tractor with off-set blade. But since the Brown Ranch Headquarters was on the highway and a scant 42 miles to the nearest refreshing beverage & diversions, I never was snow-bound for more than two weeks in a row.

There isn't anywhere prettier, to my knowledge, than Montana in the summer time. And at Brown Ranch, summer was the first opportunity to leave without leaving the outfit in a bind. They calve heifers from March 15 to June 1st and I had to protect my professional reputation and integrity. By June 1st, a fella had to be a complete slobbering idiot to leave Garfield County, Montana. Wild flowers and green grass have a rare fascination to any red-blooded Texas puncher who don't get to see such wonderments as green grass for more than two weeks in a row (West Texas variety of Texas puncher anyhow) so I hung around until August.

By then, eastern Montana was starting to "yeller up" with a drought. Also, the annual Roaring Springs Reunion & Rodeo was coming up not 20 miles from my old pard Don Karr. And I was determined to go to hell with my back broke before I put in another winter like the last two, so, before weaning became close (reputation & integrity again) I sold out & came back to Dickens County again.

With the help of Don, I got in on a relatively new aspect of West Texas Ranching, the day working. Back during the summer of '73 when I went to Montana, day workers weren't the best thought of cowboys. They were about even with a feed-lot cowboy in respectability (Ranch cowboy being on top and rodeo cowboy the lowest. Feed lot cowboy not aceing out a rodeo cowboy by a hell of a lot). But day working had become more respected in this country the six years I was up north. It has always been hard for ranches to get good help, especially in brushy country, and keep them year around. Knowing what it takes to get a cow in custody that's been running in mesquite thickets for years, I wouldn't think such talent should be wasted on cleaning corrals or fixing windmills & water-gaps. Evidently, neither does the afore-mentioned talent. All the good brush poppers I knew and/or worked with before 1973 are now either running a place or own one or have a camp job or are dead. And I, not being one to break sacred traditions, assume anyone born before 1955 has absolutely no idea how to even bring in a crippled milk cow, and do it with finesse & professional dignity.

Therefore (a much more definite word than is applicable) most big outfits have taken to hiring day help during branding & weaning time, mostly because it is probably cheaper to work capable day help 4 total months of the year than try and hang on to their own good cowboys 12 months a year. Whatever the reason, there's a good market for day help now & I take advantage of it.

I started out thinking it would be a way to survive relatively well for a long period of time until a good paying position was offered, but it's starting to look like I could go on like this forever & still enjoy a freedom I can't get with a regular job. Instead of me asking for time off, they ask me if I'm going to work. And the real sugar on the grits is that I never have to do anything that isn't ahorseback. (I am feeding cake out of a pickup for financial reasons this winter, but it's not too unpleasant, a bit de-grading maybe, but not unpleasant).

Another good thing about day working is I cover a lot of country in a short time and never leave anything but good will behind. I've worked for the Matador, Swensons, Spurs, L7, Chimney Creek, and several smaller outfits. Without day working, it would be hard to en-joy that many cattle and that much country without making some-body mad when you left.

"The Glamor of the Gay Night Life" The Classic Honky Tonk/James Ward Lee

Jim Lee and Jim Byrd

Credit: Phillip Fry and Sharon Helms

"The Glamor of the Gay Night Life" The Classic Honky Tonk

James Ward Lee

Neither of the two great slang dictionaries—Partridge[1] and Wentworth and Flexner[2]—gives any help with the origin of the word "honky tonk," and it is clear from their definitions that the compilers would not recognize a real honky tonk if they danced their shoe heels as round as apples in one. Each of the dictionaries admits that honky tonks are places of amusement and that music, dance, and drink are to be found therein. Both seem to connect such establishments with loose women and jazz—"jangling piano music" Partridge's supplement says (p. 1201)—and with low and vulgar amusements. Perhaps in the earliest uses of the term, honky tonk described Negro jazz clubs, for there is a song, "Honky Tonky Town,"[3] which tells of a place "underneath the ground" with "singing waiters, singing syncopaters" who are "dancing to piano played by Mr. Brown." Mr. Brown plays piano "queer; he only plays by ear." The implications of the song are that ragtime or jazz is the music, that Mr. Brown is what used to be called a man of color, and that the establishment—Honky Tonky Town—is operating on the fringes of the law.

But the modern honky tonk, a cultural phenomenon secure in the lore and the hearts of the folk, is a different kind of establishment altogether. There may be a few "women of questionable repute," as Wentworth and Flexner are pleased to call them; and there may be "strong drink available," as Partridge says; but "a cheap saloon" or a "low place of amusement"! Never! The honky tonk is the working man's club, his haven of rest and recreation, his place to repair— to use (abuse?) the word in two of its best senses.

The rise of the modern honky tonk is easily traced. (Its decline is not foreseeable.) When the Volstead Act was repealed in 1933, America was already crisscrossed by a network of all-weather roads and populated by a million Fords, Chevrolets, and Plymouths. There was nothing for it but to begin a crash program of roadhouse construction. A few miles outside of thousands of Southern and Southwestern towns slab-sided buildings were suddenly thrown up. Parking lots were graded and chert or caliche was spread to cover the mud surfaces. Some of the more affluent owners built a few outhouse-size "tourist" cabins in the event that men and women "of questionable repute" should decide to seek shelter from the night air.

In his book *Country Music USA*, Bill C. Malone traces the beginnings of the honky tonk in Texas and shows its connection with the oil-field boom.[4] What Malone says of Texas is true of the entire South and Southwest, even in the areas where there was no oil. Coal miners, mill hands, plant workers, and even small merchants and clerks flocked to the roadhouses being built on the outskirts of small towns and big cities alike. The working orders went to drink the recently legalized beer—10¢ for local beer, 15¢ for national brands—dance to the hillbilly music of ol' boys who worked by day and picked by night, and to mingle with their own kind. Beer was the drink and Grand Ole Opry music was the soother of savage beasts.

During the last years of the thirties, honky tonks were everywhere. By 1940 there were at least twelve roadhouses between Leeds, Alabama and Birmingham, a distance of barely fifteen miles. They ranged in luxuriousness from the Briar Patch, a rough place built of pine slabs with no finishing inside, to the Moon River Beach,[5] a large log structure with a big room for dancing and another for eating and beer drinking. The Briar Patch was about as large as a shotgun dwelling house, while the Moon River Beach must have contained over 3,000 square feet. Not only was the Moon River Beach a commodious establishment, but Clyde and Meridian Wilson, the owners, had built about a dozen tourist cabins which faced away from the highway and had covered garages—also facing away from the highway. In between the Briar Patch and the Moon River Beach, both geographically and architecturally, was the Hop Rite Inn, finished inside but built of slabs. Neat but not gaudy. The best of the lot, at least for children, was the Silver Slipper, which was built on a lot that sloped down toward a creek; the rear of the building was on pilings, some nearly twenty feet tall, and the space under the building and near it was made into a playground lighted by strings of colored lights. This was in an era when the verb "to have been babysat with" was unknown. Honky tonking parents with small children simply took them along. My parents went almost every night, and those trips, which I can remember as far back as 1936, furnish much of the expert knowledge of this paper.

By the end of the thirties, the jukebox had almost completely replaced live music except on weekends. The magnificent Rock-Ola "music-machine," an older term than "jukebox," held twelve records—5¢ a play—and were kaleidoscopes of colored lights, liquid, and moving air bubbles. The music played in honky tonks had changed. There was very little of the old Vernon Dalhart and Jimmie Rodgers, for it could not be heard above the din.[6] The new amplified music of Ernest Tubb prevailed!

If the thirties constituted the primitive stage, the forties and fifties were the golden age.[7] Better jukeboxes were built, some holding 100 records. Building materials were refined and standardized with the advent of cheap concrete blocks and the ready availability of surplus barracks buildings from World War II army camps. And by then cars were more dependable and highways better. Most important, the great honky tonk artists were at their peak during this era: Ernest Tubb, Hank Williams, Bob Wills, Hank Snow, Hank Thompson, Floyd Tillman, Roy Acuff, Cowboy Copas, Kitty Wells, and Eddy Arnold. During the forties and fifties most country and western music was of the honky tonk variety. It was during these years that all of Hank William's recording was done and most of the other great classics of country and western music written. A brief list of the songs of the forties and fifties and their chief performers will illustrate the point:

Walking the Floor Over You   Ernest Tubb
San Antonio Rose   Bob Wills
Wild Side of Life   Hank Thompson
It Wasn't God Who Made Honky Tonk Angels   Kitty Wells
Bouquet of Roses   Eddie Arnold
I'll Sail My Ship Alone   Moon Mullican
Slippin Around   Floyd Tillman
Back Street Affair   Webb Pierce
Filipino Baby   Cowboy Copas
I'm Moving On   Hank Snow
Four Walls   Jim Reeves
Have I Told You Lately That I Love You   Gene Autry
Worried Mind   Jimmie Davis
Faded Love   Bob Wills

These songs, and many by Hank Williams—"Your Cheatin' Heart," "Cold, Cold Heart," "My Son Calls Another Man Daddy," "I'm So Lonesome I Could Cry," "Hey Good Looking," "You Win Again"—are some of the standard honky tonk songs of the Classical Period.

Not much has changed since the fifties except that the parking lots are more often paved, the musical equipment is better, and the beer is more expensive. The habitues are still from the same class, the songs are still the same old country standards, and the fights still occur over the same disagreements. All sorts of pseudo-honky tonks now exist, but the real thing retains the old-time characteristics. Places Like Gilley's in Pasadena, Texas with its mechanical bull, and the newly opened Billy Bob's Texas with its capacity of 6,000 hardly qualify as honky tonks. Nor do all the so-called C&W discoes, which are usually failed rock and roll places or singles bars for secretaries and shoe clerks who want to play cosmic cowboy or cosmic cowgirl—or should it be cosmic cowperson?

No. The real honky tonk—even after all these years—is set up out on the skirts of a town. Out where men are men, women are double breasted, and property values have been ruined by junk yards, parts houses, and pawn shops. Out where the minorities dwell. Out where the noble 55 Chevy sits regally atop concrete blocks in the front yard. In short, out on those edges of towns and cities where life is real and life is earnest and the bank account is but an empty dream. Or if not in town, the classic place may be out alongside the ubiquitous frontage road, so named in loving memory of Emil Frontage, the famous Franco-American civil engineer. M. Frontage conceived of having small two-lane blacktops run parallel to great expressways so that highway noise would not drown out the jukeboxes.

The classic honky tonk ought to sit on a couple of acres of unpaved caliche or red dirt. Neither asphalt nor concrete will do. Both substances cause great distress to falling bodies, and if one frequents roadhouses, he can be almost certain of getting knocked down in the parking lot at least once. Also, squealing tires are no problem on dirt, for only on television do tires squeal on dirt and sand. The building itself should be close to the front of the lot, for some cars need to be around behind, well away from the prying eyes on the highway. Once on the lot, it's every fellow for himself. If you park unjudiciously, you can wait until closing time to get your car out.

The lot is important, but the building is crucial. The classic style is long and narrow, and many of the great honky tonks are made by jamming two World War II army barracks together behind a false store front. The false front gives the final classic touch by providing the architrave, the colonnade, and the pediment.

Inside, the building should be divided on a three-to-one basis. The front quarter is devoted to the bar, restaurant, game room, and kitchen. The other three quarters should contain the dance hall, for no really dedicated dancer can but grieve at the postage-stamp-size dance floor seen in singles bars and discoes. The front part needs a dozen tables, a dozen or so booths for serious courting, a trifling of space for a good two-bit pool table, and a long, narrow area for the obligatory shuffleboard.

Behind the bar one finds, in addition to the numerous beer ads, the usual collection of bumper stickers and glitter signs: "If You Believe In Credit, Lend Me Five Dollars." "In God We Trust: All Others Cash." "America: Love It Or Leave It." "Get Your Heart In America Or Get Your Ass Out." "Cowboys Make Better Lovers." "Truckers Make Better Lovers." "Backhoe Operators Make Better Lovers." "Cowgirls Need Love, Too." "Rodeoers Stay On Longer." And most good honky tonks have a sign that appears to contain one long Polish word, which, upon inspection, turns out to be "Quityourbitching."

The dancing room, where the real action takes place, is dimmer, bigger, and noisier. The dance floor properly belongs in the middle of the hall and should be about six inches lower than the seating area, which runs along both sides and contains tables and graveyard-style folding chairs. A rail separates the dance floor from the seating area, and various openings in the rail let the dancers issue onto the floor. I use the word "issue" on purpose, for no real dancer merely shambles out onto the floor to dance. Dancers hit the floor with that fluid, squirming motion that signifies art, style, and romance.

The band occupies one end of the hall and is separated from the floor by a rail. In a mean honky tonk, a chickenwire fence often separates the band from the dancers. The life of a customer, of course, comes cheaper than the life of a good pedal steel player. Needless to say, a honky tonk really shouldn't have any windows. People who frequent such places require privacy. And, of course, flying glass is a problem when an ejected customer decides to get even by chunking a brickbat in among the dancers.

But enough of art and architecture. How does the well-set-up honky tonk run from day to day? First, the hour of opening should be as early as possible and the hour of closing at least thirty minutes later than the legal shut-down time. There are only two kinds of people, Edwin Shrake says—leavers and stayers—"and leavers don't deserve nothing." A good stayer does not want barmaids and waitresses running around hollering "last call for alcohol" at the indecently early hour of 1:00 a.m. A honky tonk should open early for obvious reasons, for reasons of public service, public health, and domestic tranquility. Many a marriage has been saved by a neighborhood bar's being open at 11:00 a.m. and many a senior citizen has had his golden years lengthened and made blissful by morning visits to a well-run tavern.

Afternoon is a fine and tranquil time in a great honky tonk. Love has been known to blossom. Health has been miraculously restored to the halt and the lame. The ragged edge of care may have been knitted up by sleep in the medieval Scotland of Macbeth, but how much better have I seen the ragged edge knitted at the Broken Spoke in Austin, the Green Lantern in Monahans, or the Old Sadie Hawkins in Grand Prairie. The burning sun is suddenly extinguished as one steps into the cooled, darkened, and musically soothed interior of a classic honky tonk. Picture the scene. The harsh lights of day are suddenly replaced by the twinkle of neon, the gently burbling liquidity of the Hamms Sky Blue Water signs, the bubbling lava lamps regurgitating themselves inside the mighty Wurlitzer. The cooled breezes from the conditioned air machine waft across the sweat-stained work shirt. The strains of Floyd Tillman singing "Slipping Around" calm the frayed nerves. The buxom barmaid in her decollete' peasant blouse has shed a decade of hard years and looks like a gay young girl. Ah, the joys of an afternoon spent listening to Moon Mullican sing "I'll Sail My Ship Alone" as the discs from the shuffle-board make a gentle whoosh over the waxed hardwood and the ivory balls clack quietly against one another on the green baize table, and one disppointed eight ball player is heard to call another by that fine old Texas version of Oedipus Rex.

As the sun starts to set on the chert or caliche parking lot, the number of pickups and 1961 Cadillacs and slew-footed Fords starts to grow. The row of cars in early afternoon had nosed up close to the false front of the tavern like horses tied at the hitching rail of a Western saloon. Now, as dusk settles, the caliche of the parking lot is stirred by more and more vehicles inching in. The sale of beer picks up, the succulent chicken fried steak starts to add its "odors savors sweet" to the afternoon smells of the bar. The constant opening and closing of the front door shoots blinding shafts of light across the pool table. The voices quicken and the musicbox gets turned up a notch or two. And the quiet colored end of evening smiles.

As the stars come out and prance about, dancing heel and toe, the fervor builds. Tired old boys with brilliantined hair who have operated a dozer or a backhoe all day start to open guitar cases on the bandstand. Hair that has spent all day in plastic rollers as big as beer cans is now teased out and sprayed to a metallic finish. White wigs that stand as high as Dolly Parton's have been secured firmly to mouse-colored hair. Mahogany brown belts with white stitches and raised letters that say Linda Kay are threaded through loops of lavendar stretch jeans. Trembling fingers uncork precious quart bottles of Evening in Paris. A maze of wires takes order on the bandstand to connect fiddles and basses and pedal steels to computer-like boxes that blink and wink and lead to scuffed speakers with bumper stickers proclaiming that this aggregation is called, say, Floyd Durant and the East Texas Swingboys. The quiet colored end of evening smiles.

As night encompasses all, the "smell of steak settles down in the passageways"—and restrooms—and the steady thump of the bass massages the beaverboard walls. The draft beer foams to a higher head and the pecker-necked bottles of Lone Star send icy streams of moisture down their sides. The dancers whirl in stately arabesques as scores of Merle Haggards clutch to their manly chests the ample bosoms of Dollys and Tammies and Emmlous. The Swingboys go from Hank Williams to Hank Thompson to Hank Snow. The girl singer in majorette boots and pleated skirt changes magically from Kitty Wells to Patsy Montana to Crystal Gayle. The songs of Cowboy Copas and Lefty Frizzell and Jim Reeves give place to Waylon and Willie and the Boys.

Despite the changes in music, honky tonks are frozen in the fifties; they live on and on in that halycon decade of the atom bomb and the Berlin Wall and before that crazy Asian war. They live in a time when "across the deep blue water there lives an old German's daughter by banks of the old river Rhine."

When the band takes its accustomed breaks, there is a quiet time for love, for assignations to be made, for the woman whose husband is in a rig somewhere between Bangor, Maine and Opelusas, Louisiana to be, as the song says, "Almost Persuaded." Time for a hundred decisions and indecisions. Time to drop those soft words in those small shell-like ears. Words that "make the world go away and get it off our shoulders." And later there will be time to "take the ribbons from her hair, to shake it loose and let it fall." The quiet colored end of evening smiles.

As the night draws to its close, as the sounds of "last call for alcohol" echo throughout the tavern, promises are made and broken, whispered conferences in powder rooms create alibis, and time rushes toward its moment of climax. Country swains who have "not dared to dare" are left to climb into the lonely pickup cab alone. For other, luckier lads, purchases from restroom coin machines are secreted in wallets. And with the dying of the band and the raising of the lights, the quiet colored end of evening smiles—and leers.

As black night seals up all the rest, lines from the great Hank Thompson song echo in the mind. "The glamor of the gay night life has lured you" begins the second stanza of the greatest of all the honky tonk songs—"The Wild Side of Life" ("I Didn't Know God Made Honky Tonk Angels"). The word "gay," of course, is out of place in a honky-tonk song nowadays. But perhaps it is not noticed because country boys don't use the word to denote homosexuality. They use a longer word—and it doesn't begin with a "g." And perhaps even the word "glamor" is not the perfect word to use in describing a honky tonk. But the sentiment is what counts, and the sentiment of "The Wild Side of Life" is pure-and-T Country and pure-and-T honky tonk. "The places," as the song says, "where the wine and liquor flow" were made for broken promises, broken marriages, broken hearts, broken dreams, and broken heads. And who could ask for more?

Notes

1. Eric Partridge, *A Dictionary of Slang and Unconventional English* (New York: Macmillan, 1970), p. 1201.

2. Harold Wentworth and Stuart Flexner, *Dictionary of American Slang* (New York: Crowell, 1960), pp. 265-66.

3. Dorothy Horstman, *Sing Your Heart Out, Country Boy* (New York: Dutton, 1975; rpt New York: Pocket Books, 1976) mentions another song and gives a version of the spread of the term:
Ragtime, an enormously popular musical style, was born in Sedalia, Missouri, in 1890, and quickly spread throughout the South. One of its musical characteristics was the "honky tonk" piano, and, by extension, the saloons and bawdy houses where it was played became urban "honky tonks." One of the earliest uses of the term was in a song entitled "Honka-Tonk Rag," written in 1910 by Earl Jones and L. Albert. Country boys visiting these saloons brought the name home with them. (p. 221)
Ms. Horstman dates the rise of country honky tonks earlier than I do.

The best discussion of country honky tonk music is to be found in Bill C. Malone, *Country Music, USA* (Austin and London: University of Texas Press, 1968), pp. 162-70. Malone's book is the standard work on country and western music.

4. Malone, p. 162.

5. The Moon River Beach was built about 1937 on the muddiest, dirtiest, most sluggish bend of the Cahaba River. The name was suggested by a fifteen-year-old girl, Jacqueline Lee, now Mrs. James E. Lassatter of 629 Alabama Avenue in Birmingham.

6. Malone, p. 163. Malone says that Ernest Tubb "best exemplified" the new honky tonk music.

7. The Golden Age of Country Music does not completely coincide with what I consider to be the Golden Age of the honky tonk. See Malone (pp. 185-86 and p. 209) for a discussion of the Golden Age.

8. "San Antonio Rose" was first recorded by Wills as an instrumental in 1938. It was recorded again, with lyrics sung by Tommy Duncan, in 1940.

How to Have, to Hold, or Free Oneself of a Lover/*Dolores L. Latorre*

Dolores L. Latorre

How to Have, to Hold, or Free Oneself of a Lover

Dolores L. Latorre

Throughout the decade of the 1960s while my husband and I were engaged in an ethnological field study for *The Mexican Kickapoo Indians*, published by the University of Texas Press at Austin in 1975, we made our headquarters in Múzquiz, Coahuila. During our years in Múzquiz I was able, through the generosity of our two Mexican servants and their *curandera* friends, to gather much folklore of the area. My particular interests were in the use of local curative plants and the local *norteño* cuisine. The result of the latter research, *Cooking and Curing with Mexican Herbs,* was published in 1977 by Encino Press, Austin.

However, as the data was being sorted out for the latter work, I realized that there was enough other material dealing with a subject so unique and of such delicate nature that it required a separate publication, thus the material for this article.

Mexican women—like women of all stations the world over—are preoccupied with the process of getting a man, holding him, and freeing themselves from him once they have tired of his embraces. How Mexican women have discovered the potency of herbs—often in an admixture of some other rather astonishing ingredients—for controlling affairs of the heart is now available to interested readers.

When a woman desires a man she dries and pulverizes either cudweed, smooth jimsonweed or *epazote de zorillo (Chenopodium graveolens),* a variety of wormweed, and sprinkles this powder on the food of the loved one. If this formula brings less than the desired results, she buys the pulverized bones of a black cat called *Polvos de la Madre Celestina,* at a *hierbería* (herb shop) and sprinkles them on the food or beverage of the person she wishes to captivate.

If the previous formulas fail, she secures either a desiccated humming bird or a horned toad, killed when neither the killer nor the animal is angry. After powdering it, she carries it in a cloth next to her body or in a pocket in order that the desired one will fall in love with her.

To reinforce her efforts in getting a man, she may purchase a perfume called *Oriental,* bought either in a drugstore or a *hierbería* and rubs it on her hands before shaking that of the person she wishes to place under her power. This technique is even more effective when she dabs the perfume on the crook of an elbow and on her forehead. This perfume will immediately bring the desired person under her spell. My informant, a *curandera,* many of whose clients were prostitutes of the *zona de tolerancia* (red-light district), declared they had excellent results from its use.

On the other hand, when a woman desires the husband of another, she carries out a campaign to cause the man to hate his wife and leave her, thus attaining her wishes. First, she finds some excrement of the wife (not difficult in light of plumbing facilities in northern Coahuila), which she dries and pulverizes into a fine powder. In the evening at eight o'clock sharp she goes to the cemetery where she digs soil from the left side of the grave of a man who has been stabbed to death in a fit of anger.

The finely powdered excrement and this soil are mixed and sprinkled in the form of a cross inside the rival's house, on the clothing of the rival's husband or lover, or inside of his shoes. If unable to gain access to the house, the mixture may be sprinkled on the man or on the entrance to his home. The anger of the deceased from whose grave the soil was obtained will transfer itself to the spouse and cause him to hate his wife gradually and eventually to leave her.

By way of digression, our house servant's first chore after finishing the breakfast dishes was to sweep the sidewalk and note any unusual soil on it. She also sprinkled water on the sidewalk in the form of a cross to offset any overlooked signs of mischief.

The woman who related the previous information told me the following experience. When she was living with the man who had fathered her last six children (She had had eight by another.), one day she found suspicious-looking powder in front of her door. From that day onward, her *señor* who up to this time had been very good to her, paying her rent and buying provisions each fortnight, became cooler and cooler toward her until he finally left her for another woman. After leaving, he continued to buy clothing for the children, but one day he brusquely told them they were no longer his care and not to molest him further.

Once a woman has conquered the man of her desires, she contrives to hold him by all possible stratagems. If she wants her man, whether he be her husband or lover, to keep her constantly on his mind she takes the bow from inside his hat, catches a bat or a domestic dove, and ties the bow under a wing and releases the bird. If no bird is available, she hides the bow. As long as the bow remains with the bird or is hidden, her lover or husband will not be able to keep her out of his mind.

To keep him from wandering into greener pastures, a woman dries and pulverizes the leaves of *toloache* (hairy or smooth jimson-weed), and daily places a bit of it in his food. The man is then said to be "entoloachado" (jimsonweeded). He does not leave the house to spend his time in the *cantinas,* pool halls, the plaza, or out in *la zona de tolerancia.*

A woman, however, must use discretion in the amount of jimson-weed she puts in the food; for if she overdoes it, he might become in-sane or she might even cause his death, as we shall see later.

A Mexican youth who worked for us during our first months in Múzquiz refused to eat or drink anything offered him after seeing a volunteer plant of jimsonweed in the garden. Unaware at the time of the danger that this plant held for Mexican males, we had allowed it to grow luxuriously, since its fragrant blossoms at sunset helped to mitigate the nauseous odor emanating from the small pigs on either side of our home which were being fattened with table scraps for the annual *matanza* (butchering) as soon as the first norther arrived.

Shortly after the young gardener saw the jimsonweed, which we immediately destroyed, he noticed that my husband seldom left the house. We soon learned he had spread the gossip throughout the town that I had him *entoloachado.*

Not only must a husband be refrained from wandering but in the meantime he must be treated so that he will not nag. To attain this blissful situation a woman takes a few of her pubic hairs, sears them on the *comal,* and sprinkles them on her husband's food, preferably in his coffee since the dark colors mingle without detection.

If the above simple formula does not bring the results she tries a stronger one. This consists in giving him *la taza y media* (the cup and a half). She reserves a cup and a half of water in which she has taken a sponge bath when she washes her genitalia, the area behind the knees, and the armpits. She will then occasionally place a few drops of this powerful liquid in his food.

To keep her man from desiring another woman, she gathers some of his semen in a cloth and buries it in a flower pot or places it in a bottle of alcohol. In this manner, she will have control of his manliness and he cannot have intercourse or approach another woman. *"Es como dominada su naturaleza"* (It is as though his nature were tamed.). As a refinement of this method she may make a small effigy of the man, forming testicles with garlic, cloves, or chiles. Among the many names used in Mexico for the male organ, *chile* is one of them. She then places this small effigy in a bottle of alcohol where his "nature" is under her control.

If a husband or lover is given to excessive drinking, women, or other vices, but is still loved by his spouse or mistress who wants to hold him and have him go straight, she buys at the local church three prayers which she invokes, especially designed for this situation. The supplicant, while reciting the prayers at noon and at midnight is advised to wear inside of her shoes two prints of a death's-head, also purchased at church.

My informant had been given the prayers by a friend whose husband, a notorious drinker, spent his wages at the *cantina*, was seldom home and, on the rare occasions when he was, created many problems and disturbances in the family. The wife prayed for days on end and was about to give up in desperation when one day her husband confessed that on the way home the evening before, a death's-head had appeared to him. His fright was so acute it had cured him of drinking, and thereafter he was a model husband.

Prayer No. 1.
Holy Death, I earnestly implore you that, just as God created you immortal with your great power over all mortals until placing us in the celestial space where we shall enjoy a glorious day without night for all eternity and in the name of the Father, the Son, and the Holy Spirit, I beg of you and implore you to be my protector until the last day, the last hour, the last moment when your divine majesty orders me to your presence. Amen.

Prayer No. 2
Victorious Christ, vanquished on the cross, I beg with your infinite power to overcome (name of husband or lover) that he be vanquished also. If he be a fierce beast, tame as a lamb, tame as the flower of rosemary, he must arrive at our home. He broke bread with me, he drank water with me, and he permitted me to do many things. I want, Oh Lord, that your divine grace bring him to me, conquered and humiliated, to fulfill the promises he made. Since I believe, Oh Lord, that nothing is impossible for you, I earnestly beg you to concede my request, promising that I shall be your most devoted servant until the end of my life.

Prayer No. 3:
Dear Death of my heart, do not forsake me with your protection. Do not allow (name of husband or lover) to be tranquil one moment. Molest him; mortify him constantly; make him restless so he will always think of me and give up his habit.

After three prayers are invoked, the Lord's prayer is recited.

If a wife suspects her husband is in an angry mood while on his way home and is likely to abuse her, she recites the following prayer: "Lord, I see enemies approaching; they want the blood of my veins but I shall not give it to them for the wound of your side shall free me from them."

When a husband does go into a temper tantrum and begins to mumble, use abusive language, or threatens the wife and children when he arrives home, the wife recites the following prayer: "With two I see you, with three I tie you; I will drink your blood and break your heart. Christ, come to my aid and give me peace."

If a woman tires of a man and no longer wants to share his bed but does not want him to leave, she makes him impotent in the following manner. She kills a horned toad, allows it to desiccate completely, and pounds it into a fine powder. A small quantity of this powder is placed daily in his food to bring about the desired results. Another formula to make a man impotent is to place a sharp thorn of crown-of-thorns in the crack of the front door.

A wife, tiring of her husband yet not wishing him to leave her, may find a lover on the side. To prevent her husband from learning of her infidelity, she obtains a desiccated horned toad, powders and sprinkles it on his body and clothing. The cuckold man is then said to have been sprinkled with the powdered horned toad *(la echaron los polvos de camaleón),* meaning he is the only one who does not see that his wife is unfaithful.

As we learned earlier, Mexican males from adolescence live in fear of both the jimsonweeds for they know that if a wife or mistress tires of them she may resort to an overdose of this powerful drug. When a man dies in the area of Múzquiz of no apparent cause his wife is suspected of giving him *la veintiuna* (the twenty-one-day treatment with this weed). This plant is seldom, if ever, seen around Mexican homes among other medicinal herbs, although it is readily available in the fields where it grows profusely.

I regret, however, that never having had occasion to test the efficacy of the formulas for controlling affairs of the heart, I cannot give them my unqualified endorsement. I can say, nonetheless, that they are offered with the strongest recommendations of those who have used them.

Pecos Bill: His Genesis and Creators/*James M. Day*

James M. Day

Pecos Bill: His Genesis and Creators

James M. Day

Maybe Walt Disney really did give Pecos Bill to the world when he did the movie *Melody Time* in 1948. With it came Roy Rogers and the Sons of the Pioneers singing about this, the greatest cowboy of all time. Along with the telling of Bill's exploits and the caricatures of Bill and his cowboys doing what cowboys do, Roy and the Sons sing about it all so that Pecos Bill and the world he comes from are exposed.[1]

Writing in 1950, Richard Dorson labeled Pecos Bill as a fake hero, a comic demigod not a product of a "native mythology." Bill, Dorson thought, is a "native American Superman, all-conquering, all powerful, braggart, and whimsically destructive," a fake because proof of oral vitality is lacking.[2] To get at Pecos Bill's roots, young though he is, one has to look into his region, the Pecos River country of Texas and New Mexico. And he has to look into the early recorders of the legend: Alonzo Van Oden, Tex O'Reilly, and Mody Boatright.

Mody Boatright was a folklorist, a good one, who represented his region well. He first published an article on the subject in *The Southwest Review* in 1929 which he titled "The Genius of Pecos Bill." There he explained the process by which the cowboy hero, under a multiplicity of names, came to be unified under the name of Pecos Bill.[3] This method of assimilation smacks of the oral tall tale tradition. Boatright, in a taped interview, stated that he had heard Pecos Bill stories all his life among the West Texas ranch folk where he was raised. And that is all the scholar claimed for his folk hero. Boatright, born in 1890, spent some of his earlier years in the Sweetwater ranching country, and he taught at Sul Ross State Teachers College in Alpine in 1923-1925.[4]

One year after Boatright's birth, there was a Texas Ranger detachment stationed at Presidio under command of Sergeant John R. Hughes. One of the Ranger privates of Hughes' command was

Alonzo Van Oden, a young man who kept a diary. Oden made an arrest that year of one William D. Barbee, alias "Pecos Bill," on a charge of murder. Oden also was acquainted with an ethereal character named Pecos Joe, a philosopher who knew the difference between a star and a meteor. As they were riding along together, Oden asked the question: "Pecos Joe, who are you and where do you come from?" The man replied:

"Who am I? Why I'm Pecos Joe. The man you're asking about, the man who was chained to covetousness, to wealth, to reputation, the man who was chained to murderous desires because he was betrayed by the two he loved best—that man is dead, and only Pecos Joe remains. Lon, I do believe in the Eternity of Love. It's the only thing that lives: Lies die; evil rots; wealth goes; honor is dimmed; but Love lives."

Of Pecos Joe, Oden wrote:

I met Pecos Joe two years ago: he came over to Valentine from Pecos; hung around for several days visiting and swapping yarns. He talks different from the rest of us, but his ideas are the same, so we like him. Pecos Joe is all the name he will give. The second night after I met him I took him home to bunk with me. Riding home, the night was almost as bright as day, and I kept looking up at the stars. Joe noticed it, and asked me what I knew about stars. I said, "Well, if I had a beautiful lady handy, I could be influenced and aided by the stars."

Pecos Joe laughed and said, "You didn't seem to need stars to feed taffy to that coy maiden in the eating house. Now Lon," and he pointed a finger to a twinkling little star, "notice the flickering light there, and over there?" Pointing his finger at another star, "See the steady glow? Well, the twinkler is called a star, and the steady one a meteor." This started a lecture on stars and the heavens, and finally got around to religion. I'm always interested in a man's religion, and I asked Pecos Joe for his. This is his answer:

"Lon, I can't believe in a hell in some bottomless pit, where souls are burned through eternity; neither can I believe in golden stairs and harps with angels floating around; but I do believe in the brotherhood of man, in sharing here on earth, suffering, happiness, and to be brief, follow as near as possible the teachings of the greatest Master the world has as yet produced. Whether this Master was divine or not—is not to me the great question; but the life He led, and the comfort He gives is the nearest to the divine we will ever know; so I am grateful for each day life gives. I feel a song in my heart when the sun awakens me in the morning; and as I lie on my bedding roll at night, I feel a prayer on my lips; I am weary but—free. I do not try to reach into the unknown; I live each day now, and strangely, I feel it is enough."[5]

So Pecos Bill and Pecos Joe were common enough names in the mountain country surrounding the Pecos River. Bill, being the more common name, became the moniker of the hero.

Then there was Edward S. "Tex" O'Reilly, who first took Pecos Bill out of the oral tradition and put him in print. He did this in *Century Magazine* in October, 1923, in an article entitled "The Saga of Pecos Bill." He explained: "In my boyhood days in west Texas I first heard of Bill, and in later years I have often listened to chapters of his history told around the chuck-wagon by gaudy mendacious cow-boys." He went on to state that "Pecos Bill is one of my favorite heroes. He has always been a very real person to me, although I know there ain't no sich animal." A cowboy "would break his neck to get a joke on anybody, and curious come latelys are his special joy."[6] Such statements bear looking into so far as the teller thereof is concerned. The logical question, the same one asked by Van Oden, is "Who is Tex O'Reilly?"

He was born in Denison, Texas, on August 15, 1880, in the only house built there at the time. Everyone else lived in tents, if O'Reilly is to be believed. This birthing makes him an aristocrat and his parents were Irish, so O'Reilly is an Irish aristocrat. Actually, he traced the family name back to 1016 when the Irish first began to use surnames. The O'Reillys soon moved from Denison to San Saba County, where young Edward, at the age of two, was introduced to the ways of cowboys, hard-working men all right, but a little reckless with the truth when it was storytelling time. His father was a contractor, an itinerant who "took contracts" to build stone courthouses and jails for the counties in West Texas that were just being organized. Young Edward's first memories were "of wacking around in West Texas in a covered wagon, driving all day across the old free-grass, open range country." At night Mrs. O'Reilly cooked in an iron skillet in the coals and afterward she made Edward, his sister, and his brother, "learn to read from an old *Robinson Crusoe* in words of one syllable."

Tex O'Reilly never realized it, but it was his parents who gave him "the curse of the meandering foot." His father by example, forcing them all over West Texas in a covered wagon, and his mother by teaching him of Robinson Crusoe. But he also may have taken a few lessons from those knights of the cattle country, the cowboys. O'Reilly recalls an incident when he was four or five years old when a cowboy rode up the campfire one night, sat down on a log and exposed a fatal wound, and began telling his dying man's confession of how he had just killed his best friend:

"Let me alone a minute. Don't touch me. I want to tell you something. I have just killed my best friend."

He sat there and told this story: He and his friend had been out on the range hunting their cattle and branding the calves. For six months they had not seen another human being. His friend liked to sing, but the only tune he knew was "Yankee Doodle." Day after day and evening he sang "Yankee Doodle," till this cowboy got tired of hearing it.

He told his friend to lay off that tune, but he wouldn't do it.

What had happened was that they both had "cabin fever," the kind of insanity that comes over men when they are a long time together in lonely places.

They had several fights over that tune. They stopped speaking to each other. They separated their little cook outfit and wouldn't eat together. Still that fellow kept on singing "Yankee Doodle." He sang it all day while they were riding and at night he sang it by his separate campfire, till one night when they were sitting glaring at each other and he was singing the cowboy said,

"Nobody but a damn fool would keep that up. Stop it, or there'll be trouble."

He kept on singing. They had a gun fight, and the cowboy killed him.

Then he got on his horse and rode across country till he found a wagon track, and he followed it till he came to our wagon.

When he finished telling this he rolled off the log. My father undressed him and washed and bandaged his wound, but without saying anything more he died that night.[7]

O'Reilly was with his father when they saw the Oklahoma Sooners make their land run. He was eight years old at the time, but his father did not like Oklahoma, so a little later they moved to Chicago with the intent of educating the children so they would make good, steady, sober citizens. For Edward O'Reilly it was too late. He had already acquired the curse of the meandering foot. He lived peaceably enough in Chicago until the Spanish-American War broke out when he was still seventeen and he lied about his age and joined Company B of the Fourth U.S. Infantry. He fought in Cuba where his outfit took Snodgrass Hill several hundred times and El Caney more than once. After that he went to the Philippines where he contracted malaria and tried to die.[8] After his army discharge came through, O'Reilly ended up in Japan, in Kobe where, out of necessity, he founded "The O'Reilly School of English." But he tired of that after two months and went to selling water to sea-going vessels in Moji, Japan.[9] Then he became a sailor, fought with his captain, and got thrown into the ship's hold in irons. He found he was poorly equipped for being a sailor and that all those tales of horror about life at sea that he had read did not tell half the real terror of life at sea. But he finally got to Shanghai where he became bodyguard for a Chinese rent collector at four pesos a day. He only lasted half a day because the Chinese rent collector beat up a poor old woman who couldn't pay her rent and O'Reilly couldn't take that, so he beat up the rent collector and quit. Then he became a bouncer in a Chinese theater for four nights, before getting a respectable job as Police Constable #47, Shanghai International Police Department. This was good duty because he made $40.00 a month plus living quarters and meals and

he could pick up extra money as a guard at Chinese funerals. He
made good money at this because he was tall and the Chinese fan-
cied tall bodyguards at their funerals. Then he got a better offer as a
drill instructor for the Chinese Imperial Army. He transformed the
Chinese Imperial Army into the modern force it is today and then he
tired of the Orient and came back home to Chicago. He had had 15
cents when he left seven years earlier and he had a quarter when he
got back. But his brother had sent him $150.00 to Salt Lake City to
get him in and he had spent that.[10]

Then set in a year of stability in which O'Reilly received some of
the best training in the world for a folklorist. He became a newspaper
reporter, at first on the *Chicago Tribune* and later on other papers.
After a year of reporting he became an itinerant book auctioneer
through the South, in Missouri, Kentucky, Tennessee, Alabama, and
Arkansas. This led him to New Orleans, where he arrived in time to
join a filibustering expedition to Venezuela. There he became a major
in the Army of Liberty, a rag-tag outfit that got a good whipping.
Finally he got back to Galveston and landed in San Antonio about
1907.[11] There he went to work as a reporter for the *San Antonio Light
and Gazette* owned by E. B. Chandler, where he eventually worked his
way up to become managing editor. When the *Light* published its
50th anniversary edition in 1932, it paid the following tribute to
O'Reilly: "Many have come and gone through the editorial rooms of
the *Light,* but no character stands forth commanding the imagination
more than Tex O'Reilly, who counts his newspaper experience on the
Light as one of the pleasant spots in his life."[12]

During this time he married Sophia (Dixie) Blakeney of San Saba
and they lived in San Antonio from 1907 to 1915. At first they lived
on Macon Street, where they had a real estate office, and then they
lived on Devine Street. In between these dates, O'Reilly's health broke
and he and Dixie went to live near Sanderson in Terrell County on a
ranch.[13] This is the rugged country where the Pecos River lets go its
waters into the Rio Grande. This was a lonely country where the
ranch folk talked to each other a lot when they got the chance, and
O'Reilly, being the garrulous sort, picked up their stories. It is also a
country dominated by Alpine, where Mody Boatright taught a decade
later and recorded the lore of the country, and where Ranger Van
Oden knew about Pecos Bill and Pecos Joe.

When the Mexican Revolution broke out in 1910, O'Reilly was
not long in getting into it. He hired on with the Associated Press as a
stringer and he joined the revolutionary forces against the *Diazistas.*
He fought alongside Abraham Gonzalez, Pancho Villa, Pascual
Orozco, Emiliano Zapata and others on and off until 1916 when he
returned to the United States, moved to New York and started free
lance writing.[14] His autobiography, *Roving and Fighting,* was published
in 1918 and he had a biography published in 1933, one written by
Lowell Thomas entitled *Born to Raise Hell.* The title page on this one
reflects that it was "As told by Tex O'Reilly." There is a decided dif-

ference in tone between *Roving and Fighting* in 1918, where an effort is made at straight, forthright narrative, and *Born to Raise Hell* in 1933, which displays an attitude of being reckless with the truth. It was between these two, in 1923, that O'Reilly wrote the Pecos Bill article for *Century Magazine.*

O'Reilly claims to have been one of John R. Hughes' Texas Rangers for seven months and he was a major in the Texas National Guard after 1918. By 1928 he was living in Greenwich Village where he was a free lance writer. His home became a gathering place for those under the curse of the meandering foot who were reckless with the truth. O'Reilly died at the Veterans Hospital at Sunmount, New York, on December 8, 1946.[15]

But the character he left has been growing ever since, having been "passed on to a larger audience."[16] As he came to be more studied, the "fake hero" aspect of Pecos Bill came to be more controversial to those interested in the provenance of lore. Bill's companions in this labeling are Paul Bunyan, John Henry, Tony Beaver and Febold Feboldson.[17] Interestingly, Dorson was not the first to compare Pecos Bill with Paul Bunyan, for O'Reilly had stated that Bill and Paul were blood brothers by the fact that both were "fathered by a liar."[18] Boatright said that the two were dissimilar because Pecos Bill was not a giant like Bunyan, yet he thought that Pecos Bill would have supplanted his rivals as "the Paul Bunyan of the Southwest" had not industrial progress ended what he called the "heroic age."[19]

Comparison of O'Reilly's 1923 Pecos Bill and Boatright's 1929 model reveal that while both men cut their hero from the same mold, Boatright did not rely principally on the O'Reilly account. O'Reilly provides the seeds from which later writers created "the fabled demigod" aspects of Bill's character but it must be remembered that this same O'Reilly was a grand adventurer, a soldier of fortune, a member of Lowell Thomas' famed Liar's Club. He was thinking in that vein when he wrote

Bill invented most of the things connected with the cow business. He was a mighty man of valor, the king killer of the bad men, and it was Bill who taught the broncho how to buck. It is a matter of record that he dug the Rio Grande one dry year when he grew tired of packin' water from the Gulf of Mexico.[20]

After growing up with the coyotes, Bill ran into a cowboy who told Bill he was a human. To that Pecos Bill replied, "Lead me to them humans and I'll throw in with them." O'Reilly followed:

Bill went to town with this cow-hand, and in due time he got to enjoying all the pleasant vices of mankind, and decided that he certainly was a human. He got to running' with a wild bunch, and sunk lower and lower, until he finally became a cow-boy.

It wasn't long until he was famous as a bad man. He invented the

six-shooter and train-robbin' and most of the crimes popular in the old days of the West. He didn't invent cow-stealin'. That was discovered by King David in the Bible, but Bill improved on it. . . .

It wasn't long before Bill had killed all the bad men in west Texas, massacred all the Indians, and eat all the buffalo. So he decided to migrate to a new country where hard men still thrived and a man could pass the time away.[21]

Bill then headed west, tamed a rattlesnake and a mountain lion, and became head of the meanest bunch of cowboys that ever breathed. Bill staked out New Mexico for his ranch and used Arizona as a calf-pasture. He rode an Oklahoma cyclone that went "sunfishin', back-flippin', [and] side-windin'" as it skinned the earth creating the Staked Plains. When the cyclone found it couldn't throw Bill, it rained out from under him, this causing a flood that created the Grand Canyon, and releasing Bill in mid-air. He came down in California and the spot where he landed is Death Valley.[22]

O'Reilly spins these tales over and over with variations until finally Pecos Bill died. Some said it was Bill's drinking habits that killed him. Since ordinary liquor had no kick for him, he started drinking wolf bait, mainly strychnine, loaded with fish hooks and barbed wire. He liked that toddy quite a lot, but the barbed wire rusted his insides and gave him indigestion until he wasted away to two tons and then died. Another account of Bill's death states that he met a man from Boston who was wearing a mail-order cow-boy outfit and asking "fool questions about the West; and poor old Bill laid down and laughed himself to death."[23]

Boatright repeated a variation of that version of Pecos Bill's death, showing that he had either read O'Reilly's account or that they used the same oral tradition sources. Boatright presents a more plausible account of Bill's birth by having him born on the Texas side of the Sabine River and presenting him as a precocious child. When the Sabine country started getting crowded, Bill's parents, the Old Man and Old Woman, headed west. He stated that a volume would be needed to

tell how Pecos Bill was lost by the Ole Man on the banks of the Pecos River, how he grew up with the coyotes, how he all but exterminated the vicious godaphroes; how he invented ways of capturing the sly whiffle-pooffle and the shyer milamo bird; to relate his adventures as buffalo hunter, cattleman, railroad contractor, and to detail his many other exploits.[24]

Boatright passes by those to deal with variations of Pecos Bill's death, including the one that he smoked himself to death at age ninety. Bill smoked his own concoction of Kentucky homespun, sulphur and gun powder. Boatright includes the one about the wolf-bait and fish-hooks and even the account that Bill drank himself to death on whiskey, onions, and nitroglycerin. Bill might have laughed himself to death at the Boston man with the mail order clothes, but most probably he died in Cheyenne when he heard a speech by a country lawyer "just three years out of Mississippi" who made a speech about keeping "inviolate the sacred traditions of the Old West." After leaving the speech, Bill "went out and crawled in a prairie-dog hole and died of solemncholy." Boatright, in his gait and word choices followed the strictures of the tall tale on the American frontier and in so doing set himself up to be used as "wolf-bait" by later liars.[25]

The man who fully exploited the stories of Pecos Bill was James Cloyd Bowman. He had no Southwestern contacts, but took the offerings of O'Reilly and Boatright and structured a legend straight from King Arthur. In 1937 Bowman put out his *Pecos Bill: the Greatest Cowboy of All Time.*[26] Bowman is to Pecos Bill what Malory is to King Arthur. He is bedrock. A native of Leipsic, Ohio, Bowman took his bachelor of science degree at Ohio Northern University in 1905, and he studied thereafter at Harvard, receiving the doctor of philosophy degree in 1923. For most of his academic career, Bowman served as head of the English Department at Northern State Teachers College at Marquette, Michigan, he died in 1961. A statement he made one time reveals that he became interested in the folklore of America while studying at Harvard with Barrett Wendell. And it was through this study that the Pecos Bill of Van Oden, Boatright and O'Reilly took on a structure akin to the Arthurian legend, for Bowman's work is replete with classical references.[27]

At the time the wise old Coyote found Bill on the banks of the Pecos, Grandy was the undisputed leader of the "Loyal and Approved Packs of the Pecos and Rio Grande Valleys," so the wise old animal "schooled" Bill, or Cropear as he was then known, in the "knowledge that had been handed down through thousands of generations of the Pack's life." In time, all animals in the kingdom except the rattlesnake and the Wouser (a cross between a mountain lion and a grizzly bear) promised to help Bill lead a charmed life. By the time Grandy had "gone down the long, long trail that has no turning," Bill was the best of the pack, so good in fact that some brother Coyotes began to wonder if they had been wise in making Cropear a member of their order.[28]

But that was soon solved for them as Bob Hunt, known as Chuck, a cowboy, found Bill who by then had such perfectly developed muscles that he "looked like another Hercules." Through a tattoo on both of them, they discovered themselves to be brothers, so Chuck took Bill back to the I.X.L. Ranch where Gun Smith and the other cowboys initiated him into the "sacred rites of the Ancient and Renowned Order of the Knights of the Round Table of the Genus Bovine, the Cowpuncher." During the initiation, Pecos Bill took a place in the irregular circle that included Mushmouth, Fat Adams,

Bullfrog Doyle, Moon Hennessey, Pretty Pete Rogers, Legs, and Bean Hole, the cook.

After his initiation, Bill soon replaced Gun Smith as the leader of these irregular knights with Gun Smith becoming his leading knight and Moon Hennessey his most troublesome one. Still, Bill was able to unite his kingdom by inventing branding, thus establishing ranching, and being a better cowboy than anyone else. He discovered Camelot by establishing his Perpetual Motion Ranch on Pinnacle Mountain, but he soon tired of it so he and his knights looked for new kingdoms to conquer. He heard of Old Satan, the leader of the Devil's Cavalry of Hell's Gate Gulch, so Bill decided to take them in. After Bill whipped the rattlesnake and rode the Wouser, Old Satan surrendered.

Afterward, Bill conquered the Pacing White Stallion, invented chaps, and installed democracy before Slue Foot Sue came on the scene to disrupt things. Bill and Moon Hennessey argued over Sue as Moon nursed an old grudge. This marked the beginning of the end for the kingdom, but Bill still busted up a cyclone and created the Grand Canyon and Death Valley before open rebellion broke out on the range with Moon Hennessey leading the attack. After a sharp series of confrontations, Moon came to recognize Bill as being superior and Bill forgave Moon for the uprising. Thereafter Moon was a loyal subject as the cowboys set out to destroy Major Duval, Lord of the Mountain on Miracle Ranch. Duval was tough because he had the attorneys and judges on his side, but Bill was justice so he won.

Then it was all over. They drove the cattle to Kansas City, divided the profits, and celebrated by giving the first Wild West Show outside the Southwest. They went on a drinking spree during which Bill fought and annihilated Knockdown Buckner and he shot off the trigger finger of every bully in town. As a result the Kansas City police and fire departments started looking for Pecos Bill. He was a wanted man, but that did not bother him as he mounted his Pacing White Stallion, named Widowmaker, and "rode serenely off into the night." This mysterious disappearance is in keeping with Bowman's creation of his Pecos Bill in the Arthurian tradition, for just as King Arthur awaits somewhere to help his people when needed, so Pecos Bill became a "fabled demigod," near at hand "wielding the magic rope."

The meaning of this growth goes back to Dorson and his "fake hero" theory. The comic part of Pecos Bill is indeed a product of the American frontier as it manifested itself in the Southwest. Both O'Reilly and Boatright were merely telling tall tales when they recorded their versions of Pecos Bill. But it took a Harvard Ph.D. who lived in Ohio and Michigan to pour Bill into the demigod mold, and it required the movie makers with all their caricaturing skill to indelibly imprint that mold onto the minds of humanity. All writers since Bowman have stressed the "fabled demigod" aspects of Pecos Bill rather than his homespun origins. But if Richard Dorson had known enough to look at Pecos Bill's genealogy, he could not have denied the pedigree.

Notes

1. Walt Disney, "Pecos Bill," *Melody Time* (New York, 1948); Eliot Daniel (lyrics by Johnny Lange), "Pecos Bill." Recorded by Roy Rogers and the Sons of the Pioneers (New York: Victor [Album Y*375], 1948).

2. Richard M. Dorson, "Folklore and Fake Lore," *American Mercury,* LXX (March, 1950), 335-336.

3. Mody Boatright, "The Genius of Pecos Bill," *Southwest Review,* XIV (July, 1929), 418-428. Reprinted in Ernest B. Speck (ed.), *Mody Boatright, Folklorist, A Collection of Essays* (Austin: University of Texas Press, 1973), pp. 3-12.

4. Harry H. Ransom, "Biographical Essay," in Speck (ed.) *Mody Boatright, Folklorist,* pp. xi-xviii; Mody Boatright to Roger Abrahams, November, 1965 (tape recording in Folklore Archives, Wayne State University, Detroit).

5. Ann Jensen (ed.), *Texas Ranger's Diary & Scrapbook* (Dallas: The Kaleidograph Press, 1936), pp. 26-27, 36.

6. Edward O'Reilly, "The Saga of Pecos Bill," *Century Magazine,* 106 (October, 1923), 827, and unpaged following p. 800.

7. Tex O'Reilly, as told to Lowell Thomas, *Born to Raise Hell: The Life Story of Tex O'Reilly, Soldier of Fortune* (New York: Doubleday, Doran and Company, 1931), pp. 10-15.

8. Major Edward S. O'Reilly, *Roving and Fighting, Adventures Under Four Flags* (New York: The Century Company, 1918), pp. 163-167.

9. *Ibid.,* pp. 168-188.

10. *Ibid.,* pp. 189-248.

11. *Ibid.,* pp. 230-261.

12. "Famous Character Tex O'Reilly," *San Antonio Light,* February 25, 1932.

13. O'Reilly, *Roving and Fighting,* p. 262; Jules A. Appler's *General Directory and Blue Book of Greater San Antonio, 1909* (San Antonio: Jules A. Appler, 1909), p. 586; *Ibid., 1910,* p. 523; *Directory of the City of San Antonio, 1910-1911* (San Antonio: Texas Publishing Company, 1910), p. 836; *San Antonio City Directory, 1914-1915* (San Antonio: Jules A. Appler, 1914), p. 471.

14. O'Reilly, *Roving and Fighting,* pp. 263-276.

15. "Tex O'Reilly Dies; Served 8 Flags, 66," *New York Times,* December 9, 1946, p. 25.

16. O'Reilly, "The Saga of Pecos Bill," p. 828.

17. Dorson, "Folklore and Fake Lore," pp. 335-336.

18. O'Reilly, "The Saga of Pecos Bill," p. 827.

19. Speck (ed.), *Mody Boatright, Folklorist,* pp. 4-5.

20. O'Reilly, "The Saga of Pecos Bill," p. 828.

21. *Ibid.,* p. 829.

22. *Ibid.,* pp. 830-831.

23. *Ibid.,* p. 833.

24. Speck (ed.), *Mody Boatright, Folklorist,* pp. 6-9.

25. *Ibid.,* pp. 10-11.

26. (Chicago: Albert Whitman and Company).

27. "James C. Bowman Dies at 81: Author of Books for Children," *New York Times,* September 28, 1961, p. 41; Stanley J. Kunitz and Howard Haycraft (eds.), *The Junior Book of Authors* (2nd ed. revised; New York: H. W. Wilson Company, 1951), pp. 42-43; Martha E. Ward and Dorothy A. Marquardt (eds.), *Authors of Books for Young People* (2nd ed.; Metuchen, New Jersey: The Scarecrow Press, 1971), p. 57; W. J. Burke and Will D. Howe (eds.) Revised by Irving Weiss and Ann Weiss, *American Authors and Books, 1640 to the Present Day* (3d ed. revised, 2nd printing; New York: Crown Publishers, October, 1973), p. 70.

28. Bowman, *Pecos Bill,* pp. 30-37. The remainder of this paper is based on references from the same book.

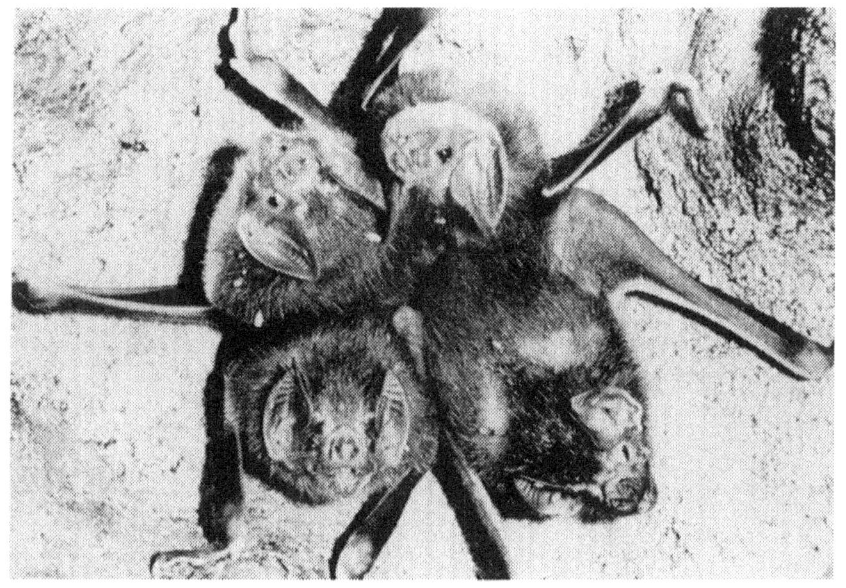

The Vampire in an Age of Technology/*Leslie M. Thompson*

Vampire Bats
credit Robert W. Mitchell

vampire, children born on Christmas Day or between Christmas and Epiphany (Greece), perjurors, persons under a curse by their parents, suicides, murdered people whose deaths went unavenged, people who ate a sheep killed by a wolf, persons who drowned or died violently, stillborn illegitimate children of parents also illegitimate, a dead person over whose coffin a cat, dog, or hen jumped, also criminals, bastards, witches, magicians, excommunicated people or unbaptized people, seventh sons of a seventh son, those dead persons whose body was reflected in a mirror, those persons born from the unholy union of a werewolf and witch (Russia), babies born with teeth, badly deformed people, and—in short—people with personal characteristics such as blue eyes, red hair or some other trait uncommon to a given area.

The vampire myth possibly originated in the belief among many primitive cultures that death consists of passing into a spirit world which, like earth, required food and water. Some Babylonian tales warn of ghosts who prey on men by eating their flesh and draining their veins. This notion likely contributed to the practice of offering living animals to satisfy the thirst of departed human beings. In *Totem and Taboo,* Freud indicates that at first most primitive cultures viewed all of the dead as having a grudge against life, but in later stages of development, ancient man ascribed malevolence only to those of the dead who had reason for feeling resentful.[1]

The concepts above, of course, rested largely upon empirical evidence as opposed to a perceptive or profound understanding of the human psyche. Contemporary theories attempt to explain this myth in light of modern psychological and scientific insights and evidence and thus to create a "vampire for the times." Interestingly, many of these theories seek not to debunk or destroy the concept but to explain it in believable terms. Such attempts, coupled with the continued popularity of vampire stories and movies, must tell us something about ourselves.

A plausible theory which in part helps explain the rise of vampirism concerns premature burial. Inadequate medical knowledge enhanced the likelihood of premature burial, and such a circumstance does help explain the fact of the uncorrupted corpse. If a vampire or other scare caused superstitious people to open the grave to discover a recently buried corpse not yet decomposing, with a frightful expression on its face and blood on its hands, then vampirism would be the logical explanation. Instances of premature burial crop up even today, and the number of such cases must have been magnified during the time before modern medical technology. Also, there exists the possibility that under certain conditions the corpses might have remained intact for long periods of time. Instances such as these might well give rise to vampire stories among ignorant people.

Numerous theories relate to the vampire's need for blood. Webster's International Dictionary, for example, defines a vampire as "a bloodsucking ghost or re-animated body of a dead person believed to

The Vampire in an Age of Technology

Leslie M. Thompson

Progenitors of the vampire go far back into history, and myths and folktales of such bloodsucking figures as Ekimmu, Lillith, Lamia, Aluka, and Strix dot the landscape. The word vampire, however, did not enter the English language until the 1730's, but within the next few decades, the interest in vampires increased rapidly. Accordingly, vampire stories proliferated, and the late eighteenth and early nineteenth centuries saw this motif come into full bloom in European literature. It seems strange that this crude motif would blossom in literature at such a late date and that it would continue to maintain a profound hold on the modern imagination. Obviously, this widespread popularity reveals a great deal about nineteenth and twentieth century sensibilities, fears, and anxieties. This paper, therefore, will briefly discuss early folk, mythological, and other attempts to account for vampires, and then shift its attention to modern definitions and theories about vampires and what these notions reveal about some prominent modern concerns.

The terror inspired by vampires has prompted numerous theories as to the definition and origin of these malign and bloodthirsty creatures. These theories, which reflect the obvious ignorance of earlier ages, usually depict vampires as the personification of evil. Modern psychology and sociology provide a better basis for understanding the true nature of these fears, but—lacking these insights—early writers postulated ideas on the basis of current wisdom.

Numerous theories developed as to how one might become a vampire. The causes expanded over the years until it became much easier to become a vampire than not to be one. Vampires, it came to be generally accepted, resulted from either a demon entering a dead body, or from the spirit of the dead person himself inhabiting his own body. The most frequently mentioned way of becoming a vampire is to die in a state of sin without the blessings of the church. Wicked people would likely become vampires as would people bitten by a come from the grave and wander about by night sucking the blood of persons asleep, causing their death." While earlier vampires may lack all the accoutrements popularized by Hollywood, almost all stories about vampires emphasize their blood-thirstiness. Thus, unwittingly, these tales underscore an idea very prominent in modern theories: namely, the kinship of this theme and concerns about life, death, and immortality. Early hunters discovered that as blood flowed from a wounded man or animal, life, too, drained away. Blood was the source of vitality, and accordingly, men sometimes smeared themselves with it or drank it. Such ideas certainly relate to the vampire's attempts to gain vitality by drinking blood, for as Dracula, quoting from Deuteronomy 12:33, tells us in Stoker's novel, "The blood is the life." Blood, it should also be noted, serves a healing function in many primitive customs.[2]

Modern psychologists recognize that when the drinking of blood occurs among civilized people, it generally involves sexual pleasure to the probably seriously neurotic or psychotic person engaging in the practice. The vampire's bite, according to Freudian psychology, represents a sado-erotic kiss; in addition, even the vampire's thick red lips, unusual hairiness, and other features correspond to widely-held folk beliefs about excessively sex-oriented people. Leonard Wolfe, in *A Dream of Dracula,* says of the attraction of blood: "Hot red blood, with its thick smell, its extraordinary changeability. The pulse in the throat marking an endangered rhythm is the place to kiss. The perfumed skin, beneath which surges the fountainhead. So long as it throbs, there is life."[3]

Hope Robbins postulates the theory of a "rare and abnormal" disorder that produces a maniacal hunger for blood. An example of such a blood mania appears in Robert Bisler's *Man Into Wolf,* which recounts the history of a British vampire who in 1949 killed nine people and drank their blood.[4] Of course, such a rogue's gallery must also include the real Count Dracula, known as "the impaler," Elizabeth Bathory, who took beauty baths in the blood of young girls, and the Italian Vincent Verzeni, who committed his crimes between 1867–71. Verzeni achieved orgasm by grasping his victim by the throat, choking her, inflicting a wound with his teeth, and then sucking her blood. Other human vampires include Fritz Haarmann, the Hanover Vampire, who committed most of his crimes in the early 1920's, and the American Albert Fish, born in 1870. The latter was described by examining psychiatrists as a polymorphous pervert who indulged in such perversions as coprophage, or eating of excrements, masochism, sadism, vampirism and cannibalism, as well as lust murders. Without doubt, these extreme examples lend at least a certain credence to some of the psychological theories about vampirism.[5]

Late in the nineteenth century Madame Blavatsky in *Isis Unveiled* discusses vampirism and other crude superstitions in terms of theosophy. The author, who finds the subject repulsive, attempts to define vampirism in terms of astral forms, and she concludes:

If we are forced to believe in vampirism, it is on the strength of two ir-refragable propositions of occult psychological science: 1) The astral soul is a separable distinct entity of our ego, and can roam far away from the body without breaking the thread of life. 2) The corpse is not utterly dead, and while it can yet be reentered by its tenant, the latter can gather sufficient material emanations from it to enable itself to ap-pear in a quasi-terrestrial shape.[6]

Madame Blavatsky's work continues to be very influential in some circles, and her belief in psychic vampires who drain energy from others manifests itself in numerous later theories and works.

The late nineteenth century occultist Franz Hartman says of the psychic sponge or mental vampire that they unconsciously vampirize every sensitive person with whom they come in contact, and they in-stinctively seek out such persons and invite them to stay at their houses.[7] In many ways Coleridge's Geraldine fits into this tradition,[8] and Bram Stoker frequently mentions Dracula's ability to drain peo-ple of their psychic energies. Interestingly, both modern writers of fic-tion and theorists about the vampire myth are attracted by these ideas.

Peter Penzoldt, for example, asserts that both psychic and literal vampirism represent not mere allegory but rather the outbreak of deeply rooted subconscious fears. Thus, the clue to the vampire, a sucking monster, lies in the oral stage of development. The child receives pleasure and gratification from sucking its mother's breast, and he soon begins to suck his thumb and all sorts of objects for what becomes erotic pleasure. The child, in short, desires to become one with the beloved object by incorporating it. Of course, the child eventually realizes that eating a thing destroys it. When applied to persons, this desire produces a guilt which leads the child to replace oral tendencies with other modes of affection. The vampire, therefore, represents but one of those horrors that an imagination tormented by retaliation might invent.[9] Karl Menninger further points out that a love-hate ambivalence characterizes this stage of development, and he illustrates this theory by the story of a woman who in early life suffered serious oral thwarting. Accordingly, despite her numerous successes, she was never satisfied. "She was actually voracious in her relationships with other people. People could not but like her, because she would make herself so agreeable, but they soon became aware of the fact that she was encompassing them with love—smothering them, as one person put it, like an octopus."[10]

Other possibilities suggest themselves, for the vampire might, as Hope Robbins suggests, be interpreted as a projection of oral sadism.[11] Like Penzoldt, Robbins identifies the vampire's tendencies with repressed sexual wishes and guilts which devolve from the un-conscious world of infantile sexuality. These views reflect in part the complex Freudian approach to vampirism which delves into the mind to investigate closely such instincts and emotions as love, hate, fear, and the will to survive. The Freudian, Ernest Jones, explains the vampire as a nocturnal spirit who embraces a sleeper to suck his blood; such a creature is obviously a product of the nightmare. In addition, he points out that a belief in vampires derives from complex, fundamental emotions concerned with early parental relationships. These feelings manifest themselves in anxiety dreams which apparently mold such aspects of the vampire superstition as:

The Vampire's capacity for transformation, his flight by night, his appearance in animal form and, finally, the connection between the belief and that in the return of dead relatives. The belief is, in fact, only an elaboration of that in the Incubus, and the essential elements of both are the same—repressed desires and hatreds derived from early incest conflicts. The main differences are that hate and guilt play a far larger part in the Vampire than in the Incubus belief, where the emotions are almost purely those of desire and fear.[12]

Vampirism, Freudians tell us, begins in infancy but reaches its strongest during the stage of oral development. The Freudians further contend that a belief in vampires arises from peoples' universal fear of death. Bernhardt J. Hurwood says of this theory: "Although they tell us that this fear comes from repressed guilty love and hate, all of which generates fear, it seems much simpler to bypass all of this and pay more attention to the fact that those who believe in vampires, ghosts, and other revenants, fear them because they don't want to be prematurely forced to join the dead."[13]

Dr. Lawrence Kayton, a psychiatrist at Michael Reese Hospital in Chicago, suggests that many of history's vampires were merely schizophrenic youth manifesting their craving for love and affection. We can appreciate the vampire's dilemma, says Kayton, if we imagine ourselves obsessed with a need to love and be loved while also possessed by enormous oral needs which dominate our lives.[14] In light of these psychological assertions, it is little wonder that the British author Maurice Richardson describes the vampire as a kind of incestuous, necrophilous, oral-and-sadistic all-in-all wrestling match.

Even in this century some rather esoteric theories have been promulgated. In *The Vampire*, Reginald Hodder creates a living character, the member of a secret sisterhood, who must exercise her powers as a vampire to prevent the loss of her vitality. Since the vampire exercises her power through the medium of a metallic talisman, the story hinges on the struggle for control of this object.[15]

Some modern theorists see vampirism arising from some disease, and British microbiologist David J. Garwes suggests rabies as one possibility. He also indicates that exhumed bodies still unaffected by decomposition might be intact as a result of poisoning, because the strong chemicals would also tend to kill the bacteria which cause the decay. Dr. Garwes further speculates that microbiology might account for other characteristics associated with vampires. He notes, for example, that many slow viruses act years after the time of original infection. Such occurrences might well lead to strange symptoms and accordingly promote vampire scares among the ignorant.[16]

Richard Matheson develops such a general theory of bacterically induced vampirism in his science fiction tale *I Am Legend*. The book's protagonist, Robert Nevill, says that vampirism is "a bacillus, a cylindrical bacterium. It creates an isotonic solution in the blood, circulates the blood slower than normal, activates all bodily functions, lives on fresh blood, and provides energy. Deprived of blood, it makes self-killing bacteriophages or else sporulates."[17] This blood disease kills and then resurrects its victims until only Nevill remains as the last living human being. Being an affront to the newly developing vampire society, he must die and thus become legend.

Another famous science fiction work, A. E. van Vogt's "Asylum," explains vampires as victims of an accident on an interstellar flight, as one of the vampires explains:

We were among several thousand holidayers who were caught in the gravitational pull of a sun, afterward called the Dreegh Sun. Its rays, immensely dangerous to human life, infected us all. It was discovered that only continuous blood transfusions, and the life force of other human beings could save us. For awhile we received donations; then the government decided to have us destroyed as hopeless incurables. We were all young, and in love with life, of course. Some hundreds of us had been expecting the sentence, and we still had friends in the beginning. We escaped. We've been fighting ever since to stay alive.[18]

This story stresses the recurrent themes in modern works on vampires of their loneliness, their inordinate desire for immortality, and their incessant demand for energy, i.e., blood. In *The Space Vampires*, Colin Wilson also stresses the vampire's great need for energy and his desire for life. In fact, the creatures found floating in an apparently dead space vehicle are "energy vampires," and as one of the protagonists declares, "All people are energy vampires to some extent." Wilson eschews most of the trappings usually associated with this motif, and while he does have one character imply the similarity of the vampire to the occultist view of astral projection, Wilson primarily stresses the link between vampirism and crime. In *Dracula*, Dr. Von Helsing makes this analogy in reference to Count Dracula. The professor says, "To begin, have you ever studied the philosophy of crime? . . . You, John, yes; for it is a study of insanity . . . The criminal always works at one crime—that is the true criminal who seems predestinate to crime, and who will of none other. This criminal has not full man-brain. He is clever and cunning and resourceful; but . . . he be of child-brain in much."[19] Thus, as one character in Wilson's novel states, "'You see, the vampire is basically a criminal. He is like a thief in the night.' "[20] Later a member of one of the superior ruling races of the universe explains that the vampires were scientists who had vanished fifty thousand years earlier, and he further indicates, "'The criminals were creatures like ourselves, members of the Nioth race, in whom the impulse of protection towards the weaker races had been perverted into a kind of sadism. . . . '"[21] One of the vampires speaks in his defense, and his cry certainly echoes not only a universal aspiration and fear, but it also poignantly underscores one of the basic sources of the vampire myth: "'The Nioth-Korghai, like the human race, are mortal. We of the Ubbo-Sathla have achieved a kind of immortality. Is it nothing to have discovered the secret of living forever? You will say that we have achieved it by destroying lives.'"[22] Naturally, this immortality involves direct exploitation, but other more indirect examples of exploitation crop up.

Indeed, numerous writers use the vampire as a generalized metaphor to explain some kind of exploitation. Voltaire, for example, discussed vampires primarily as a means of attacking the clergy of whom he states, "The true vampires are the monks, who eat at the expense of both kings and people."[23] In *The Consequences* from the *Disasters of War,* Goya pictures war as part vulture, part vampire sucking blood from the breast of man. In his work entitled *The Phantom versus the Multinational Vampires,* Julio Cortazar depicts multinational corporations such as AT&T and GM as vampires who drain other nations of their resources and metaphorically of their blood.

The most appealing explanation of vampirism to me is the thesis postulated by Leonard Wolfe and others that this myth relates to man's search for immortality. To a society dedicated to defying aging and death, Dracula's situation, as bad as it is, seems infinitely appealing. Dr. Devendra Varma, an authority on the vampire motif, told the Count Dracula Society: "Dracula stands as the symbol and essence of all philosophies of the East and the West. He represents resurrection, transmigration, rebirth, renewal, and immortality."[24]

Medical technology already reveals to us the risks of immortality in this world, but many people gladly cling to any idea, concept, remedy, or machine that will perpetuate even a vestige of this life. Like cryonics or some other modern theories, the vampire myth seems to offer at least a limited triumph over death. Unfortunately, as Leonard Wolfe points out, Satan not God, provides the energy. Thus, the "vampire's quest becomes an infinite extension of death; his resurrection has ghastly conditions imposed upon it; and his promised eternal life is an animated corporeality that stinks of the grave."[25] The vampire's existence would hardly seem to tempt anyone, but the earliest myths, including those in Genesis, underscore man's apparent compulsion to defy God and to grasp for eternal life. Leonard Wolfe cogently asserts that Dracula is *the willing representative of the temptations, and the crimes, of the Age of Energy. He is huge, and we admire size; strong, and we admire strength. He moves with the confidence of a creature that has energy, power, and will. Granted that he has energy without grace, power without responsibility and that his will is an exercise in death. We need only to look a little to one side to see how tempting is the choice he makes: available immortality. He has collected on the devil's bargain: the infinitely stopped moment. What does it matter that his flesh is dead? He can move, he can kiss and kill. With only a moderate intake of blood, he can stay young.*

Nor is that all. The vampire fascinates a century that is as much frightened as it is exhilarated by its rush toward sexual freedom. Slowly, but in recent years more unambiguously, his message has been filtering down from our movie screens. In the vampire's embrace, any number of sexual dilemmas are outwitted. His kiss permits all unions: men and women; men and men; women and women; fathers and daughters; mothers and sons. Moreover, his is an easy love that evades the usual failures of the flesh. . . .[26]

The theories discussed in this paper cover a wide range, and obviously they differ considerably in merit. I believe that they speak very eloquently about numerous contemporary fears and anxieties. We can understand why primitive man would come to believe in vampires, and certainly such factors as premature burial, fear of the dead, belief in blood as the life force, and other notions would give rise to and perpetuate this myth. What is more difficult to explain, however, is why this rather barbarous motif would gain its greatest literary currency during the time of the Industrial Revolution and the advent of the modern scientific world.

Microbiology and other areas of medical research provide intriguing clues as to how the masses might adopt a belief in vampires. In addition, the insights of Freud and other psychoanalytic theoreticians—to the extent that their work is true—indicate why certain individuals believed themselves to be vampires and why society accepted them as such. But do large masses of people then respond to this myth because of latent sadistic, erotic, necrophilic and other urges? Since most people surely do not literally believe in vampires, do such stories evoke some atavistic urge or trigger some Jungian archetype? Do these stories merely represent allegorized versions of inner conflicts, or do they reflect the terror of the soul which we have been taught to hide? There may be an element of truth in each of these suppositions, but primarily I believe that this myth bespeaks of our overweening desire for life, our ominous fear of death, and our uncertain status in an increasingly depersonalized world. Under such circumstances, even the vampire's immortality, power, and energy seem appealing.

Vampires may have a circumscribed and tenuous existence, but at least they do not die. Even the Greeks, moreover, found Hades better than no existence at all. In addition, vampires do not concern themselves about those moral distinctions that make life difficult in an era of rapidly changing ethical and moral values. Perhaps if we were more certain about this life and the next, were more assured about the meaning of our existence, were less worried about the pressures of society, felt less lonely, did not fear a God who might exist, did not feel the need to defy authority, and acted rationally, then the vampire myth might become a mere colorless, emotionless footnote to literary history. It is ironic indeed if at a time when we have less reason than ever to believe in vampires that we concomitantly might have a greater need to do so.

Notes

1. Douglas Hill and Pat Williams, *The Supernatural* (New York, 1967), p. 202.

2. *Ibid.*, pp. 198-199. See also: Bernard J. Hurwood, *Vampires, Werewolves, and Ghosts* (New York, 1968), p. 51; Raymond T. McNally, *In Search of Dracula* (Greenwich, CT, 1972), p. 144; Dudley Wright, *The Book of Vampires* (New York, 1973), pp. 13-14; R.E.L. Masters and Edward Lea, *Sex Crimes in History* (New York, 1963), pp. 108-9; anonymous, "Bibber of Blood," *MD* (November, 1965), pp. 323-328; Leonard Wolfe, *A Dream of Dracula* (New York, 1972), pp. 77, 105-34; Ornella Volta, *The Vampire* (New York, 1962), pp. 17-34.

3. *Ibid.*, p. 77.

4. Hill and Williams, p. 202.

5. See Hurwood, pp. 109-14, 141-146; Masters and Lea, pp. 95-114; McNally and Florescu, passim; Wolfe, pp. 41-74, 241-259; and Wilhelm Stekel, *Sadism and Masochism* (New York, 1965) II, Chapter XVII, "Cannibalism, Necrophilism, and Vampirism," pp. 248-330.

6. H. P. Blavatsky, *Isis Unveiled: A Master-Key to the Mysteries of Ancient and Modern Science and Theology* (Pasadena, CA, 1960), I, p. 459.

7. *Borderland,* 3 (July, 1896), pp. 353-58.

8. See especially the chapter "Vampires and Medical Demonology" in Arthur H. Nethercot, *The Road to Tryermaine* (New York, 1962), pp. 59-79.

9. Penzoldt, *The Supernatural in Fiction* (New York, 1965), pp. 37-40.

10. *Man Against Himself* (New York, 1938), p. 40.

11. "Vampire" in *The Encyclopedia of Witchcraft and Demonology* (New York, 1959), p. 525.

12. "The Vampire" in *Nightmares, Witches, and Devils* (New York, 1931), pp. 129-130.

13. Hurwood, p. 61.

14. Daniel Green, "Human Vampires Exist Among Freaks, Deviates," *The Houston Post,* October 3, 1974, p. N/1.

15. Wright, p. 196.

16. Hurwood, "Introduction," pp. 9-19.

17. *I Am Legend* (New York, 1954), p. 100.

18. A. E. van Vogt, "Asylum" in the collection *Away and Beyond* (New York, 1963), p. 184.

19. Bram Stoker, *Dracula* (New York, 1965), p. 286.

20. Colin Wilson, *The Space Vampires* (New York, 1976), p. 135.

21. *Ibid.,* p. 199.

22. *Ibid.,* p. 200.

23. *The Works of Voltaire* (Akron, 1904), XIV, pp. 148-149.

24. Daniel Green, "Dracula is a Gothic Superstar," *The Houston Post,* October 3, 1974, p. N./1.

25. Wolfe, p. 129.

26. *Ibid.,* pp. 302-303.

Pull Rings, Kidney Machines, and the Oral Tradition/*Lawrence Clayton*

Lawrence Clayton
Credit: Matt Mitchell

Salinas, Cal: Science teacher Charles
Monteith surveys heaps of aluminum
beverage can flip-tops turned in by junior
high students. (World Wide Photos)

Pull Rings,
Kidney Machines,
and the Oral Tradition

Lawrence Clayton

In our media-oriented age, we sometimes fail to appreciate the continuing prominence and power of the oral tradition. Two recent examples show that more than shady stories and Aggie jokes are alive and well in this mode of communication. Both involve the saving of an apparently useless item to be turned in for something valuable to someone else. One is the collecting of pull rings from metal drink cans. The second, and slightly more recent, of the two hoaxes is the saving of decals made up of numbered lines printed on the labels of canned goods. The purpose of these decals is actually inventory control and a means of charging customers for goods at checkout counters in markets, where an electronic device "reads" the information coded in the decal. These items were to be turned in to provide time on a dialysis machine for an underprivileged child with a kidney disorder. Both of these collecting drives turned out to be false and have an amazing degree of similarity as well as considerable geographic distribution, thanks to oral tradition.

I first became aware of the label "scandal" in March of 1977, when my parents, who live in deep East Texas, visited me in West Texas, some three hundred miles away, and asked if we knew where to turn in the labels to help the child on the kidney machine. I had heard of the scheme but had never thought of its being widespread. At the same time my wife, then the principal of an elementary school, said that students in the junior and senior high schools in Clyde, near Abilene, were saving pull rings for the same purpose but that she did not know where to turn them in either. We were evidently one hoax behind.

Things did not really begin to fall into place until April 7, 1977, when enroute by automobile to a joint meeting of the Texas and New Mexico Folklore Societies in El Paso, I heard a national radio news service announcer read a statement from the National Kidney Foundation and other agencies stating that the collection of labels to be traded for time on a kidney machine was a baseless hoax. I then began to wonder how such a thing could get started and become widespread and not be discovered immediately for what it really is, a hoax at work in the oral tradition. The resulting study proved immensely interesting and reminded me that oral transmission is alive and well and is being used to dupe gullible people who would like to perform some worthy service, especially if the deed seems both noble and inexpensive.

The widespread coverage of these two phenomena was easily documented from friends and students at Hardin-Simmons University. I have talked with informants from as far away as Nevada and California who are quite familiar with the idea and, in September of 1977, almost five months after the label hoax was revealed in various media, one of my informants had not yet heard that he was the victim of a joke. I was informed in April of 1978, when I read an early draft of this paper to a meeting of the Texas Folklore Society in Nacogdoches, that in the basement of Parlin Hall on the campus of the University of Texas at Austin, a machine dispensing canned soft drinks had taped to it a large envelope and a sign asking that the rings be deposited in the envelope so that they could be turned in for time on a kidney machine.[1]

Young people, particularly college students, church and other youth groups, and even public school students appear to have been particularly susceptible to this hoax. Two of the occurrences that I investigated involved church groups, and another was noted in a high school, but the source even in this latter case was a local church.

The pattern for the exchange of labels or some kind of coupon for goods or services is not unknown. During 1977, Post Cereals and the Campbell Soup Company sponsored a program whereby one could exchange box tops and labels from the soup cans for playground equipment. This was a bonafide offer of which many schools took advantage. An earlier program involved the saving of coupons from cigarette packages, particularly Old Golds. The coupons could be traded for valuable merchandise, and at least two brands—Sir Walter Raleigh and Bel Aire—continued for some time to offer this incentive to smokers.

One precursor of these two hoaxes was relayed to me by a local pastor who said that "about ten years ago" there was a similar ruse involving the saving of cellophane wrappers on cigarette packages, but it was not for time on a kidney machine.[2] He could not recall what one was to receive for the wrappers, but I learned from another informant that the wrappers were to be traded for a wheelchair.[3] That this ploy was used during the polio period is not surprising. Even earlier people saved tin foil during World War II to help in the cause by providing bullets and bombs.[4] Another ploy was the saving of tea bag tags. One informant recalled seeing on a counter in a cafe a small jar with a slot cut in the top in which patrons were to deposit the tags.[5] The foibles of man take many forms, it appears.

The source of the kidney element of the most recent hoax may have arisen from a program concurrent with the collecting. In a widespread program in the media, people were asked to sign donor cards so that when the person died, the organs would be available for transplant. As part of the drive, the National Kidney Foundation also used billboard advertising specifically for kidney donation. I even saw one such advertisement on the back of a bench of a bus stop in Abilene. Another motivation may have been stories frequently appearing in newspapers and on television of persons who must spend time on a dialysis machine. These stories usually emphasize cost and complication of a person's life because of the treatment. A donor could thereby contribute to a fuller life for one of these people and provide a kind of life after death for himself, thus stimulating an emotional response that might well lead to an overt act of donation.

One of my best informants turned out to be a small-town home economics teacher, who was not reluctant to talk about her experience with pull ring collecting. Not all of my informants were so open as she was. Many just dropped their eyes and turned away when I asked about the collecting. This teacher was told by a student that for 1,000 pull rings, which were to be turned in "somewhere" in Abilene, the nearest large city, a needy person would be given one hour on a kidney machine. My informant was told to turn in what her students had collected at the local high school to one of the four Baptist churches in town, but the specific church was never named. Her informant was a young woman who got her information from a youth director of a local church. He in turn had received the idea from a young woman who had visited the church on a lay witness mission. When I called the mother of one of the girls who was quite active in the local effort, she denied that she or the girl knew anything about it and hung up abruptly. I knew that someone's ego had suffered. Another interesting turn came in Jacksonville in East Texas where a checker in a Safeway store, when asked about the decal on canned goods, responded that they were "for the little girl," apparently believing that this use was the only reason the decals had for being on the goods.

A search of the back issues of the Abilene *Reporter-News* turned up a story, datelined Austin, which cited a report by the Texas Medical Association denying any validity of the exchange of labels for time on the dialysis machine. Steve Carrell, Assistant Communications Director, indicated that the idea was prevalent all over Texas and, to prove his case, reported inquiries from Jasper, Center, Marshall, Giddings, Longview, Houston, Pflugerville, and Nacogdoches. He cited one incident in which a local grocery store thought that the local hospital was redeeming the labels. The hospital thought the grocery store was. Carrell closed by saying, "It's an easy community project. People are quick to get together and help in things like that, especially in the spring."[6]

In each instance of this collecting hoax, some common

denominators are visible. First, a worthy cause is served, usually helping one struck down by a dreaded and incurable disease such as polio in the case of the cellophane wrappers and kidney dysfunction with the rings and labels. Second, the item saved is worthless. Third, the items pollute the land and create a public nuisance and eyesore when scattered over the landscape. I still see the idea behind these hoaxes as essentially positive if not humorous. It is comforting to see that people will still support a common cause when a need arises, and even though we are duped, we can still laugh at ourselves and not lose faith in one another.

Notes

1. Michael Licht, Interview, Nacogdoches, Texas, March 24, 1978.
2. Rev. Don Connors, Interview, Clyde, Texas, March 10, 1977.
3. Ferrell Newton, Interview, Clyde, Texas, March 15, 1977.
4. Joyce Roach, Interview, Nacogdoches, Texas, March 24, 1978.
5. Dr. Melvin Mason, Interview, Nacogdoches, Texas, March 24, 1978.
6. April 8, 1977, p. 8 A.

Folklorish Remnants of Peyote
Ceremonialism/*Ernestine P. Sewell & Charles E. Linck*

The Trip of the Shaman

The Hunt for the Peyote

Folklorish Remnants of Peyote Ceremonialism

Ernestine P. Sewell and Charles E. Linck

Scientifically, peyote is *lophophora mamillaria*, one of forty hallucinogens known to the pre-Columbian cultures, a small bluish-green plant with nipples at the top, which, as it matures, flatten into sharply defined ribs. Hidden under bushes, it appears to sink into its root during the dry season, but when the rains begin, it surfaces. *Los indios* say the flowers come in the same colors as corn: yellow, blue, red, white, and black, but commonly the blossom is white or pinkish-red. The thick outside skin has a woolly appearance, some say, but is recognized, rather, by a few scattered fleshy bristles. It is found between and on both sides of the Pecos and the Rio Grande, in the desert country, as far east as Corpus Christi.

Historically, the ritualistic use of peyote by the Aztecs was recorded by Spanish missionaries and reference is made to condemnation of the practice by the Spanish Inquisition—without stopping the native rituals however.[1] Interestingly, peyote is not found around Mexico City. That fact added to the Aztecs' story of migration to Mexico City from some undetermined place north suggests they could have inhabited originally the area where peyote grows and could have continued their ritual by making annual pilgrimages to harvest a supply of the peyote buttons.

Anthropologically, according to Weston La Barre, the Huichols still observe the ancient peyote ritual. Living now near Lake Chapala in the state of Jalisco, in extended family organization instead of in communities, they have been subjected to less change than most indigenous peoples. They still make an annual pilgrimage: "Their route to the Real de Catorce is full of religious associations, since formerly the gods went out to seek peyote" and now meet the pilgrims "in the shape of mountains, stones, and springs."[2] The landscape leads man to his gods. Wirikuta proper, one of the sacred places where the peyote grows, is demarcated by boundaries invisible to an outsider. A flat stretch at the base of two sacred mountains, it is a kind of Eden to the ritualists. Before the peyotists reach the holy ground, they have purified themselves by abstinence from sexual relations, by confession, and by changing names, identities, speaking nonsense, in short, reversing their habitual modes to be ready to leave the profane world for the sacred.

Among the Huichols, the hunt for Father Peyote is a dramatization of a hunt for the blue deer, because the peyote, the deer, and the corn are their trinity. The maraakame, the head man, stalks the peyote to reenact the feats of the gods and find favor and protection. When he finds it, the pilgrims gather around in complete silence. He approaches on tiptoe, soundlessly parting branches of the mescal, where it is likely to be found, so as not to frighten it away. He takes his praying arrow (for it was when a god dipped his arrow into the blood of a female deer that arrows became strong enough to be useful for hunting) and penetrates the peyote, causing rays of color like the rainbow to spurt upwards. Everyone weeps silently as he dips his arrow into the peyote's blood and anoints each pilgrim by stroking foreheads, cheeks, eyes, and breasts. He carefully cuts out the peyote, taking care to leave the root in the ground. Then the pilgrims scatter out to find the elusive peyote to fill their own baskets. When they return home, the women are allowed to partake of the sacramental peyote, children are initiated to the mysteries, and riotous and even orgiastic dancing concludes the ritual.

Fernando Benitez wrote, "With the magical associations of the Holy Land, [the pilgrims] had at last become one with the landscape. . . . They had left the profane world behind." The peyote is a god that makes visible "in a series of dazzling epiphanies" its association with the other gods.[3] It is the accelerator of a magical process by which the true order of the universe is made manifest. And the symbol of that order is the *tsikuri*, the god's eye, with its center and four points, a rhombus of wool stretched on a cross of two slender sticks. On a pilgrimage the searchers take many god's eyes and leave them in sacred places, an offering to their gods. Mountains speak, cactuses are transformed into flowers bursting with gorgeous color. Magic birds vibrant with bright plumage and mythical little animals float in space. The Blue Deer is the teacher of ecstasy that sings the shamanic songs. Such images are transferred to yarn paintings by the Huichols. The bark paintings available to tourists likewise may be religious picturizations of a chain of visions created by chewing the buttons or drinking a bitter tea brewed from the peyote. Including preparation for the pilgrimage and the return, the entire ritual takes thirty days.

With reference to myth, there remain to be gathered the stories of the Huichols. Some are recorded but the ethnologists, who did not become interested to any extent until the 1960s when the Flower Children brought acid to the attention of the scientists, admit that each maraakame changes the stories and only remnants, individual experience, and imaginative re-creations are available now. In this country, it is told that in the 1870s or 1880s Quanah Parker left Oklahoma to visit the Texas relatives of his mother, Cynthia Ann, who wished to educate him. But he became dangerously ill. When the white doctor's remedies failed to help him, his grandmother called in a Mexican curandera, who had a brush arbor built, laid the ailing Quanah on a pallet with his head to the east, dosed him with a bitter tea while she sang songs, smoked corn husk cigarettes, and prayed. In four days he began to recover. The curandera told him the secrets of the peyote tea, warning him that it must never be used except for healing and religious purposes. And she told him about the woman who had first brought peyote to the people.

It could be a story from the Tarahumara, the Yaqui, or the Otomi. A woman dreamed she was lost from her tribe, having fallen back from the hunters and gatherers because of being with child. Alone, she gave birth, cut the navel cord with her stone knife, and lay helpless under a bush, watching the buzzards swoop and soar lower and lower. Then a voice spoke: "Eat the plant that is growing beside you. That is life and blessing for you and all your people." Barely able to turn her head, the woman reached for the plant, and ate. Feeling her strength return, she lifted the child, fed it from breasts now full, and by evening had found her people. Her uncle heard her story, and, being a wise man, said, "We must share the blessing of Father Peyote with all the people."[4]

The Taosenos seem to have borrowed a Kiowa story that a warrior heard singing, and when he approached the sound he found a small round plant, symbolic of the female, that invited him to come inside. As he entered, the hole became larger and larger until it was a big hollow in the ground like a kiva, and there a wise old man told him about the blessings of peyote.

The Shawnee, the Kickapoo, and other plains peoples conceive of peyote, not as Father, but as a goddess whose wisdom one can catch in her songs if one listens closely.

Another story of the introduction of the cult into the Southwest is that the Apache who escaped the cavalry to hide out in Mexico learned about it from the Tarahumara and that Quanah Parker, on a hunting foray into Mexico, learned from them. Whatever the truth, the Comanches spread the use of peyote as a surrogate for the warrior way of life and today it is the basis for the theology and rituals of the Native American Church, perhaps the greatest force for unification within the American Indian consciousness.

Every October Native Americans make a pilgrimage to Laredo to buy their supply of peyote. Unfortunately, they must pay a fee to search the fields of their Eden. The Woodlanders buy their supply from traveling vendors, often hippies who have gathered it illegally. Then a ceremony may be arranged at any time for any occasion. A teepee is set up, large enough for thirty or forty persons. In the center is a fire, whose ashes are shaped into the image of a bird, the cormorant. Father Peyote is placed on a bed of sage and a crescent—a half moon drawn on the ground to represent the pathway of man from birth to death. The leader, the Man of the Road, has a drum, a gourd rattler, a staff, a bag of peyote, and cedar incense. His box, to carry his paraphernalia, like the medicine bag of the shaman, is also a holy accoutrement for the ritual. The drum is animal skin stretched over a metal pot filled with symbolic water.

At the entry the fireman and the water bearer stand. Offerings of meat, fruit, corn, and water are placed before the fire. The ceremony, which begins at nightfall, consists of smoking or praying together. This is followed by an incense-blessing ceremony, for which the cedar man sprinkles his dried cedar on the fires. Then the peyote bag is passed, always clockwise. Before the people chew, they crush sage or mesquite or whatever is native between their palms and rub themselves with it. This done, they eat, with much spitting, some nausea. It is said the more sinful a man, the more nausea. Singing follows the eating of the peyote, each man singing to the drumming of the man on his right. A musicology of the peyote cult has developed, but like the art, it is spontaneous and individual. By the time the drum has been passed around the circle, several hours have lapsed. At intervals a man will pray aloud; someone may break into sobbing. Anyone may call for more peyote at any time, as there is no agreement about how many are consumed. Perhaps for the women, as few as three or four; for a man, up to thirty or more. A Winnebago tells that he was skeptical about the power of the peyote to create a vision so he continued to eat the buttons until he had masticated sixty. He did have a vision—and became a faithful peyotist.

At midnight cedar is put on the fire again for incense and as all join in singing, everyone blesses himself in the smoke. After this, the singing continues until dawn at which time the woman who is to bring water is summoned. Peyote makes one thirsty and to go without water is to perform an act of abstinence in honor of Father Peyote. This is followed by the ritual breakfast. While the women busy themselves preparing food, old men lecture the young about their behavior; visitors are given an opportunity to express their gratitude, and informal geniality prevails. Anglo visitors are rarely seen because the hippies abused the use of peyote and made it difficult for the Indians to obtain it except at exorbitant prices. The ritual forms a strong bond for the Native American with the aboriginal past, the bits and pieces of which emerge as cultural remnants manifested in their paintings, their crafts, and their music. The original belief system can only be pieced together by the folklore that has arisen.

The Navajo Henry Tsosie told us, "My sister Dorothy she married Charley Begay. They belong to that peyote church. That stuff'll make you crazy," he continued, "make you do crazy things." Henry brought the Begays to our campsite. Charley spoke hardly any English but smiled as Dorothy handed us some of his paintings: one a blue deer, the other of a woman bringing water to peyotists after a night of ceremony. Charley let us know he was painting a picture of the "medicine bag" of the Man of the Road. Would we want that one? Dorothy explained that if we had been in camp a day sooner we could have gone to a special service to honor her son who was leaving for the army. It had been a traditional Navajo giveaway in addition to the regular peyote service with special prayers that the power of the peyote protect him. We would have been expected to give him a handsome gift of money. The custom indicates the way an adopted ritual will become acculturated and altered to incorporate the local ritualistic giveaway. Now Dorothy added, "We try to get Henry to join the church but he won't. Charley used to drink but now he goes to peyote church and he won't drink that other stuff any more."

We were to hear other Navajos and Kiowas and Delawares and Seminoles say the same thing. "I used to drink that old whiskey until I started going to the peyote church," as if Father Peyote did indeed have magical power.

Another time we were with Navajo Andrew Bia in his pickup. We knew he belonged to the Church because he had sold us paintings of a peyote tent. I asked, "Do you think Carlos Castañeda was telling the truth in *The Teachings of Don Juan?*" Andrew, eyes straining into the distance of the canyon ahead, said in verification, "I saw my mentor in Taos run after the deer and catch it with his bare hands." After a time, he asked, "Do you know *Chariots of the Gods?*" I said yes. He turned the truck off the road to bump across a flat expanse of rock. He stopped. We got out to follow him around as he pointed to con-figurations on the rocks. If one stood back to get perspective, lines and colors, not man-made, formed the shape of the constellations. "The gods have visited earth and left signs for us. This is a holy place. Only the Navajos know where it is." Andrew was confiding in us his belief that the gods had indeed left their people gifts that would guide them, protect them, and give them power.

Former hippies from Jemez Springs, Linda and Nick S___________, described the sensations of using peyote; they had journeyed with friends into the mountains south of Albuquerque where, with no trouble, they found the buttons. There is no necessity for a pilgrimage to Laredo to get the peyote? Their response was "You can find it anywhere in New Mexico." Linda said, "It's bitter; I'd rather drink the tea than chew it. But peyote makes you feel good—except for the nausea at first." "The Huichols," I said, "fast in advance of a ritual to avoid nausea." "They can fast as long as they want, they will still get sick at first," she laughed.

I said, "The Navajos consider the nausea a cleansing ritual." And she said, "That's just their way of making the whole experience have some religious meaning." She continued, "After the nausea, you have good feelings. You just sit for eight or nine hours and feel good. We sat wrapped in our sleeping bags and just felt good. And there are no after effects."

"Why do the Indians wait until morning to drink water? The peyote must make one thirsty." "That's an easy one to answer," she said; "if you drink water, you dilute the effects of the peyote." "What is the effect really?" I pursued. "You sit and sit and talk and talk. It's pleasant. I've made up poems and songs—but when I read them later they were stupid."

"And visions? Did your thoughts take the shape of a cormorant and fly heavenward in search of a vision?" "No, the nearest I ever came to having a vision was one time when I looked out over the distance and concentrated on White Sands and I thought, What if God were to come down and leave a giant footstep in the sands!"

"I have heard some Indians say the image of Christ appears to them in the visions." Linda said, "Whatever you believe, whatever you have inside you will be intensified. It's like any other drug: whatever the person is will be manifested in an exaggerated manner. If a person is a thief, he will go steal something; if he is a potential murderer, he will go murder; if he is inclined to suicide, he'll commit suicide."

Linda continued, "I've heard there are two kinds of peyote. One tribe of Apaches uses a kind that creates monstrous visions; the only kind we know just makes you feel good." (We have since learned that there are not two kinds of peyote: some Apache medicine men developed this fiction to maintain their power and instill fear in their people.)

"Is it an aphrodisiac?" "Is it ever!" And she added: "I can have an orgasm every ten minutes. It intensifies all the feelings. It's like this: I could take a book and see into the layers that make up the cover. One's senses are more aware. I can literally feel the sounds of the guitar touching me. It is great. But not mescaline; it's dangerous and datura is worse than that. Deadly. The Indians avoid both of those unless they want to take a chance and get drunk on mescal. Peyote is different." "The Mexicans around Mora tell a story about peyote causing some men to die." "Sure," Linda said, "if you mix it with alcohol or acids but by itself it's harmless. And there's no hangover."

As with other religions, a musicology and an art movement have been developed that represent bits and pieces, the cultural remnants of an earlier organized belief system. In sculpture, metalwork and beadwork, peyote and art design reach a high level of artistry. Among the Woodlanders, influences of Christianity are found; in one of Andrew Bia's paintings, a vision of Christ rises from Father Peyote. Among the Southwesterners the tortured man, the sacrifice of man or animal to appease the gods, the attempt to rise spiritually to commune with one's god, the contest of good and evil forces for the soul of man are artists' universals, conceived intellectually by both primitive and civilized man.

The accompanying photographs of Huichol yarn paintings demonstrate how beliefs of the primitive remain in the mysteries of the mind until such time as they find expression, whether the artist is conscious of that residual memory or not.[5]

Notes

1. Weston La Barre, *The Peyote Cult*, Enlarged Edition (New York: Shocken Books, 1969), p. 23.

2. La Barre, p. 30.

3. Fernando Benitez, *In the Magic Land of Peyote* (New York: Warner Press, 1975), pp. 72-73.

4. Alice Marriott and Carol Rachlin, *Peyote* (New York: Mentor, 1971), pp. 14-15.

5. For general reference, see *El Arte de los Huicholes*, by Ramon Mata Torres (Guadalajara, 1980).

Animal Metaphors & Verbal Abuse/*Glen E. Lich*

Glen E. Lich

A Rural Texas-German Family
Lilly Smith Schuchardt Collection, Boerne

Animal Metaphors & Verbal Abuse

Social Relations & Values Among German-Speaking Farmers on Cypress Creek, Kerr County

Glen E. Lich

While watching *Anatevka* in 1969 in Munich, I was struck by the wealth of humorous description in the folk language of the village. Particularly the Yiddish tradition, it seemed to me at the time, had accumulated a wide range of descriptive metaphors that under closer examination yielded a surprisingly complex order of physical and psychological categorization. My later studies suggested that this richness which I had first observed in the Yiddish was characteristic of peasant languages throughout central and eastern Europe. The idea to examine shared understandings and social consensus in the language spoken by descendants of German colonists in Texas developed after further field studies in the lore and local history of the German province of Hesse.

There, it seemed, as I scouted for material and personal resources, my childhood knowledge from Texas of remnants of this peasant language that "they don't teach in the schools" opened many doors and re-formed a link of ethnic identity which, for all practical purposes, had been broken over a century earlier by emigration.

The community I selected for this study of German verbal abuse in Texas was the valley where I had grown up. The German spoken there today is in a state of fairly rapid decline, but the comparatively late settlement of the valley afforded a large number of second and third generation informants. The diverse European backgrounds of the families had necessitated the speaking of standard non-dialectal German without many of the peculiarities of place or class that mark the German of more homogeneous enclaves in Texas. This language, cut off from its linguistic source two and three generations ago, has been modified, of course, by English bilingualism, the new environment, technology, and the culture of the surrounding Anglo-American majority. In many respects, the German spoken in this small valley between Comfort and Kerrville exemplifies in syntax, vocabulary, and development the modified standard German spoken throughout central and southwest Texas.

Patterned by cluster migration, westward dispersal, political and economic assimilation—the settlement in the rural valley above Comfort transpired over a period of forty years. Early German farmers from New Braunfels who began settling in 1852 in the fertile valley of the Cypress Creek, which winds for fifteen miles through the hills of southeastern Kerr County and crosses into Kendall County about a mile above its confluence with the Guadalupe, made the first organized settlement within the confines of what is today Kerr County. By the turn of the century, four family complexes of sixteen surviving surnames had formed. The population by 1900 was slightly under 150. All these families engaged in agriculture on farms and ranches fronting on the creek and accessible by a road running along the creek. Over half of the families, however, descended from burghers removed by a generation or two from the land in Europe. Among these were a Freemason, a student radical who drifted into the area after the failure of the commune at Bettina, a royal Bavarian forester, a pharmacist, several teachers, a notary, several artisans, an officer political refugee, and one couple from the royal Hanoverian court. Fewer than half had been workers of the land in Europe. The families of this smaller group, however, evolved into the largest landholders.

Despite this diversity of background, the families uniformly favored education and professed hostility toward religion and politics. Consequently, a school was built early in the community's history, but a church has never been formed. The families independently organized their own militia, harvesting and marketing cooperatives, and other means of mutual support, but they remained apolitical except for the period when the Civil War changed them into imprudent unionists.

Life in the community derived from the home, the extended family, the livelihood of the men, and the landscape. The community itself, to use Howard Becker's terminology, was a modified "sacred society," not very far progressed toward becoming a "secular society." Social contacts were primary; tradition played a large part in individual life; "sacredness" dominated even the economic sphere; there was a simple division of labor, along with a mutual effort to sustain self-sufficiency; the forces of gossip and tradition were powerful tools of social control; and the value system was impermeable.[1] In general, the families were patriarchal and people were age-oriented. For example, the gradual transition of active management of home and land was based on physical capability, and, furthermore, it was often said that when an older relative died a child was born to take his place. This sequence of death and birth was discussed by older people so often and sometimes with such urgency that as a child I had the literal impression of a one-for-one replacement. Since the population of the valley has remained fairly constant since 1900 (because many of the children have moved away and their offspring do not count toward the replacement of the older generation), one can see how this superstition was fed by fact. Perhaps this notion relates to the prevailing non-religious outlook of the valley.

Christmas and Easter were celebrated as secular occasions, and the most important social events were birthdays, dances, and weddings. The menfolk took part in a local shooting club which assembled near the cemetery, while the women belonged with few exceptions to a small German literary society. Apart from cards and dominoes, the most prevalent pastimes at social gatherings were games of mimesis, pranks, and joking. These were especially popular among the men also during harvest, which—like barn-raising, butchering, canning, and quilting—took on secondary social functions.

Large families were favored. At the turn of the century, eleven couples along the creek had a total of ninety children. Women in the extended families not only cleaned their houses and cooked for work crews, harvested their vegetable gardens and orchards, and fed penned livestock, but also worked in the fields—a practice which Anglo-Americans (whom these Germans derisively called "biscuits") considered repugnant. With the transition toward fewer children and the breakdown of the self-sufficient extended family, women also began to drive trucks and tractors in the field and to help with round-ups. The men, however, never worked in the houses or yards, although the boys helped with such chores as chopping wood, butchering chickens, and feeding penned livestock. The German men worked the fields, tended the pastured or range livestock, and did the fencing, building, and shopping.

For most people there, the landscape was imbued with the qualities of the early settlers. Since title to the previously unsettled land in the valley had been acquired either directly from public domain or indirectly as railroad land, they viewed it as an extension of self and identified it with their own names in everyday speech and in story-telling. Land division among heirs regularly caused the only serious strife that ever arose in these families.

The farmsteads along the creek presented a picture of uniformity. Although house and barn were not under the same roof as they were in a German farm village, the house and surrounding outbuildings (barns with lofts, pigsties, smoke house, chicken house, milking shed, blacksmith shop, outhouse, windmill and tankhouse, covered dipping vat, and garages) formed a tight cluster interlaced by pens, corrals, and fences leading out to fields and pastures.

The early houses were rough log cabins (which the Germans despised as Anglo-American, or "biscuit," architecture), but these were replaced by substantial limestone or frame farmhouses as soon as possible. Most of these rural houses used Anglo-American floor plans (five-room, L- or T-shaped, large kitchen on which most activities centered, and cellar) and for the most part were not identified by German construction methods such as half-timbering. Many of the houses had half-stories accessible by outside stairs, where the children slept, and all of them had large front and back porches called "galleries." Without exception, these farmsteads were situated on slight rises or hillocks overlooking the creek and out of reach of seasonal flood waters. The homesteads reflected few socio-economic or cultural differences among the people.

Other differences among the early families, however, led to two peculiar social conventions based in part on pre-Texas considerations and in part on the character of the original settlers whose descendants populate the valley. One of these, still spoken of today, though I know of only one instance in 1912 when it was strictly observed in practice, is the notion of "family rank." Any marriage which brought together a man and woman of different ranks was viewed ambiguously. For the spouse who was marrying "up," such a marriage was advantageous, while for the other spouse it involved a certain loss of face which could be ignored if one chose. The second convention is the frequent practice by both men and women of explaining away other people's behavior by ascribing to them the mentality and habits of those people's ancestors. Since by now nearly everyone in the valley is related through blood or marriage, this practice often involves using one's own ancestors or, better, those of his wife to victimize siblings, cousins, or other neighbors. Marriages, which effected alliances between families and which circumscribed commercial ties in the valley and in the town, could, by implication then, produce offspring of the man's type or of the wife's type.

This second convention, one of several humorous social correctives in the valley, is accompanied by the retelling of stories from the lives of uncles, aunts, grandparents, and other early settlers. Such stories are often linked spatially to certain landmarks, giving an egocentric self-identification to the land: like the shortcut Uncle Henry took down the bald hillside in his wagon when he got angry while building a fence, the valley where someone was frightened by some wild animals, the buzzard roost where Uncle Louis sent city-slickers one night to poach "turkeys" on his brother's land, the road where a rattlesnake struck the first county commissioner's Model-T tire and blew up as the escaping air inflated the snake's body through its fangs, or the curve near the local Rigi where Tante Emilie caused the car to roll off the left embankment because she sat in the back seat behind her husband.

Apart from such stories told to preserve the atavistic character of the community and to impart personal attributes to the land, another type of folk humor which contributes to the symbolic self-portrait of these people is the complex set of animal metaphors. Here, in its most succinct form, the observer secures an insight into the humor of the village and the ongoing construction of social reality. These terms, in particular, constitute shared understandings and social consensus retained from the Old World, but like the language in general in the valley, they have undergone modifications in Texas.

The humor of these expressions is strikingly apparent when one observes but is not otherwise involved with their use. Even though many of the abusive terms now can be used ambiguously in joking, they are still more than just humorous if they function therapeutically to manage tensions and reinforce social values at the moment when they are employed. For the victim to overlook or laugh at the insult, or for the metaphor to be used in a cold rather than a heated way, would deviate from the normal, contextual use and inflict serious injury on one or both of the participants. Consequently, in order for the metaphor to be effective, it must be delivered as an insult, and for it to be metaphorically pejorative it must be contrary to fact. For example, a person can deliver the expression "That's folklore!" as an intended insult, but the expression is not metaphorically pejorative if the subject is indeed folklore. Animal metaphors should be, by definition, contrary to fact.

Underlying all the terms are an assumption and an analogic mapping of the animal world onto the human community in the form of an unexpressed simile. For example,

The donkey is a dumb, laughable animal. *(assumption)*
You are as dumb and laughable as a donkey. *(unexpressed, analogic simile)*
"You donkey!" *(animal metaphor)*

Of course, these metaphors can be employed indirectly ("What a donkey!"), as well as directly. Both usages have the effect of actualizing two sets of relationships, analogous to saying, "A donkey is to other animals as you are to people."

The German of the Cypress Creek community abounds in such animal metaphors of verbal abuse. During two months of intermittent research I was able to collect eighty-eight expressions from twenty-six male and female informants. The project evoked a humorous reaction from each informant, as the recollection of one expression of verbal abuse led to another, and so forth. The best interviews were those involving several informants at once because then the chains of association were stimulated by mutual rub-off and the informants acted as correctives on each other.

All the metaphors were uniformly rated by most informants according to relative abuse. The informants seldom expressed any uncertainty regarding what type (age and/or sex) of person was the *normal* target of the abuse, although they were not always that certain of what types of people were excluded by particular metaphors. By considering the entire set of metaphors as a collection of folk wisdom used as social correctives, I thought it might be possible to construct a composite from the wide range of physical and psychological descriptions of what aberrations and deviations were not tolerated.

To study their structure and pattern of meanings, I began by dividing all the terms into generic groupings. Each grouping, then, consisted of general or differentiated terms listed under a *generic category* heading (e.g., cat, sheep, ape). Usually the generic heading was also a verbal abuse, but four (bird, cattle, hedgehog, bird of prey) were not known as verbal abuses and these headings had to be added artificially. Once all the pig terms and dog terms were grouped, for example, I divided the generic categories spatially, functionally, and by male and female spheres of influence. Generally, descending order of animal categories indicates increasing pejorative intensity.

[KEY: German animal metaphor (literal translation): type of metaphor (i.e., *diminutive, modification* including sex differentiation and age, *compounds* of nouns and nouns with adjectives, and *hybridization*). English equivalent meanings; target of metaphor.]

1. *HOUSE AND YARD*
    Close proximity to family, pets and pests, female sphere of influence
    4 generic categories: mouse, cat, vermin, dog
    22 terms of which 8 apply to females only, 13 apply to males only, and one is a collective term

    Maus/mouse   general category & pet name
    Honey, dear; girlfriend, wife
            Mäuschen/little mouse   dim. & pet name. var. of the above
            die Mausie/little mouse   dim. & pet name
            She's my honey, dear; girlfriend, wife, usually used with a third party
    Katze/cat   general category & mild verbal abuse
    False deceitful woman
            Kätzchen/kitten   dim. & pet name
            Sweet thing; girl
                    Schmeichelkätzchen/sweet-talking kitten
                    mod. & dim.
                    Coquette, flatterer; girl
            Kater/tomcat   sex diff.
            A male on the prowl, skirtchaser; mature, single man[2]
            Gickelkatz Gockel·/rooster-cat   var. sex diff. & hybrid
            A strange bird, twisted chick; girl or young woman
    Ungezierfer/vermin   general category
                    richtiges Ungezierfer/real vermin   mod.
                    What scum! What a pack! a horde; collective term, in-discriminate
                    alte Spinne/old spider   mod. Vague term from one in-formant
                    old woman who causes bad luck
                    Mädchenschnecker/girl-snail   comp.
                    Girlchaser; young boy
                    Lausbub/louse-boy   comp.
                    Smart-aleck, sassy adolescent; young boy

Dreckkäfer/dung-beetle   comp.
Unclean, unkempt; man
Hund/dog   general category & a verbal abuse
Mean, spiteful, miserable man
grober Hund/gross dog   mod.
Fat-head, mean man
närrischer Hund/crazy dog   mod.
Foolish, strange, peculiar man
Lumpenhund/rag-dog   comp.
A man who has "gone downhill," mentally and physically, no longer trustworthy
Misthund/dung-dog   comp.
Mean, insidious man
Hundearsch/dog-ass   comp.
Extremely vulgar term, mean, sickening man
Hundefutz/dog-vulva, dog-fart   comp.
Extremely vulgar term, repulsive, deceitful man
Schweinehund/swine-dog   hybrid
Extremely vulgar term in Germany but weakened in Texas through frequent use, a very mean character, repulsive, reprehensible; man
Sauhund/sow-dog   hybrid & sex diff.   Var. of the above but less frequent
morally bad, a man who takes advantage of women

2.   *FARM AND RANCH*
Reduced proximity to family, penned and loose livestock upon which the family's livelihood depends, male and female spheres of influence
7 generic categories: fowl, horse, ox, donkey, sheep, cattle, swine
46 terms of which 6 apply to females only, 28 apply to males only, and 12 apply to males and females

Trombeltier/doddering animal   comp.
A general term meaning weak, old, perhaps bloated; an old person
Vogel/bird, fowl   general category
   Spatz/sparrow   general term
   A small man, one not taken seriously
   Dreckspatz/dung-sparrow   comp.
   A dirty child
   alte Klucke/old hen, cluck   mod. & sex diff.
   A somewhat overbearing or dumb woman
   alter Gickel/Gockel/rooster, cock   mod. & sex diff.
   An old man, senile, slightly crazy
   dumme Gans/dumb goose   mod.
   A dumb, affected, or narrow-minded woman

>*dummes Hinkel/Hahn*/dumb rooster, cock   mod. & sex diff.
>Crazy, not overly bright; young man, though apparently sometimes used for women
>*verdrehtes Hinkel/Hahn*/twister rooster   mod. & sex diff.
>Crazy, a strange bird, queer; man, though apparently sometimes used for women to mean "twisted chick"
>*Zankhahn*/quarrel-rooster   comp. & sex diff.
>Wrangler, squabbler, bickerer, one who picks fights; man

Pferd/horse   general category and mild verbal abuse
Old work-horse; woman

>*Schimmel*/gray or white horse   color diff.
>Generally an older person of either sex with thick gray hair, can also be used for a young tow-headed person
>*Krack/Kracke*/old, weak horse   age diff.
>Old work-horse, almost with connotation of reliability, steadiness; man

>*Dorfhengst*/village stud   comp. & sex diff.
>A man who ruts indiscriminately

Ochs/ox   general category & verbal abuse
Dumb, primitive, coarse, clumsy, slow-witted, oaf, boob; man

>*Hornochs*/horn-ox   mod. Var. of above, lummox

Esel/donkey, ass   general category and verbal abuse
>Dumb, crazy, laughable; man
>*Steinesel*/jackass   comp. Var. of above, somewhat more derogatory through reinforcement of compounding

Schaf/sheep   general category and verbal abuse
Simpleton, dumb, naive, helpless; man

>*alter Schaf*/old sheep   mod. Var. of above, depending on intonation either slightly more tolerant or more abusive
>*Schafbock*/sheep-buck   sex diff. Slightly stronger than "Schaf," but without the ambiguity of "alter Schaf"
>*Hammel*/wether, mutton   sex diff.
>An extremely abusive term meaning unclean of body or clothing, immoral, indecent, coarse, obstinate, thick-headed, boorish, uncouth, rough; man

>>*Streithammel*/quarrel-mutton   comp. & sex diff. Quarrelsome fellow, picks fights, irritable, in addition to the agglomerate "Hammel"; man
>>*Neidhammel*/envy-mutton   comp. & sex diff.
>>Envious, jealous, petty in addition to the agglomerate "Hammel"; man
>>*Misthammel*/dung-mutton   comp. & sex diff.
>>Var. of "Hammel," but with a decided emphasis on coarseness and obstinacy; man
>>*Dreckhammel*/dirt-, shit-mutton   comp. & sex diff.
>>The most abusive term of this category, meaning physically dirty, morally come down or depraved, boorish and af-

fected, mean and contemptible; man
Schafskopf/sheephead   comp.
Dumb, foolish, uninteresting, boring man
Rindvieh/cattle   general category, not a verbal abuse in standard
High German pronunciation
Kalb/calf   dim. or age diff.
Foolish, silly, dumb, dense, good-natured or easy-going; a
person of any age or sex
Kuh/cow   sex diff.
An indolent, idle, fat, stout woman
Viech/Vieh/beast   general term
Beast; indiscriminately used against any category of
humans or domestic animals
Hornviech/-vieh/horn-beast   comp. Var. of above
Mistviech/-vieh/dung-beast   comp.
Contrary, thickheaded, bad, wicked, vulgar; woman
Rindsviech/-vieh/cattle   substandard pron. of general
category
Dumb, flabby, ungainly, clumsy, slow, boring, uninteresting
person of either sex
Schwein/pig, hog, swine   general category
Seldom a verbal abuse other than as a quick rebuke to a child for
making a mess while eating or playing in mud. "Schwein haben"
(to have a pig) is used in Germany to connote "good luck"
Ferkel/piglet   dim. or age diff.
A person who is dirty or wears dirty clothes, mischief-
maker; a young person, not as derogatory as the follow-
ing word
Sau/sow   sex diff
A very abusive term applied to a person who is filthy or
wears filthy clothes, immoral, obscene, indecent, bawdy;
a person of either sex, any age
Saufratz/sow-face   comp. & sex diff.
An ill-mannered, naughtly or disobedient young per-
son, more abusive than "Fratz" by itself
Saupans/sow-belly   comp. & sex diff.
Glutton, potbellied from food and drink, sloppy;
man or woman
Mistsau/dung-sow   comp. & sex diff.
Dirty, very immoral, unscrupulous, degenerate,
depraved; man
Drecksau/shit-sow   comp. & sex diff. Var. of above
Saukerl/sow-fellow   sex diff.& hybrid.
Miserable, despicable, lamentable; man
Saumensch/sow-slut   sex diff. & hybrid.
A coarse, shameless, vulgar woman
Sauhund/sow-dog   sex diff.& hybrid.
Intensification of "Hund" used for a mean, spiteful,

pitiful man
*Ewer/Eber/*boar   sex diff.
Meaning similar to "Sau," but more restrictive and less
frequent; primarly a man who is filthy, perhaps also im-
moral
Hundeewer/-eber   sex diff. & hybrid.
Sometimes applied to old male dogs, the
term (when used for people) is an intensifica-
tion of above
*Schweinigel/*swine-hedgehog   hybrid.
A dirty unkempt man, not as abusive as
"Schweinehund."
*Schweinehund/*swine-dog   hybrid.
Extremely vulgar term, but overused and frequently used
in joking, meaning a very mean, unprincipled, repulsive,
reprehensible, contemptible man

3. *FIELD AND FOREST*
Wildlife, animals which are hunted or avoided, male sphere of influence
11 terms, not divided into generic categories because the terms
are too random. Of these eleven terms, one applies to females
only, 3 apply to males only, and 7 apply to males and females

*Fasan/*pheasant   general term
A good-natured, but shy and quiet girl
*Fuchs/*fox   color diff.
A person of either sex, young or old, with thick reddish hair
*Hase/*hare   general term
A word used inclusively to designate German-speaking natives of
Fredericksburg, with a connotation of cowardice, indecisiveness,
ignorance (not stupidity); when used for an individual man the
word generally means unduly shy and unaffirmative
*Sandhase/*sand-rabbit   comp.
Var. of above, "sand" refers to the soil of Fredericksburg and
the Llano Basin
*Bock, Hirschbock/*wild buck, stag   sex diff. A good-natured coun-
try bumpkin, willful and stubborn, horny or sensuous; man
*Igel/*hedge hog   general term, never a verbal abuse
*Schwinigel/*swine-hedgehog?   hybrid. The pronunciation of
this word varies so much in Texas and in Germany that it is
unclear whether the affix is "Igel" (hedgehog), "Ekel" (puke),
or "Nickel" (a little, mean man)
As used generally, however, the word means dirty, unkempt,
maybe immoral, but never as abusive as other "Schwein"
words; man
*Stinkkatze/*skunk   general term
A person of any age, male or female, who enjoys pestering people
or causing dissention

       Stinkkater/male skunk   sex diff. Var. of above.
Wildsau/wild sow   sex diff.
Intensification of "Sau" used for a person who is filthy or wears filthy clothes, immoral, obscene, indecent, bawdy; a person of either sex, any age
Watz/wild boar   sex diff.
Intensification of "Eber" used for a man who is filthy, perhaps also immoral, generally refers to the odor of body excretions
Geier/bird of prey   general term
       Aasgeier/buzzard, vulture   comp. An uxorious husband, an excessive sycophant, an adult of any age or sex whose greed is disguised as kindness.

4. *FOREIGN*

Remote, animals which are known but have not been seen in natural habitat, outside of spheres of influence
3 generic categories: elephant, ape, camel
9 terms of which one applies to females only, 4 apply to males only, and 4 apply to males and females

seltsames Tier/strange animal   general term and a moderate verbal abuse
A phrase used without strong feeling for a strange, peculiar, queer, cranky person
Elefant/elephant   general term and a mild verbal abuse
Fat, flabby, huge, ungainly woman
Affe/ape, monkey   general term and a mild verbal abuse
Dumb, silly, idle, boring man, a buffoon
       Äffchen/little monkey   dim.
       A pet name for a hyperactive, imaginative, mischievous youngster
       Moosaffe/moss?-monkey   comp. Etymology uncertain, not used outside Cypress Creek, var. of "Affe"
       This mild, joking abuse connotes silliness and buffoonery
       Affengesicht/ape-face   comp.
       A person who constantly grins, someone with an ill-favored, primitive, Cro-Magnon face or head
       Affenschwanz/ape-tail   comp.
       An intensification of "Affe"
       Affenarsch/ape-ass   comp.
       An intensification of "Affe"
Kamel/camel   general term and a severe verbal abuse
Blockhead, numbskull, dolt; also used like "Affengesicht" with a variety of connotations meaning physically ill-favored in appearance, unpleasant or offensive to look at

    The terms themselves are interesting from a technical viewpoint. With the single exception of diminutives (e.g., kitten, piglet, little monkey), *any tendency* toward specificity corresponds with increasing pejorative value. Although the diminutives are animal metaphors, they are not verbal abuse but rather pet names applied to wives, sweethearts, boys and girls. Specificity is effected structurally by modifying, compounding, or hybridizing the general base metaphor. Obviously, the most clearly defined characters are the most hostile. For example:

   a.   general base metaphor *Hund/dog*
       mean, spiteful, miserable man.
   b.   modification (can include sex and color differentiation) *närrischer Hund/*crazy dog
       foolish, strange, peculiar man.
       Adjectives most frequently used for modification include "old," "gross," "dumb," and "strange."
   c.   compounding *Hundefutz/*dog-vulva
       extremely vulgar, repulsive, deceitful man.
       Compounding is usually accomplished by adding some form of the words "dirt" or "shit" or some body part or lower orifice to the base metaphor.
   d.   hybridization *Schweinehund/*swine-dog
       extremely vulgar, very mean, repulsive, reprehensible man.
       Hybridization always is effected by joining some form of "swine" or "pig" with the undifferentiated "dog," resulting in swine-dog, sow-dog, or dog-boar.

My approach toward interpretation of the metaphors basically follows these patterns of structure and meaning. The fundamental questions were, if such expressions function as social correctives and equalizers of tension, what do they attack? who uses them? and what is the underlying social consensus? In summary, what are the values they enforce?

First of all, we must assume that people, like the animals of the two more proximate categories, have highly determined, unavoidable functions or roles.[3] Furthermore, traditional views of social reality are predicated upon the maintenance, within certain ranges of deviation, of those functions or roles. What we have then in some of the animal metaphors is an extended set of analogies. In that sense, the metaphor is a social corrective used as we employ many familiar proverbs.

In the pig metaphors, for example, we see that outward appearance is considered indicative of inner deficiencies. Being called a *Schwein* [pig] is not too bad. *Sau* [sow], on the other hand, connotes filth, immorality, obscenity, indecency, and bawdiness, while *Eber* [boar] implies mainly filth. The hybrid *Schweinehund*, describing a marginal being which derives its power from its potentiality for danger or disruption, brings to bear the strong abusive connotations of both *Schwein* and *Hund*. In Germany, it is probably the single most abusive animal metaphor in any context, but in Texas the word has been so overused that it is now completely acceptable in a joking context. Outside that context, though, *Schweinehund* is abusive in Texas, but its relative frequency here (where such words have become stock and trade in a shrinking bilingual heritage) far exceeds its frequency over there. I have only to think back to a cultural tour I directed one summer for nineteen Texans—ages 23–84, seven men, twelve women, two retired nuns—through German-speaking Europe to be reminded of the salty potency of the Texas-German idiom. The extreme incident which I observed occurred at dinner in a comfortable Swiss hotel. There a puny restaurant proprietor upbraided a six-foot female cousin of mine (who had a large collection of abusive animal metaphors at the tip of her tongue and a correspondingly adept command of German) for ordering a fourth basket of breads and pastries. Obviously the type of person who would take no impertinence from a Brahman bull, much less from someone waiting our table, she shot back her order, reinforcing it loudly and clearly with *"Du Schweinehund,"* the moral equivalent in stodgy Switzerland of "You loathsome goddamned bastard," as only a Texan can draw out those words. The result was that after a short while—as soon as others could gulp their *Schnitzels*, down their wine, and exit—we had the entire restaurant delightfully to ourselves and enough beer to not let it bother us.

Especially intriguing are the two strange animal metaphors used by the Cypress Creek and Comfort Germans against the German-speaking natives of Fredericksburg. Both *Hase* [hare] and *Sandhase* [sand-rabbit] connote cowardice, indecisiveness, ignorance, undue shyness, and reticence, but the obvious differences between the people of Cypress Creek and Fredericksburg are that the Fredericksburgers are more homogeneous, speak an inferior German, and are despicably religious. Otherwise, only the Anglo-American "biscuits" have been victimized in this manner, suggesting that, among the early settlers, only two groups outside the community were viewed with sustained hostility: the "other" Germans (i.e., the Fredericksburgers as opposed to Germans of Sisterdale, Boerne, San Antonio, and New Braunfels) and that other larger and more indiscriminate group, the Anglo-Americans.[4]

In deriving a world-view from these metaphors, we must ask again, what do they attack? By and large, these metaphors of Cypress Creek attack four deviations. Sex differentiation in the metaphors is linked with impotence, immorality, or promiscuity. On the point of sexual immodesty, a very strong double standard is apparent. To be a *Kater* [tomcat] or a *Dorfhengst* [village stud], whether those words are employed by a man or a woman, is never as low as the female equivalent *Saumensch* [sow-slut]. Second, the metaphors attack physical deterioration and filth as outward states indicative of inner deficiencies. Third, the expressions stressing ungainliness are attacks on that which is unsettled and graceless, on that which is not in control of itself. Most striking, finally, in view of our stereotype of traditional German culture, is the recurring implicit attack on age. I suspect this results from the ambiguous passing on of home and farm to the control of the younger generation. Although the ancestor stories seem to counter this view, the metaphors suggest that the older people, who "must die so new people can be born," are seen perhaps as stifling influences because no clear transitions of control or inheritance have evolved. Lingering anti-religious tendencies in the community doubtlessly intensify the ambiguous and threatening nature of transitional or marginal states like age and death.[5]

Like the ancestor and landscape stories told so frequently in the Cypress Creek valley, these animal metaphors constitute part of the collected folk wisdom. The values enforced by the metaphors are the positive values belonging to the group's symbolic self-portrait. Whatever deviates too far from this underlying social consensus and thus causes tension—that is, whatever draws attention to itself, is not right, not good, not pleasing, intemperate, unmeasured, ill-favored, unclean, unpleasant, or improper—becomes the target of these traditional social correctives.

Notes

1. Howard Becker, *Through Values to Social Interpretation: Essays on Social Contexts, Actions, Types, and Prospects* (Durham, North Carolina: Duke Univ. Press, 1950), ch. 5.

2. The animal metaphor *Kater* [tomcat] recently acquired a new vogue since its local pronunciation makes it a homophone of the Germanicized pronunciation of "Carter." Thus, while national cartoonists singled out the President's teeth, or smile, or peanut warehouse as the butts of their humor, in the German-speaking parts of Texas he invariably came across as a prowling tomcat.

3. It is amusing to note some of these naming practices. Despite the abusive severity of the dog metaphors, dogs were generally given warm and affectionate names like *Prinz*, reflecting the sex of the animal. More recently, there has been a tendency to give dogs satirical names like *Spiro* from American politics. Cats, as a rule, were not named, probably because most families had too many. Milch cows, bulls, rams, and billy goats usually were given humorous or abusive names. Cows were often named in jest after women in the neighborhood; male breeding livestock got such names as *Tojo* (used during World War II) or *Bildo* (a more recent bull's name). All horses usually acquired affectionate names as colts. Pigs, unless they were show animals, never had names; neither did chickens, geese, ewes, or nannies.

4. A German folklorist, Wilhelm Heiland, observes, "In der 'guten alten Zeit' war es Brauch, dass jedes Dorf zu seiner amtilichen Ortsbezeichung einen volkstümlichen Beinamen bekam. Dieser 'Spitz- oder Unnamen' wird nicht von den Dorfbewohnern selbst gewählt, er wurde ihnen von den 'lieben Nachbarn and Freunden' als Schimpfnamen beigegeben." *Nivora-Nauborn. Beiträge zur örtlichen Geschichte* (Wetzlar: Zunn, 1978), p. 190.

5. Although he is not saying the same thing, Emile Durkheim's comment on the tribal soul is interesting to note in connection with

193

what may here be a vestige of an extremely old folkloric motif: "The primitive does not have the idea of an all-powerful god who creates souls out of nothing. It seems to him that souls cannot be made except out of souls. So those who are born can only be new forms of those who have been; consequently, it is necessary that these latter continue to exist in order that others may be born. In fine, the belief in the immortality of the soul is the only way in which men were able to explain a fact which could not fail to attract their attention; this fact is the perpetuity of the life of the group. Individuals die, but the clan survives." *The Elementary Forms of Religious Life* (New York: Free Press, 1965), p. 304.

Within the Walls/Texas Prison Folklore/*Martha Anne Turner*

Until Director O. B. Ellis formulated and implemented sweeping reforms in the 1940's, the Texas Prison System farms depended on mules and oxen. (Courtesy, Texas Department of Corrections)

The Walls. Old Death Row was located behind the corner. (Courtesy, Texas Department of Corrections)

Within the Walls
Texas Prison Folklore

Martha Anne Turner

It was Robert Frost who said

> *Before I built a wall I'd ask to know*
> *What I was walling in or walling out.*

Founded in 1849, the Huntsville branch is the oldest of the fourteen units comprising the sprawling Texas prison system. Because of the forty-foot-high enclosure surrounding the compound, the unit is known as the Walls. Behind the vine-covered barrier in the heart of Huntsville, under its leafy canopy of East Texas pines and liveoaks, approximately 1,700 inmates man industries and discharge essential service operations.[1] These consist of the prison hospital, cemetery, automobile license plate plant, a textile mill, print shop, a cardboard box factory, and a machine shop. Here the prison rodeo arena and the death house occupy compatible positions on the site. Here within the Walls the prison publication, *The Echo*, founded in 1928, is edited and published by a competent staff of inmates.

Today the system—now identified as the Texas Department of Corrections—ranks as number one among the penal institutions of the nation.[2] Only thirty years ago, however, before the advent of sweeping reforms dramatically instituted by O. B. Ellis (1948-1961) and subsequently continued by Dr. George Beto (1962-1972) and his successor, Director W. J. Estelle, Jr., the system was one of the most decadent.[3]

John Greenway's definition of folk community—"an un-sophisiticated, homogeneous group living in a politically-bound culture but isolated from it by such factors as topography, geography, dialect, economics, and race"—[4] applies particularly to the penal enclave. Furthermore, in the special community, created by society but operating outside of it, folklore plays a far more vital role than it does when its members inhabit the free world. Within the Walls in

Huntsville, there exists a way of life comprised of material indigenous to the Texas penal system per se, to mores native to general prison culture, and to phenomena from crime and other free world folklore.

Criminologists recognize three categories of prison society: the *non-criminal*, the *thief*, and the *convict*.[5] Even though they may vary from one institution to another, the categories are basically the same. Naturally all three groups are composed of men serving sentences for crimes, but their differences add dimension to prison folklore.

The *non-criminal* group includes men whose attitudes and orientation concern values and goals of a non-criminal society. These men have committed a single crime under extraordinary circumstances and will not likely repeat themselves. The category is composed of a large proportion of homicides, political prisoners, and civil rights agitators. Inside prison and out they have little connection with the underworld or with organized crime. Customarily they avoid inmate society and ignore prison rackets. Infrequently they may go over to one of the other groups, especially if they are under long-term sentences. But such conversions are rare.[6]

A notable example in the Texas Department of Corrections was a former judge of the Court of Civil Appeals. At sixty the man had become a hopeless alcoholic and, while intoxicated, murdered a young secretary. A physical wreck but brilliant, the inmate was first assigned to a teaching post at Harlem Farm, now renamed Jester. Since he had been assessed only three years for the heinous crime and other inmates had drawn much stiffer sentences for less serious offenses, they rejected him. Prison Manager Lee Simmons reassigned the man several times but still thought he could make better use of him.

At the time the state penitentiary owned 73,000 acres of land but the boundaries were inexact and some of the titles obscure. The convict-attorney was made a trustee and put to work on land titles. By the time he had finished his job every acre of the land was validated and mapped and the state had recovered 800 acres of land in the operation.[7]

The *thief* culture is composed essentially of public officials and businessmen and is numerically the smallest of the three categories. Members engage in everything from misappropriation of public funds to floating phony stocks to commercial assassination. But their motive is money and has nothing to do with criminal life. They are the golfers, the country clubbers, whose wives' names fill the social register.

A classic specimen was the Texas politician convicted of land grabbing. All Huntsville was agog when the millionaire came to town in a chauffeur-driven gold Cadillac, stopped at a filling station, and inquired of the attendant the address of the Walls, where all incoming felons were processed before the Diagnostic Center was built in 1964.

The *convict* group poses the greatest problem to authorities and penologists. This culture provides the largest proportion of the recidivists. As the hard core of prison subculture, members find their reference groups inside the institution and seek status through penal environment. Whereas the *non-criminal* class try to do their time as quietly as possible and the *thief* opts for comforts that will make incarceration easier, the *convict* seeks privileges that will enhance his position in the inmate hierarchy and the chance to "jump" for freedom to continue his life of professional crime on the outside.

Only incidental relationships exist between the *convicts* and the *thieves*. In fact, the *thieves* consider themselves socially superior. Since many of the *convicts* attain their apprenticeship in juvenile institutions, where the *thief* culture is practically nonexistent, the two have little in common. While the *non-criminal* and the *thief* eschew prison argot, it is the natural idiom of the *convict*.[8]

The *convict* culture in Texas penology is laced with the legends of such daring gunmen and hardened criminals as Clyde Barrow, "Pretty Boy" Floyd, Raymond Hamilton, and Joe Palmer—and of an earlier day, John Wesley Hardin, who accumulated forty-two notches on his .45 before he cashed in his chips in an El Paso saloon in 1895. More recent candidates of the subculture include the gangster dope pushers who were involved in one of the most tragic shootouts at the Walls in all penal history.

In the old days within the Walls, when the Code was law, the term *convict* commanded respect. To be called *convict* meant one was loyal to the prison community as opposed to the authorities and prison officials. The *convict* kept his mouth shut, did not inform, and tended strictly to his own business.[9]

Argot is one of the most distinctive facets of prison folklore. Even though inmates from the upper strata of free world economy avoid it, they understand it. For that matter, to officials and inmates alike a *stool-pigeon* is an informer; the *tank*, the cell block; *a jump*, a prison break; *a buck*, a mutiny or mass refusal to obey a work order; and a *knockout*, a prisoner so senile or otherwise incapacitated that he is unable to do manual labor.

Correspondingly, the expression *to be put on the ground* means "to be awarded a full pardon." Such a case was that of one of Clyde Barrow's gang whose family helped to set up Barrow and Bonnie Parker for the ambush in Arcadia, Louisiana, when they were liquidated by Ranger Frank Hamer on January 16, 1934. Lee Simmons had arranged with Governor Miriam A. Ferguson "to put" Henry Methvin, the son, "on the ground" in exchange for the assistance from his parents.[10]

For the inmate, however, prison terminology is frequently more connotative than denotative; and it is the very word association that excludes the outsider. One example is *big bitch*—a life sentence under the habitual criminal act. Others are words with multiple meanings. *Joint*, for instance, which has a Phallic origin, in Texas may refer to a marijuana cigarette, the paraphernalia for injecting narcotics, a saloon or house of prostitution, and the male sex organ. *Rap,* which is usually preceded by the modifier *bum* because of its adverse connotation, may mean the criminal charge or sentence, a protest against an inmate's release, or even a report for violation of rules. One of the most compelling specimens of connotative argot is *Old Sparky,* the electric chair, installed in 1924 and banned by court action in 1964, after a total of 365 executions.[11]

In Texas there is also language peculiar to farm work. *Turn-row*—the road forming the boundary of a *cut* or single crop area—is a keyword. *Fire on the turnrow* means the warden is coming. *Thunder on the turnrow* indicates that the prison director is near. *Side line* refers to working on one side of a row. *Flat weed* means getting everything out of a field; *catch up tight*—work closely together—and *don't leave a comeback*—get everything out of a row so that it won't be necessary to rework the other side.[12]

An anecdote originating at Ramsey Farm concerns a released prisoner and his first free world haircut. When he sits down the barber looks at his head and asks if he has been in prison.

"Why, no," the ex-con protests. "Why do you ask?"

"No reason in particular," says the barber, "I was just wondering." Then he asks his customer how he wants his hair cut.

"Sideline the sides. Flat weed the top. Catch up tight and don't leave a comeback."[13]

Nicknames for inmates and officials are common in the Texas system. Though stereotyped, the nicknames are likely to be more original than prison slang or vernacular. Sometimes the intimate names originate from a favorite saying or custom. More often they derive from a physical characteristic or personality trait. Thus inmates were identified as *Looking Down Red, Big 40, Blabbermouth, Applehead, Marble Eye*, and *Hog Jaw.*[14]

Two black inmates carried the extraordinary labels of *Lead Belly* and *Clear Rock. Lead Belly,* who later gained fame as a ballad singer for the noted ballad collector John Lomax, was said to be able to eat anything without injury to his stomach. *Clear Rock*, also a talented balladeer, explained the origin of his nickname characteristically: "Ah throwed three Nigguhs wid rocks. Dat's how come dey calls me *Clear Rock.*"[15] He meant that he had committed three different murders with three rocks!

Since the nicknames were employed essentially for reference, the real name was frequently forgotten. In one unit some of the inmates were taking up a collection for a convict about to be paroled. Money trickled in until it was explained that the fund was for *Hucklebuck.* Few knew the felon by his real name.

One day a prison board member visiting Wynne Farm inquired if a certain prisoner was a member of a particular squad and the captain said "no." Then recognizing the man, the board member said, "There he is." The inmate had been in the squad twelve years, but his captain knew him only by the name of *Stricknine*.[16]

Derision had its effect particularly in names chosen for officials. Two were rechristened *Boss No-Socks* and *I Killem Kelly*, respectively, for diverse but obvious reasons. The latter's initials were *I. K.* and inasmuch as the inmates considered him trigger-happy, the *K* designated *Killem*.[17] On one guard was hung the cognomen of *Sundown* because he refused to recognize quitting time in the fields by turning his back on the sun. Another, *Stud Horse* Tom Hennessey, a familiar figure at Clemens in 1929, got his sobriquet from his mount.

Although there are exceptions, it is the *convict* category that enjoys homosexual jokes and is most likely to engage in deviate behavior. Before his first imprisonment, the average inmate has not had extensive homosexual experience. He may be familiar with such terms as *fag, fairy, queen,* and *gay*. But in prison he learns two new words—*punk* and *wolf*—and a whole new concept, cold and hard as steel. Furthermore, he learns that a large proportion of inmate population tends to be exceedingly solipsistic in its interpretation and assessment of perversion.

In general, the attitude is that free world homosexuals are acceptable because they are overt, honest and admit what they are. On the other hand, prison catamites, or *punks*, are viewed with contempt because they are covert and weak.

As a rule, administrators play down this aspect of prison life, and its incidence varies from system to system. Despite this fact, some authorities insist the incidence of participation runs from ten to twenty percent in some institutions and as high as ninety-five percent in others.

It is of record that one convict in the Texas system was supposedly killed for informing, whereas the real reason for his murder was jealousy in a homosexual relationship. It is likewise true that a young prisoner killed in an escape attempt could no longer tolerate the mistreatment to which other inmates subjected him. Not only did the *wolves* violate his body, they took his pocket change, and forced him to wash their underwear and socks and perform other unsavory duties.[18]

In some instances jokes dealing with perversion are adaptations of those from the free world wearing prison garb. A typical example bears the Jesse James stamp.

Jesse James was robbing a passenger train. As he relieved the passengers of their money and valuables, he said, "I'm gonna rob this train and then I'm gonna f—k all the men."

Whereupon a lady stood up and said, "Mister Jesse James, you mean all the women."

And there's this punk on the train who arose and said, "Hey, lady, who's robbin' this train, you or Mister Jesse James?"[19]

Still other jokes involve a knowledge of the penitentiary locale. A specimen undoubtedly circulated by deviates themselves is the following:

Say, did you hear about the guy who did thirty years in prison? He finally went out. Yes, the old boy finally got a parole. Now after thirty years everything changes, you know. And this ex-con is kind of leery of the new way of life. When he went in they didn't even have a streetcar, a bus, or anything like that.

So he's standing there outside the prison walls with his cheap suitcase in hand, his release pay in his pocket, and wondering what to do. Then a civilian comes down the street carrying a sack lunch. Seeing the civilian, the ex-con decides to do what he does. So he matches stride with him, and the civilian says, "Good morning." The ex-con repeats the greeting. The two continue talking and a bus arrives.

The civilian enters first and drops a nickel and a dime in the slot. The ex-con does the same. The civilian finds a seat and so does the ex-con—beside him. The bus takes off, stops, takes off again. Suddenly a good-looking blonde gets on.

Civilian ogles her and nudges the ex-con. He doesn't know he's an ex-con, you know. "Hey," he says, "Look at that pair of legs!"

Ex-con says, "Yeah, nice. Very nice. But look at the ass on that bus driver."[20]

Material folklore is a vital phase of the subculture. This aspect reached its height in the Texas penitentiary in the 30s and early 40s and gave new meaning to folk ingenuity.

Foremost in the segment is the convict's knife. In some institutions inmates make knives by shearing a piece of sheet steel at a diagonal. In Huntsville during the period the convicts made theirs in the automobile license plant in shapes to fit the places of concealment. Some carried them inconspicuously in jacket linings, in pockets, or strapped to a leg. However, many of the felons carried the contraband weapons in the extra fold of cloth over the trousers' zipper. It was the one place the guards did not pat when they searched an inmate.

Rarely was a Texas prisoner without his knife. There was one whose instrument was so dull that it would hardly cut anything, but the inmate carried it, felt insecure without it. Nevertheless, most of the prisoners kept their knives razor-sharp and did not hesitate to use them. In 1938, one morning at Eastham when a drunk officer got a little too close to his squad, the inmates mugged him and slashed him unmercifully. Eight of them disarmed him and left with his guns. Eventually the escapees were recaptured and six were killed in the process.

Between 1935 and 1940, when the bat and bullwhip were symbols of authority, inmates used their knives to sever their heel tendons and otherwise mutilate themselves. As one inmate explained it: "A bunch of convicts would decide that the next morning a certain number would cut their heel strings. They drew straws to see who would cut. If you got the short straw, you either cut your heel strings or got killed. None of the tough guys ever cut theirs . . ."[21]

Although criminologists and authorities believed the inmates mutilated themselves to keep from working in the fields under the scorching Texas sun, the felons claimed the mutilations were a protest against prison brutality. Certainly the notorious Clyde Barrow did not cut off his toe at Eastham, before Governor Ross Sterling paroled him in 1932, to escape work. He did it in hopes of being transferred to the Walls in Huntsville, where he considered the possibility of escape more realistic.

Texas convicts resorted to another type of demonstration—one against prison authority and particularly the searching of the tanks by guards. They secretly smuggled water moccasins and rattlesnakes into the Walls and deposited them in their lockers and cabinets.[22] To get the reptiles into the building they wrapped them in their coats or tied a string around their necks to prevent them from biting and brought them in taped to their legs. There were definitely fewer searchings after several guards had been bitten by the reptiles.

During these chequered years, when food was scarce, some of the inmates of the Walls maintained a restaurant in the East building to supplement the usual fare of peas, beans, sow belly, and cornbread. They called their project the "Greasy Spoon" and either stole most of the food from the steward's department or paid guards to procure groceries for them in town.

Gambling and drinking within the Walls were rampant during these atrocious years. There was always a lot of cash in the main building in Huntsville and the felons gambled it off at poker or at shooting craps. According to one inmate, "There was no effort to control the gambling. The prisoners placed the gambling tables in the prison yard in front of the buildings in full view of the guards so that they could watch and keep down killings."

Texas convicts distilled their own liquor. They called whiskey *chock* and produced it by fermenting ingredients in containers from a discarded swamp boot to an unused commode. For their operations they stole sugar by the barrel or bribed the steward to look the other way as they replenished their supply. Said to have had a variety of flavors, the concoction was tested by putting a piece of fresh meat in a batch. If the meat turned green the whiskey was considered unsafe for drinking.[23] One convict stated that the guards and officials could not care less about their making *chock*. He elaborated further:

I ran a still on Retrieve. I made pretty good whiskey. I even sold some of it to guards. Once I had run off a batch and was taking a jelly glass of it to a boy in another tank. The picket guard came over and asked what I had. I said, 'whiskey, want some?' He said 'Yes,' and I gave him the glass. After that, I gave him some every run.[24]

All prisons have their miscellany of stories circulated by officials, anecdotes orignating with the incarcerants themselves, along with legends of monumental breaks and the exit of infamous desperadoes. The Texas system is no exception. Some of these merely typify facetious commentaries, whereas others are designed to portray facets of penal routine.

Three disseminated by prison personnel are of interest. Twenty-five years ago when a new guard joined a unit, the old officers initiated him. One Saturday ten or twelve dressed in convict clothes, with the approval of the warden, and went with the new man to the fields to hoe a patch of corn. Beforehand the officers had removed the lead from the bullets in the guard's gun without his knowledge.

Soon after they arrived at the field the men impersonating the inmates threw down their hoes and started to run. The guard began shooting. After emptying his gun, he reloaded it with bullets the officers did not know he had. When the real bullets began whizzing over their heads, the masqueraders tried to explain that it was just a trick they were playing on him. The trick backfired. The new guard worked his "squad" until sundown.[25]

One warden liked to tell about the good luck he had at the Retrieve unit in 1948. The number three picket guard noticed a bird looking down a hole and pointed to it. Upon investigating, the warden found an inmate's coat in the hole and also discovered that the convicts had dug a tunnel from one of the tanks to the building. There were lights in the tunnel, along with wide places to permit passing. The inmates had flushed all the loose dirt down the drains. The means of escape was completed and the convicts would no doubt have made the break that evening had a bird not "stooled off" the possibility.[26]

The third yarn concerns a black man's request for clemency. Old Mose, the aged Negro who had been in prison many years, was employed as a domestic by Captain Buck Flanagan of Central. When he heard that Governor Pat Neff was coming for a visit, Old Mose prevailed upon Captain Flanagan to obtain for him an audience with the governor so that he could petition for a pardon.

Permission was granted, and the black inmate approached Governor Neff, with cap in hand, servilely. He reviewed his record in detail. He had been in the penitentiary longer than he could remember; earlier he had given trouble, had attempted to escape twice, but now he had reformed . . . . "An' the Cap'n knows ah's been a good Niggah foh a long time, an' please Moster Guvnor, won' yo' he'p dis ol' Niggah convict?"

Governor Neff, who was not noted for granting clemency, asked how much time the convict had. Old Mose had two life sentences to serve and just didn't see how he could make it. Then the governor of Texas said: "Mose, tell you what I'll do. When I get back to Austin I'll take one of those life sentences off you."[27]

A few stories emanating from the convicts themselves bear scrutiny. Some have to do with food. No doubt most are unfounded.

There was the incident of the felon who discovered the leg and foot of a mouse in his stew. He complained to an official. With exaggerated mock sympathy, the officer replied, "What in hell, do you want —a whole rat?"

At Central Farm every time a malingerer requested a lay-in (sick excuse), his captain would repeat his words almost verbatim. If the prisoner said, "My head hurts," the captain would invariably say, "Mine too, me too." If the convict said, "My leg hurts and I have a stomach ache," the answer came right back, "Me, too. My leg hurts. My stomach aches."

So one day the inmate vowed, "I'm gonna get me a lay-in." "Captain," he began, "I want to lay-in."

"What's the matter with you?" asked the captain.

"I got the clapps in the ass." The captain started to repeat. Then, thinking better of himself, said, "Lay-in!"[28]

The inmate's aversion for the prison guard is universal. A favorite story from the Walls in Huntsville involves a cathouse and a certain guard who patronized it. The guard was a regular customer, saw the same gal every Saturday night. One Saturday night she was not there. When he demanded to know where she was, the establishment informed him that she was taking time out to have a baby.

Whereupon the guard exclaimed, "I didn't know whores had babies!"

"Sure," the madam told him. "Where do you think these prison guards come from?"[29]

Before reform was initiated in 1948, there were more prison breaks from the Walls in Huntsville in a month than in some federal prisons in an entire year.[30] Frequently the success of a raid or break was largely due to the negligence or disobedience of officials or to inside assistance of a guard willing to accept a bribe. Two such breaks occurred in a single year during Lee Simmons' administration and both were related.

The first was a raid near Eastham Farm at nine o'clock on the morning of January 16, 1934, when Clyde Barrow and Bonnie Parker freed three members of their gang—Raymond Hamilton, Joe Palmer, and Henry Methvin. By invitation another convict—Hilton Bybee— joined the trio.

Simmons had placed the members of the Barrow gang and others of their caliber at Eastham, a unit designed for maximum security risks. Located in Houston and Walker counties on the Trinity River, five miles from a main highway, the isolated site recommended the unit as such a place of incarceration. As an additional precaution against escape attempts, the prison manager assigned a special guard as a "backfield man" to take a position around the edges of the area where convicts were employed and to keep his presence and whereabouts concealed. Qualifications for the job included excellent marksmanship, unquestionable discretion, and extreme courage.

At the time of the raid 200 convicts were cutting timber about two miles from camp. Thus several squads and guards were merged in the single work detail. At the outset Hamilton "jumped his squad" to join Palmer's. This should have aroused suspicion, but the guard ignored it. Worse, the special guard, who should have been out of sight around the perimeter of the area, had joined the group in direct disobedience to his orders. As the workers entered the wood, the guard of Palmer's squad called the special guard over to him. When the latter rode up, Hamilton and Palmer, each armed with a .45 automatic smuggled to them the night before by a trusty, opened fire on the two. In the exchange of shots the special officer was fatally wounded. As the guards' horses wheeled and reared at the sound of gunfire, Clyde Barrow moved in with a machine gun to cover his men's escape. With the machine gun chattering and the whine and zing of direct and ricocheting bullets above their heads, two of the guards panicked and fled, while another ordered the remaining convicts to lie flat on the ground.[31]

Only a short time later Hamilton and Palmer were apprehended and tried for killing the guard. They were convicted and given the death penalty. In Texas, before 1965 when death row was moved to Ellis, inmates assessed a death sentence were assigned to the death house—a one-story brick building equipped with eight five-by-ten cells in the courtyard of the Walls. Fronting the death cells is a forty-five-foot corridor separating the cellblock from the opposite wall. At the right end is the barber's chair, plainly visible, where inmates may see a condemned man get prepared to "go down" by having his left leg and a spot on the crown of his head shaved to accommodate the electrodes. At the opposite end is the entrance door. To the left of the cell doors is "the little green door" to the death chamber.

The second incident, which occurred on July 22, 1934, was the only successful death-cell break recorded in Texas penal history.[32] In the spectacular break, enacted during a Sunday afternoon baseball game, Hamilton, Palmer, and Blackie Thompson scaled the Walls on a fire ladder to shortlived freedom. Two getaway cars driven by women awaited the escapees. Although the break was masterminded by a lifer friend of Thompson—who was himself shot off the ladder in the escape attempt—a guard had smuggled in three automatics with which the break was staged. The guard, who accepted a bribe of $500, reentered the Walls on August 13, 1934, under three five-year sentences to run consecutively.[33]

Recaptured, Hamilton and Palmer were remanded to death row. As their time was running out, it was Hamilton—whose sentences, before the death penalty, totaled 263 years[34]—that lost his nerve. From the outset Palmer, who dared to attend Clyde Barrow's funeral with the electric chair staring him in the face, accepted his fate stoically. Up to a few hours before his execution, Hamilton was hopeful that his lawyers would get his sentence commuted. At four o'clock that afternoon he insisted that Prison Manager Simmons call Austin.

As the Reverend Hugh Finnigan, who went along for confirmation, and Simmons left the cellblock to telephone, Hamilton called out wildly, *"I'm not in the chair yet!"* When Simmons and the chaplain returned to inform Hamilton that no official action in his behalf had been taken, he faced the reality of his execution for the first time.

At five o'clock the two men were moved to the same cell next to the execution chamber. Fear consumed Hamilton. Only Palmer's adept counseling and faith in the hereafter helped to calm him. At their trials Palmer had attempted to save Hamilton from the chair by taking all the blame for killing the guard. Now he assumed another responsibility—that of trying to help his friend face the inevitable end with courage.

It was thought best to have Palmer go first. When the warden asked him if he had anything to say, Palmer read a prepared statement in which he expressed admiration for the chaplain and asked forgiveness of those he had injured as he himself forgave those who had injured him. He closed with this remarkable assertion—

I ask God to accept my ignoble death [here Palmer interpolated: "Let's get that word right, boys; that is 'ignoble' and not 'noble.'"] in atonement for my sins.[35]

Five minutes later when Hamilton followed Palmer through "the little green door," he was a different man. He crossed himself and stated that he was glad to pay his debt and atone for his sins. He mentioned Joe's farewell and requested that the chaplain tell his mother and his girlfriend that he "was happy to die this way."[36]

So on May 19, 1935, the two members of Clyde Barrow's gang walked the proverbial "last mile" to keep their appointment with "Old Sparky." Their cellmate Thompson, with whom they had escaped, had preceded them, having lost in a running gun battle with an Amarillo posse on December 16, 1934.

In Huntsville there is an old wives' tale that the city's lights dim when the executioner throws the switch. But the prison has its own generators and dimmed lights are seen only within the Walls. . . .

> *Something there is that doesn't love a wall,*
> *That sends the frozen-ground-swell under it,*
> *And spills the upper boulders in the sun.*

Notes

1. "The Huntsville Unit, Texas Department of Corrections," 1: *History of Corrections; History of The Texas Department of Corrections,* Manual No. 21, Property of the Texas Department of Corrections Officers' Training School.

2. Austin MacCormick to W. J. Estelle, Jr., May, 1977, Letter. Official Prison Archives, the Walls, Huntsville, Texas. See also *Texas*

Department of Corrections: 30 Years of Progress, Official Prison brochure (Huntsville, Texas, 1978), 12.

3. Austin MacCormick, *Survey of the Texas Penal System*, 1944, Official Prison Archives. See also Austin MacCormick to Dr. George Beto, February 28, 1968, Letter. Official Prison Archives.

4. John Greenway, *Literature Among the Primitives* (Hatboro, Pennsylvania, 1964), xii.

5. John Irwin and Donald Creesy, "Thieves, Convicts, and the Inmate Culture," Howard S. Becker (ed.), *The Other Side: Perspectives on Deviance* (New York, 1964), 225-245.

6. *Ibid.*

7. Lee Simmons, *Assignment Huntsville: Memoirs of a Texas Prison Official* (Austin, 1957), 190-193.

8. Becker, *The Other Side: Perspectives on Deviance*, 225-245.

9. Bruce Jackson, "Prison Folklore," Reprinted from *Journal of American Folklore*, October-December, 1965, Vol. 78, No. 310 (Cambridge, Massachusetts, 1965), 320.

10. Simmons, *Assignment Huntsville. . . ,* 127, 132.

11. "The Huntsville Unit: Texas Department of Corrections," 4; *History of Corrections; History of the Texas Department of Corrections,* Manual No. 21.

12. Jackson, "Prison Folklore," 328.

13. *Ibid.*

14. *Texas Department of Corrections: 30 Years of Progress,* 16.

15. Simmons, *Assignment Huntsville. . . ,* 112.

16. *Texas Department of Corrections: 30 Years of Progress,* 16.

17. Jackson, "Prison Folklore," 328.

18. *Texas Department of Corrections: 30 Years of Progress,* 20.

19. Richard M. Dorson, *American Folklore* (Chicago, 1959), 241-242.

20. *Ibid.*

21. *Texas Department of Corrections: 30 Years of Progress,* 22.

22. *Ibid.,* 21. Story also verified by Rosemary Heinsohn, public affairs coordinator, to author, May 21, 1978.

23. *Texas Department of Corrections: 30 Years of Progress,* 22.

24. *Ibid.*

25. *Ibid.,* 13.

26. *Ibid.*

27. Simmons, *Assignment Huntsville. . . ,* 192-193.

28. Dorson, *American Folklore,* 241-242.

29. *Ibid.*

30. A matter of common knowledge. See also MacCormick's *Survey of the Texas Penal System* as previously cited and official prison correspondence and records, Texas Prison Archives.

31. Simmons, *Assignment Huntsville . . . ,* 114-117.

32. Don Reid and John Gurwell, *Eyewitness* (Houston, 1973), 17.

33. Simmons, *Assignment Huntsville. . . ,* 158.

34. Record for Number 74125, Texas Prison Archives.

35. Simmons, *Assignment Huntsville. . .* , 162.
36. *Ibid.,* 163.

Oil Field Jokes from the Llano Estacado/*Jim Harris*

Oil Field Jokes
From the Llano Estacado

Jim Harris

It's 3:00 p.m. Thursday. You're ten miles north of Hobbs, New Mexico, at a place called Dan's. Four filthy roughnecks enter. They wear heavy boots, jeans, longsleeve shirts (even though it's July) and hard-hats. At the bar, they join a driller who has been on the stool since 1:30. The driller wears shiny cowboy boots, khaki pants, and a western shirt with bolo tie. One roughneck acknowledges the driller, who is talking with the bartender. The roughneck then turns to his friends who have taken their cans of Coors to a pool table in the rear of Dan's.

"That was a bitch," the roughneck says to his friends.

"I hope so," says another roughneck laughing.

The second oil hand has made reference to a joke heard frequently in the oil fields: A pack of dogs is running down a dusty oil field road. One male dog at the back of the pack says to another, "Boy! Ain't this a bitch?" The other male dog says, "I hope so."

To an outsider who has not travelled the dusty oil field roads, the joke is not especially funny, but the telling of it initiates a round of jokes among the oil field workers, a round that is matched only by rounds of Coors. Each man tells at least one joke about the business he carries with him to the hundreds of small town and rural bars that circle the oil fields. In his study of fights and fight stories in bars, "Fists and Foul Mouths," James Leary writes of the American bar: "Contemporary fights occur most frequently in and around barrooms. Although little scholarly attention has been given it, the barroom is an important locus of much of the social activity in small American towns and rural areas."[1] Leary's conclusion seems justifiable in oil regions: the bar is the center of much social activity. But Leary also writes that the fight story is the dominant tale in the bar. In those bars near the oil fields the oil joke is dominant. (Incidentally, much of my scholarly work was done, at great hazard to my personal safety, in places like Dan's, The Caprock, Fifi's, The Buckaroo, The Half-way

Bar, The Starlite, and Glenn's, where on one afternoon I was there the FBI man was still measuring distances between dried pools of blood.)

In Dan's bar this Thursday afternoon many of the jokes told by the oil hands will be scatological, even though Dan has placed several "No Cussing" signs about the walls. Most of the stories will be about the oil worker's life. For the oil field joke is alive and well in west Texas and eastern New Mexico. In his book *Gib Morgan: Minstrel of the Oil Fields,* Mody Boatright notes that "there is a unity in the lore of oil that transcends state lines."[2] The stories I have collected during the last two years substantiate Boatright's statement. Many of the stories he published from East Texas now regularly appear in the Permian Basin, and many of his generalizations about the oil stories of East Texas and the east coast apply to the stories coming out of the oil fields of the Llano Estacado. For instance, the stereotyped oil characters Boatright found in the eastern fields a few years ago and wrote about in *The Folklore of the Oil Industry* are still present in the west in the 1970s. There are still plenty of jokes about the driller, the tool pusher, and the roughneck. One oily told me about a person he called the "Paul Bunyon" of the oil fields and related a Gib Morgan story, although he did not call him Gib.

But many changes have taken place in the industry in recent years. Arab oil, Alaskan oil, out-of-sight prices have permanently changed the business; and the folklore of the oil industry reflects these contemporary changes. For instance, many stories of Arabs now circulate in the oil field.

Rich Arab
There was this rich Arab who, with the help of an American friend, made a lot of money from an oil field. As the Arab was leaving to go back to Arabia, he asked his friend what he could do to show his appreciation. The American replied that he would like a set of golf clubs. So the Arab said he would see what he could do and left for home.

About a year later he showed up at his friend's house with a briefcase full of papers. The Arab apologized, saying, "I couldn't get you a full set of golf clubs, but here are the titles to ten of them."

Arab's Gifts
At Christmas time one year this Arab couldn't think of what to get his three boys. So he decided just to ask them what they wanted. The first boy said all he wanted was a toy plane. So the Arab went out and bought him a 747. The next little kid said all he wanted was a toy boat. So the Arab went out and bought him a yacht to sail around the oceans in. The third little boy said all he wanted was a Mickey Mouse outfit. So the Arab went out and bought him Conoco.

As you can see with the above examples, the Arab has replaced the rich Texas oil man in variations of jokes told a few years ago. And as is the case with many occupational jokes, many versions can be found in settings other than the oil fields. Aggie jokes or hippie jokes are sometimes told as if they originated in the oil fields.

The emergence of different American lifestyles in the 1960s also has had its impact on oil field lore. Gib Morgan might have been the character to reckon with in the legends, tales, and anecdotes of a few years ago. For sheer frequency of appearance, the hippie has taken Gib's place in oil field jokelore. The hippie appears over and over in stories like the following.

Californian

There were two men who met riding motorcycles. One was from Texas and the other was a hippie from California.

The man from Texas asked the hippie why he was heading for Texas.

"Well," replied the Californian, "because I heard that they have five gallon cans of dope, thirty foot joints, a pusher on every rig, and they take a trip every day."

Most of the jokes I have collected center around stereotyped characters. Among these are the roughneck, the engineer, the ignorant outsider, the farmer, the driller, the worker's wife, and the prostitutes. The following stories are about roughnecks.

Intelligence

These two roughnecks were working real hard on a drilling rig one day. Their boss was sitting on a hill under a shade tree. One roughneck said to the other, "Why do we have to work so hard while the boss sits under a shade tree?" The other said, "Why don't you go ask him?" So he went and asked him. The boss said, "See my hand?" He had it in front of a tree. The boss said, "Hit it." So the old roughneck drew his hand back and just as he swung the boss pulled his hand away and said, "It's just a matter of intelligence."

Roughneck and Toolpusher

Difference between a roughneck and a toolpusher: all the roughneck wants to do is sit on the bottom of the hole and circulate and all the toolpusher wants to do is come out of the hole and check the bit.

Lest you don't follow that version here's another:

Driller's Wife

A driller's wife and a roughneck's wife were talking about their husbands. The driller's wife said, "All he wants to do is come out of the hole." The roughneck's wife said, "All mine wants to do is just get on bottom and circulate."

Roughneck and Marbles
The research center was doing a survey on three men. One was an engineer, one was a mathematician, and one was a roughneck that works on a drilling rig. They take the engineer and put him in a padded cell and the only thing in there with him was three steel marbles. When the doctor came the engineer had put the balls into a triangle. They took him out. They put the mathematician in there and he figured the distance between all three marbles. They took him out. Then they put in the roughneck. When they came back he had busted one, lost one, and had the other in his lunch bucket.

The moral of the story is that what a roughneck can't tear up or lose, he'll steal.

Not Much
An engineer is man who knows a great deal about very little and who goes along learning less and less until finally he knows practically everything about nothing.

A salesman, on the other hand, is a man who knows very little about many things and keeps learning less and less about more and more until he knows nothing about everything.

A production man starts out knowing everything about every-thing, but ends up knowing nothing about anything, due to his association with engineers and salesmen.

Don'ts
When I broke into the oilfield, my driller told me that there are two don'ts. You don't hurry on the boss's time, and you don't shit on your own.

Depression Work
Back during the Depression the hands in the oilfield had to reach out and get it. At the time a new hand came on a job. It was his first day on a drilling rig. After what he thought should have been lunch time and he was so hungry his stomach thought his throat was cut, he asked the driller,

"What do we get off for lunch?"

The driller said, "One glove."

Some stories deal with outsiders coming to the oil fields.

Daylight Crew
Late one afternoon a member of the clergy came out to visit a rig. After he had talked with the hands a short time, he decided they didn't know anything about religion. He asked one of the hands about the Bible.

"Do you know who crucified Jesus Christ?"

The hand thought for a minute and then said, "It must have been them daylight SOBs. They messed everything else up."

Farmers appear in many of the stories.

Back to the Farm
One time a fellow from a farm hired out on a drilling rig to work.
After he had worked a few days he told the driller he was quitting the
job. The driller liked the fellow and wanted to know why he was
going to quit.

The fellow said, "Ever since I've been working all you people
have talked about is getting enough money to buy a farm so you can
leave the oilfield. I've already got a farm."

Deep Hole
There was a farmer who had a well drilled right behind his barn, but
as luck would have it the hole came up dry. The foreman of the drilling crew came up to the farmer and said they would come back the
next day to cement the hole over. The farmer waved him off saying
he would take care of the hole. So the next day he constructed an
outhouse over the hole. That night at dinner someone asked where
grandpa was and one of the children said he was in the outhouse.

"Oh my God," said the farmer, "Grandpa always held his breath
until he heard it hit bottom."

The prostitute contributes much to the body of jokes.

Chippy Talk
One time two of the chippies who worked in the local cathouse were
talking. One told the other,

"I've had only three customers today. A toolpusher, a driller, and
a roughneck."

The second said, "I haven't been here long enough to tell how to
tell them apart."

"That's easy," said the first girl. "The toolpusher thanked me and
left ten dollars. The driller left ten and walked out. The roughneck
grabbed his clothes, jumped out the window, and hollered, "I'll see
you payday."

And in conclusion here is a story about an offshore oily:

Baby Kraut
There was this man that worked on off-shore drilling. His wife's baby
was due any day. He had taken about all the kidding he wanted to
hear from his working buddies. So he told his wife to send a telegram
when the baby came. He told her just to write "Kraut" on it so he
would know but his buddies wouldn't. The next week he received a
telegram. It read, "Kraut, Kraut, Kraut, one with wiener, two without."

Notes

1. James Leary, "Fists and Foul Mouths," *Journal of American Folklore Society,* Vol. 89 (Washington, D.C., 1976), 27.
2. Mody C. Boatright, *Gib Morgan Minstrel of the Oil Fields* (Dallas: SMU Press, 1945), p. xi.

Happy Jack and the Booger Man/*Roy W. Lawson as told to his daughter Mrs. Patt Roach*

Happy Jack
and the Booger Man

*Roy W. Lawson   As told to his
daughter Mrs. Patt Roach*

Roy Lawson was born on Easter Sunday, 1899, in Courtney Flat,
Oklahoma Indian Territory. His parents moved across the river into
Montague County, Texas, where he lived until 1920. It was while he
was growing up in Montague County that he first heard "Happy Jack
and the Booger Man" from an older brother, Virgil, now deceased.
"We had a good coon dog, and when we went coon hunting, we used
to build a fire, and we'd sit around telling tales, while we let our coon
dog do all the work." "Happy Jack and the Booger Man" was one of
them, and if you've read the Jack tales—or many other folk tales—
you will recognize the stories as old familiars in the lexicon of world
folk tales.—Mr. Lawson died May 8, 1980.
Editor.

Well, old Happy Jack was sorta bachelor like and a mean old guy and
nobody liked him. You know, he just stayed to himself. He killed
hogs, and you know, it's customary for a guy to give his neighbors
some of the fresh meat when he killed a hog, but he didn't. So the
neighbors decided Happy Jack was a mean old cuss and they'd get
rid of him. But he suspicioned something. Every time he looked up
one of the neighbors was watching him. So that night he got an old
hog bladder, filled it with blood, laid it on his pillow, and sneaked out
to the barn and slept. And during the night, sure enough, they came
up, and one of them eased the window up and jabbed Happy Jack in
the head. They were going to try to cut his throat, but they got blood
on the knife, and decided that was good enough.

The next morning one of them said, "Well, old Happy Jack won't
bother us no more. I got him last night. I cut his throat."

Then one of them said, "Who's that out there whistlin' and chop-
pin' wood?"

And it was old Happy Jack.

Dry times, wasn't no grass, hadn't rained in a long time. They didn't have no feed for their milk cows. The trees were trying to bud out a little. And old Happy, he was always smarter than anybody else, he was cuttin' those trees down and let the cows eat on them. You know, that would help a little bit. And the others got started at it. So Happy Jack accidentally cut a tree down on his old cow and killed it. Well, he decided he couldn't lose all that, so he skinned the cow and carried the hide to town to sell it. But hides wasn't bringin' much, and going to town, he noticed a bunch of crows flyin' over. He thought, "Well, he might as well take a chance." He stretched the cowhide over his wagon like a wagon sheet, stopped up the ends and cut a hole in the top of it and sprinkled corn down in there. The crows flyin' over would see that corn, fly down in there and couldn't find a way out, and he'd get 'em. He got a *whole* wagon load of crows and took 'em to town and sold 'em for chickens.

Coming home, the neighbors ran out to see if Jack had any luck in gettin' rid of his cowhide. He said, "Yep, sure did." He was just whistlin' and unhookin' his team.

"How much did you get for her, Jack?"

Said, "I got a dollar for each hair that was on it."

So they grabbed their axes and here they went, killed their cows, you know, carried them in and couldn't get a dollar for a hide. Well, that made 'em mad. And Happy Jack was just going on makin' money all the time, even when times was bad.

They sent for the old Booger Man. They had put up with Happy Jack as long as they wanted to. They'd tried to kill him and hadn't had no luck. They knew the old Booger Man could outwit him.

So the Booger Man came around and went over to see Happy Jack. Said, "What could I do, Happy Jack, to make a little money?"

"I'll tell you what we can do." Said, "Let's farm on the halves. We'd make a good team."

He said, "Sounds good to me. What will we raise?"

Said, "We'll raise sweet potaters."

Doggone, they had a good crop. Prettiest vines. The ground was just covered, you know. They got ready to gather them, and old Happy Jack said, "Well, Booger Man, it's time to harvest our crop. What do you want? Tops or bottoms?"

Said, "What do you mean, tops or bottoms?"

Said, "What's on top of the ground or what's under the ground."

The Booger Man said, "Hm. I want what's on top of the ground."

So he got the old vines, and they wasn't any good. Jack got the bottoms and all the taters. He outwitted the old Booger Man.

Next year Happy Jack said, "What do you say we make another crop?"

Booger Man said, "All right." Said, "What are we goin' to plant?"

Said, "Oats."

They made a good crop. It rained, you know. Good crop of oats and they got ready to gather them. Jack said, "Well, Booger Man, it's 'bout time to harvest the crop." Said, "Whatcha want? Tops or bottoms?"

Said, "I want bottoms. I took the tops last year and didn't get anything."

So Happy Jack took the tops and got all the crop that year.

The next year Happy said, "Well, Booger Man, do you want to work together again?"

Said, "Yea, if I can fix it where I can get some money out of it."

Happy said, "Well, we'll divide just as equally as we can." Said, "Let's raise hogs this year."

They did and they had a big crop of hogs, all fat and all. They had one great old big papa hog in the bunch.

Happy Jack said, "Well, Booger Man, let's go down and build some pens, and tomorrow we'll start dividin' our hogs."

Booger Man said, "How're we goin' to divide 'em?"

Said, "Each one of us will build a pen at the end of the big pen, and tomorrow morning when the clock strikes eight, all the hogs that each man throws in his pen is his."

Booger Man said that was good. He knew he had Happy Jack this time, 'cause the Booger Man was pretty stout, you know.

So Happy Jack went down the night before, after everybody had went to bed and got some axle grease and went down to the pens and greased his old papa hog *all* over. Just *all* over. He knew the Booger Man would make for him first.

So when the clock struck eight, Happy Jack was throwing hogs in his pen just as fast as he could get one by the leg and throw him in. Then another and another.

Meanwhile the Booger Man would get this old papa hog and he'd slide right out of his hands. And he'd take hold again and almost have him in his pen and he'd slide right out again. Pretty soon, he seen there were only two left. Happy Jack was gettin' all of them.

Booger Man said, "When you get through there, Jack, if you'll help me get this hog in my pen, I'll give you half of him."

Happy Jack said, "All right. Back off." And he spit in his hands and reached down and got a handful of dirt, grabbed that old hog up and slammed him right in the pen.

So all Booger Man got for three years' work was half a hog.

The neighbors decided that wasn't any good. They'd get rid of Happy Jack. They caught him in bed that night and got a wagon sheet and rolled him up in it. There was an old dug well, one of those big ones, about six foot across over there in one of them fields. And they throwed him in that old well.

The next day Happy Jack was hollerin' and takin' on down in that well, and a cowboy came along drivin' a big herd of cattle. Jack kept hollerin' for help. The cowboy looked around and found Jack and Jack asked him to help him out of there. The cowboy threw his lariat down in the well and drew Jack up to the top. As soon as Jack got out, he pushed the cowboy down in the well, got on the cowboy's horse, and begin to drive the herd of cattle.

So here came Jack ridin' a good saddle horse and a new saddle and drivin' 150 head of cows. He was just whistlin' and ridin' along.

The neighbors couldn't believe their eyes. Said, "Jack, where in the world did you get all of them cows?"

Said, "Over there in that well."

Said, "Is there anymore?"

"Lots of 'em."

Said, "Can we get some?"

"Yes, but I'll have to go with you."

They got over there and Jack got them all lined up. Said, "Now when I count to three all of you go together so you'll get equal shares."

You know, there is always one crook or greedy one in every bunch. Every time Jack would get to "two" he'd have to push this big greedy man back. Finally Jack said, "Now this is the last time. All of you stay in line." When he said "two," this old greedy man ran ahead of the others and jumped in. He was a big man and as he hit the side of the well, he kind of grunted.

Someone said, "What'd that guy say?"

Said, "Come quick; he had a *cow* by the tail."

So they all jumped in the well.

Jack got rid of all of 'em and he had a good saddle horse, a new saddle, and 150 head of cattle.

"Happy Jack and the Booger Man" appeared in *Southwest Folklore*, II, No. 1 (Winter, 1978), pp. 19-22, and is reprinted with the permission of the author and editor.

When You Call Me That, Smile!/*Francis Edward Abernethy*

When You Call Me That, Smile! or Folklore, Ethology, and Communication

Francis Edward Abernethy

It was now the Virginian's turn to bet or throw in his cards, and he did not speak at once.

Therefore Trampas spoke. "Your bet, you son of a ________!"

The Virginian's pistol came out, and his hand lay on the table, holding it unaimed. And with a voice as gentle as ever, the voice that sounded almost like a caress, but drawling a very little more than usual, so that there was almost a space between each word, he issued his orders to the man Trampas: "When you call me that, smile!"

The Virginian by Owen Wister

The basic premise for this paper is that much of folklore is a cultural response to genetically implanted behavior patterns which man holds in common with all his animal kinsmen, and that communication is one form of this folklore.

The Ethological Approach
Our physiological kinship with the rest of the animal kingdom is amply supported by a study of evolution and comparative anatomy. Our behavioral relationship, the study of which is ethology, is equally supported by an observation of the basic drives or instincts that most animals hold in common—those of sociality, dominance, territoriality, and sexuality. Man's folklore is his cultural response to these drives. For example, the customs and traditions and religious beliefs which a group holds in common enforce the sociality drive, or herding instinct, and bind them together in a strong, survivable unit. The dominance drive for the establishment of a pecking order is illustrated in all folk contests and in folk tales of Hercules and Jason and their ilk who must overcome obstacles to take their places at the top. Territoriality, so necessary for an animal's procreation and survival, is illustrated by games, both intellectual and physical, by chess

and football, in which teams struggle to penetrate and gain new territory while protecting their own. And sexuality, which the females of the various species control for the continuation of the species, is a basic ingredient of all kinds of folk song and literature and of folklore itself because the folk have always known that without continuing fertility and the sexuality that operates it all other factors of life are meaningless.

This brings us to communication, which is one kind of folklore, and which will be discussed from the viewpoint of the ethologist, that is, as one aspect of inherited behavior patterns that all animals hold in common. The bases for all human communication are behavior traits that man shares with other animals, and these traits have been genetically transmitted throughout the human race. Man has, however, gone beyond the lower animals, primarily because he has a better memory and therefore a higher ability to reason, to choose among courses of action. He has chosen instinctive communication signals—such as touching, waving, or crying—he has modified them to suit his culture, and he has passed these new distinctive hand shakes, peace signs, and love songs along through later times and other spaces. This is his folklore, most of which is putting his genetic drives into symbolized forms.

Communication by Signs and Symbols
Communication is the voluntary and involuntary transmission of information (includes feelings, attitudes, states of mind, reactions) from one animal to another. The four ways animals communicate are by smell, touch, sight, and sound.

Communication is achieved by means of signs (or signaling) and symbols. Theoretically the lower animals communicate by signs only. Their signs—their cries, gestures, and scents—are the results of genetic reactions and conditioned responses to internal feelings or external situations. Other animals hear them, see them, feel them, or smell them and react or respond to their signals. One dog enters another's territory, smells the signs the home dog has left on the fireplugs and utility poles, and loses some of his confidence. Mourning doves in the springtime romantically lean against one another and bill and coo. Bees return from a scouting expedition and do a dance indicating the direction and distance from the hive of a new pollen source. And whales moving in groups keep continual "songs" going that keep the group in contact with each other.

People communicate by signs also. They emit odors that communicate to those nearby that they have been under nervous or sexual tension. They touch, slap, grab, and shove each other to attract attention or to announce their moods. They smile, frown, blush; their bodies are continually moving in response to their own feelings and external conditions. And they laugh, cry, moan, and sigh according to their moods. These genetic responses and conditioned reflexes are signs and signals man holds in common with other animals and with other people, whether they are members of his culture or not.

One of man's distinguishing characteristics is that in addition to being a sign user he is a user of symbols in his communication. A symbol is dictionarily defined as something that is used in place of, stands for, or represents something else. The "something else" can be abstract (feeling, state of mind) or concrete (a person, place, or thing). Communication within a human group is accomplished mainly by means of cultural symbols which are meaningful only within the particular group. To English speaking people the word *table* represents a piece of furniture with a flat top and enough legs to keep it up and stable. To the Spanish, *mesa* stands for the same thing. The Eskimos communicate tactilly by rubbing noses; Americans touch lips. The association of the idea with the symbolic response is conditioned by the culture which uses it. These symbols are his culture's folklore, traditionally circulated and continually changing.

Man and the lower animals share four different methods of communication. They are olfactory (smell), tactile (touch), visual (sight), and acoustical (sound).

Olfactory Communication
Olfactory communication is the transmission of information by use of scents. In the evolution of communication among animals it is the simplest and most primitive form, first used by the female of the species to announce sexual readiness.

The one-celled paramecium usually reproduces by cell division but it may also reproduce sexually by conjugation. At the time of sexual readiness it emits a chemical attractant which will call in a mate and at the same time repel those that it cannot mate with. On a much higher evolutionary plane, among mammals the female in a state of estrus sends forth a chemical or olfactory signal when she is ready to copulate. Females among humans at the time of physiological readiness also broadcast an estral odor, but man's olfactory sense is too undeveloped and blunted to perceive it, except vaguely.

The estral odor, along with other odor stimuli secreted by the apocrine glands during sexual arousal, are signals in the olfactory communication system. They are genetic and/or conditioned responses to situations. Olfactory symbols are scents that he has created to stand for certain desirable olfactory signs, usually sexual signs. Perfumes with a musk base are used by females as aphrodisiacs (consider My Sin, Aphrodesia, Intimate, Tabu, Wild Desire, Soul Kiss); that is, the female removes her natural odor by washing and substitutes a manufactured scent that is recognized as titillating in her culture. This substitute scent is an olfactory symbol.

Although the sexual musk base is the dominant odor, there are many variations of the blended secondary odors of spices and flowers, and various groups express their own folk preferences. Mediterranean peoples lean to heavy, oil-based odors, while Asiatics traditionally prefer flower scents, and the Nordics use the lightest scents of all. The Atakapan Indians of the Texas Gulf Coast boiled the oil from alligator tails, allowed it to get rancid, then coated their bodies with it. The resultant bouquet was their socially distinguishing smell and also kept off mosquitoes.

Olfactory communication in folklore has purposes that are other than sexual. It is one way of communicating with the gods in some cultures. The burning of incense and aromatic woods during worship services is to attract the gods' attention. This holds true with the Greeks' sacrifice of hecatombs as well as with other burnt offerings, especially among the early Hebrews. Noah, when he finally came to land "took of every clean beast, and of every clean fowl, and offered burnt offerings on the altar. And the Lord smelled a sweet savor" and leaned out and looked down upon him and blessed him.

Tactile Communication
Tactile communication is the transmission of information through touch. The primates, especially the large social primates, such as the chimpanzees and baboons, are continual social touchers who spend much of their time leaning against one another and grooming one another. The initial result is comfort and cleanliness; the principal result is the strengthening of the social bond. Another tactile signal among primates is mounting, which communicates dominance. In a contest for territory or sexual favors, the weaker male, in order to appease the dominant male, will present himself as if for copulation. The dominant male will mount him not for direct sexual purposes but to demonstrate his dominance. This is ancestral to hugging or the formal *abrazo*. The hugger is dominant; the huggee is sub-dominant.

Man communicates tactilly through both signals and in symbolic communication. Tactile signals include any type of touching that has as its purpose the gaining of attention or the expression of a mood. One person taps another on the shoulder so that the tappee will look in the tapper's direction. Or one leans against another person for comfort or touches him or straightens his tie to demonstrate affection. This is grooming similar to cats licking one another. The folklore that evolves from this need to communicate by touch includes the formal handshake and *abrazo* and all the modern ways of swapping skin. Rubbing noses, western kissing, and the religious practice of the laying on of hands are also tactile symbols; that is, each kind of physical contact represents more than merely the touching of skin, and each is a formalized representation of something else, usually an emotion.

Visual Communication
Visual communication is the transmission of information through movements, postures, and other externals which can be seen. Visual communication among most mammals, especially the primates, occurs in three ways—by gross movements, or the stance of the entire body or its parts; by raising of the hair over the whole body, down the

back, or on the head and face; and by facial expression. These are genetically implanted signals which man holds in common with his animal kinsmen. We bow up or cower, smile, frown and pout, back our ears and flare our nostrils; and even though we don't erect our hair as well as our furrier friends do, we still have the physiological mechanism to do it; and sometimes the hair does stand up on the backs of our necks or we get goose bumps that raise what little hair we have. Man's visual signs include blushing, smiling, frowning, and all sorts of gestures and body postures which are informal, non-traditional, and are the immediate results of a situation or state of mind. This is body language, and is a holdover from our evolutionary past. For example, the smile is the relique of the baring of the teeth in a defensive posture.

Visual symbols are those gestures which a culture has formalized into traditional and recognizable patterns. This is our folklore. Included in it are all sorts of sign language, including the peace sign and the black power sign as well as the insulting signs such as the stuck-out tongue and the extended middle finger. (The flashed middle finger as well as the Italian thrusted forearm are both sexual symbols asserting male dominance in the same way as in the primates' mounting signal, and these gestures are technically improper when used by females.) Also included is the dress style that cultures and subcultures affect to announce their membership in classes, clubs, groups, and lodges.

Acoustical Communication
Acoustical communication is the transmission of information through sounds. Among humans this includes telegraphy, hand clapping, and whistling, along with communication by voice or any instrument that is an extension of the voice (a saxophone as well as a telephone).

Most of the mammals communicate vocally, and this vocalizing functions as a result of the sociality drive, holding the herd of cattle or whales together; of the dominance drive in voicing aggressive intentions; of the territorial drive, as the herd bull paces his territory bellowing both an invitation to females and a warning to other males; and of the sexuality drive, as the birds and mammals whistle and howl their readiness. As the most complex of communication methods vocalization is highly elaborated in some animals, even to including learned dialectal differences that exist among certain species of birds and seals, to mention two.

Vocal communication is man's most highly developed skill. Vocal signals are those cries, sighs, laughs, and moans which a person emits under internal or external stimulation. All humans cry and laugh, and they yell when they are hurt and growl when they are angry. Each culture, however, selects about thirty phonemes from the 10,000 sounds the human animal can make and with these phonemes creates words, or sounds which stand for something in particular. These words are vocal symbols, because they are substitutes for the thing itself. The word *cat* is a traditional way of arranging sounds in order that one in our culture might transmit the idea of a cat. The word is a substitute, a vocal symbol, and it is our folklore, being continually shaped and reshaped, corrupted and refined as we use it and pass it on to our progeny.

Conclusion

Communication among humans consists of folklore, conditioned reflexes, and inherited behavior patterns. And probably folklore is the least of these. Spinning off the studies of Albert Mehrabian and using his figures, the Total Impact of Communication is 7% verbal (the word itself) + 38% acoustical (the sound of the word) + 55% visual (the gestures which go with the word). The verbal part, the words we use, mean very little by themselves, but the sound of the words said and the stance of the sayer—all these together communicate. There are many ways to say "What a lovely dress" or "I hate you." Both can be spoken in a way to mean the opposite of the explicit meaning of the words. Hamlet asks Ophelia, "Are you honest?", meaning "Are you chaste?" She answers, "My lord?" with two, simple, one-syllable words whose meaning—anger, embarrassment, amusement?—depends entirely on tone of voice and whatever visual signals she might send. And it was all right for Trampas to impeach the Virginian's maternity as long as he smiled when he said it.

The folklore is the word said, the figure of speech, the language and dialect, and whatever traditional gesture, smell, and touch that accompanies the word. These are the symbols that one generation of a culture passes on to the next, and this symbolic communication is consciously performed. But underlying and amplifying this level of communication are all his years of being conditioned in his culture and all the blood, bones, and nerves that are a part of his genetic makeup. And here is where most of the sound of his words comes from and the look on his face and the movements of his body as he speaks. And it is on this level that he meets his past and all those animals he came down the evolutionary road with. On this level, he howls and snarls and stomps his feet in threat or cringes in submission, tail between his legs. And on this level he becomes *almost* as honest about what he really means as his animal kinfolks.

Folk Stories From the Elmdale Community

Nancy Patrick   Student Contest Winner

This paper is the result of a collecting project which I did for a folklore class at Hardin-Simmons University under the direction of Dr. Robert Fink.

The control group for the project was the senior adults at the Elmdale Baptist Church just outside of Abilene. My specific aim was to collect folk stories, but most of the information I gathered falls into the category of personal or family lore. Some of Milton Antilley's stories go beyond this. I used the personal interview method of collecting in all cases but one. One man preferred to tape his stories alone at his home.

Two of my best informants were Callie and Ray Antilley, a couple in their early eighties, who live close to the Abilene Municipal Airport. Ray's parents helped establish Elmdale Baptist Church in 1904. Callie was anxious to tell me her stories, but Ray was reluctant. He said that he couldn't think of any, but when Callie was talking, he would interrupt and tell a story of his own. The first story is Callie's.

"When the Alamo fell, what armies Texas had left started runnin' in front of Santa Anna tryin' to get away from him or back to their families. Most settlers were in southeast Texas. The women and children started leaving Texas any way they could. They didn't wait for their men. It was mostly on foot or horseback. And my grandmother—they lived somewhere below LaGrange—I can't remember just where. My grandmother was two years old and her mother had a tiny baby. Now there was an old Mexican couple that lived right close and they'd been helpin' her out through this war. And this old Mexican man made a sled and he loaded bedding on there and had her and this tiny baby on that sled and the woman carried my grandmother who was two years old on her back. And they were trying to get them out of Texas, and them too, 'cause any Mexican National that helped, why they was in trouble too. And they got way off down there.

"Well, there was this old lady in the group who was always mad at somebody. Well, this morning she'd had a quarrel and she was pouting and had gone off a little ways from camp and was sittin' on a log a-poutin' and this man he comes ridin' up on horseback. He stopped and talked to her a minute and she suddenly got up an' she just started dancin' and shoutin' up and down that log. Said she'd go up one end and down the other. Then he rode on into the camp and told 'em Santa Anna, he'd been captured. That he'd fought the battle of San Jacinto and had been captured.

"My great-great grandfather and two of his sons' names are on that monument at San Jacinto. They had been captured. They were led by a man named Dawson and they'd all been captured and after they'd surrendered and turned over their arms and everything, the Mexicans were marchin' them along and commanded them to stop and turn around and stand in a row, and they started shootin' at 'em. They was just goin' to shoot 'em all and be done with it. And of course they started runnin' and everybody run for any horse that was close and one of my great uncles run to grab a horse—his name was Gonzales Woods—and somebody from right behind him yelled 'My God, Gon, don't get my horse' and he looked and one of his neigh- bors was right behind him and a Mexican right on him with a weapon. It was a long thing with a sharp spear-like thing fastened onto the end of it, so he run past this horse and thought he'd let this man get it since it was closer, so he went on and the Mexican killed the man he was after and come on then after the uncle and had it raised up to kill him with it. Well, he turned around and reached up and grabbed it and wrestled it away from the Mexican and killed him and then got out of there."

This is Ray Antilley's first story.

"I had three fishing poles. This is a true story. I wanted to go to Joe's and fish, and one of the poles was down there on the tank set- tin' out. I went down to look at it and there was an old mud hen on the end of it. Do you know what a mud hen is? It's kind of like a duck but they'll go down to the bottom huntin' for something to eat. Well, I got that mud hen off that pole and come to the house. I had two poles in the pickup and Callie looked out there and saw that cat come along and that hook hooked that cat in the side. He had that hook in his hide so far—I tried to pull it back up and I couldn't get it out so I went and got me a pair of pliers and taken and caught the pliers on the hook and I raised the cat up over my head and I throw'd 'im just as far as I could and I jerked the hook out of him. I came on back and got up here close to my pickup. Well, the last time I was fishin' I had a grasshopper on the end of my pole, and it was stickin' out of the back end of my pickup. And the old chicken ran up and swallowed that grasshopper and she set back and just threw her head and broke the line right off with that grasshopper. She swallowed it hook, line, and all. You've heard of swallowing it hook, line, and sinker. That hen did. Well, I got a mud hen, a house cat, and a chicken all on three poles."

Another informant was Faye Daniel, a seventy-six year old widow whose father built what is known as Griffith Lake in northeast Abilene. She told this story about her grandfather.

"We used to go to North Park School in Abilene. It's called Ben Milam Elementary now, but then it had first through twelfth grades. One day in our geography class the teacher told us about how the sun sometimes draws fish out of the water and stores them in the clouds; then when it rains, it rains fish. Well, my grandpa lived in San Angelo at the time and he was building a house. He told us this story and he wouldn't lie for anything. Anyway, there came a great big rain —rained four or five inches, so he couldn't work on the house for a few days. After it had time to dry up some, he got on the roof to work on the house and there was dead fish all over the roof. Now they didn't live anywhere near a river or lake. You tell me, where did those fish come from?"

W. H. Blackburn, Jr., a third informant, runs the gas station at Elmdale. His parents also helped settle the Elmdale community in the early 1900s. His stories concern some land he owns near Baird.

"We own a farm down near Baird that I raise cattle on and a few crops. Legend has it that the man who lived in the house many years ago was a money lender. He never let the borrowers see his money, though. He would find out how much they wanted and send them away while he got the money. Well, two fellas decided they were going to get all that money, so they shot and killed the man. They never did find the money. People still come and ask me for permission to go on the land with metal detectors, trying to find where that money is buried.

"On this same piece of land there is a grave marker made out of sandstone that reads: 'John Reynolds born on such and such a date was killed by the Indians, 1863.' This young boy who had lived there had gone to the creek to gather wood that might have washed up on shore so the family would have fire wood. The Indians saw him and killed him before he could make a run for the house. Ruth and I saw a picture of this tombstone at the World's Fair in San Antonio."

My most colorful source was Milton Antillery, a retired highwayman. He recorded his stories privately, but he is the kind of yarn spinner any folklorist would love to meet. The first story is about his dad.

"This happened about ninety years ago when my dad was about seven years old. They lived about fifty miles west of Midland on a ranch. One day when his dad (my grandad) was gone to Midland on business, it was just his mamma and the boys on the place. The boys was out playin', followin' a bunch of dogs, and the dogs had stirred up a big rattlesnake. Well, the snake bit my dad on the leg. They said it caught him in the leg with his fangs and just held on. It finally got off, and they run and got his mother and told her that he'd been bit, so she got a butcher knife and come up from the house. He had on buckskin boots that laced up so she had them take the boot laces and cord up his leg. Then she cut his leg where the snake bite was and bled it. They carried him to the house and put him on the wagon to carry him to Midland. Now on the way there was ranch houses about fifteen miles apart, and even back in those days there was telephones so each house would call ahead to the next house and tell 'em that they was comin' so to have a fresh team of horses ready. At each place somebody from the house would get on the wagon to help take care of him. Each one of them had their own remedy for snake bite— usually it was whiskey. Some of 'em say, I don't know how true it is, that he drank eleven pints of whiskey in the time it took to get from the ranch to Midland. His daddy met them when they got to Midland and they took him to the doctor. He was in pretty bad shape, and the old doctor said, that after so much time the only thing he knew that might save him—which he didn't know about—was this poison he had that had come from Germany. It was in a little vial and he didn't know how poison it was, but if my grandparents wanted him to, as a last resort, he would inject some of this poison into my dad and see if it would counteract the snake bite—which they had no snake bite venom back then. They waited as long as they could, and then told the doctor to go ahead and try it, so he injected some of this poison into my dad's leg along by where the snake had bit him. The first thing you know big blisters popped up and they let some of these burst, but wherever the poison run the hide came off his leg, so they started using a needle and draining the poison out. Then he started getting a lot better. They say the poison counteracted the snake bite, but the poison had to come out.

"I'll tell you a Halloween story that happened to a neighbor of ours. He was a very conscientious man—wanted to protect his family. He had a long shotgun and didn't mind tellin' people that he'd shoot 'em. So there was a bunch of boys in the community that had rigged up an old dummy and made him look pretty real. Course they was no electricity in those days so everybody used coal oil lamps. Well, these boys brought this old dummy up to the man's house at night and set it inside the fence over by the gate and hollered—'Hello, Hello, Hello.' This man came over to the door and just enough light came out that he thought the dummy was somebody. So he said, 'Hello, what do you want?' Well, this went on for a time and after a while he got pretty vexed and he said 'I'll tell you what you'd better do. You better say something.' So he told his wife to go get the shotgun. I'll make the gentleman talk. So she goes and gets the shotgun and he says to the dummy, 'Now Mister I've put up with this as long as I'm going to. You better tell me what you want or I'm going to shoot. I'll tell you what I'll do. I'm goin' to count to ten and if you don't talk, I'm goin' to shoot you.' So he starts countin' and he counts real slow to ten because he didn't want to shoot the fella. And he'd say I'm goin' to give you one more chance and he'd count to ten again. Well, after about thirty minutes he told his wife to call the law. She called the law and he kept the gun on this gentleman till the law drove all the way out from town to his country home and as they turned in he saw that this was a dummy. Well, he didn't do nothing but turn around and go into the other room and lock the door and wouldn't come out.

"I'll tell you a story about the butter. It seems like this lady was churning back in the Depression. She turned around to do something and a mouse fell in the churn. Well, then a pound of butter was a pound of butter. It was worth ever bit of fifteen or twenty cents. She got something and got the rat out of the churn real quick and went on and gathered the butter. Well, she just couldn't make herself eat this butter, so she got to thinking she'd just carry it up to old Mr. Piggly Wiggly, and she told Mr. Piggly Wiggly, 'I had a little accident with this butter. A mouse fell in the churn, but I got it right out. It didn't hurt the butter. I just thought maybe you'd trade me a pound of butter for my pound of butter. What the other folks don't know won't hurt 'em.' So he takes the butter and goes back in the back and got to thinking about it. He just brought her pound of butter back and gave it to her and said, 'What the old sister don't know won't hurt her.'

"Used to all the folks would go to a party. They'd take all the little kids in one room and put 'em on the bed. Some of the boys would slip around and get in this room where the babies were sleepin'. If they had a baby in a pink blanket, they'd just put it over in a blue blanket and after a while the party would get over and everybody would come and gather up their kid in the blue blanket and load him in the buggy and drive five or ten miles home and get home and go to take him out of the blanket and say 'Well, that's not my kid. It's somebody else's kid.' So they'd have to go back to the place where they started from and see if somebody had their kid. Well, it got to where it happened so much, they'd just go ahead and keep the kids to the next party."

These are only a few of the many stories that I collected, but as you can see, Elmdale has a very interesting history. The people are very proud of their heritage and take great pleasure in talking about how their families have prospered over the years. One thing that I learned from my experience is that I have only scratched the surface of a deep store of folklore in the Elmdale area.

1. Mosaic — 12" sq

2. Yankee Pride — 11" sq

3. Fish Tails — 11" sq

4. Flock of Birds — 16" sq

5. Dutch Windmill — 9" sq

6. Dolly Madison Star — 18" sq

7. Mill Wheel — 12½" sq

8. Double Irish Chain — 20" sq

9. Tree of Paradise — 13" / 17"

10. Rocky Road to Dublin — 13" sq

11. Drunkard's Path — 13" sq

12. Lady of the Lake — 12½" sq

same pattern, name changes with color arrangement

12. **Grandmother's Flower Garden**
diagram represents center of quilt

Piecing Patches and Quilting Up a Storm/*Gail Y. Litton*

Dutch Doll
applique

2. Southern Bell
applique

3. Clown Quilt
liquid embroidery by C.

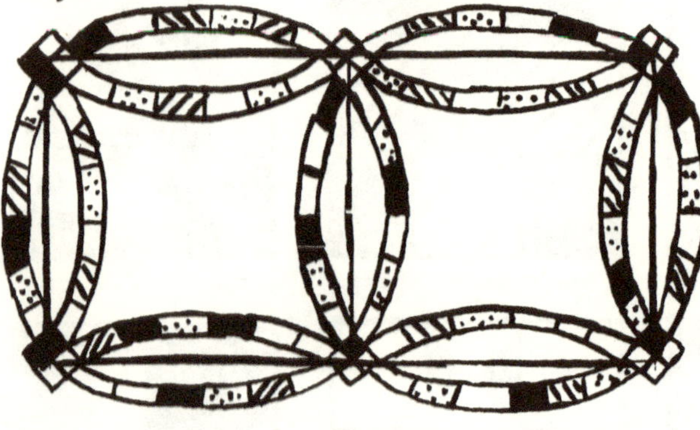

4. Double wedding
ring. usually
56

5. "glittering star" covers almost
entire center of quilt. Diamonds
are 5¾" long.

6. cat or square stich

8. running stich

7. Chain

9. Feather
stich

10. Outline
stich
some-
times
used to
attach
applique

Piecing Patches
and Quilting Up a Storm

Gail Y. Litton   Student Contest Winner

Grannie sits in her oaken chair
The firelight flits o'er her silvery hair,
The silent children around her sit,
As she pieces her patchwork coverlet;
She tells them the story of London Town,
And shows them the scraps of her bridal gown;
Each fragment there is a printed page,
With mem'ries written 'twixt youth and age.

from the old song, "Patchwork"[1]

This portion of verse from an old song gives a beautiful illustration of
the way patchwork quilting has been done for many years in
America. But as holds true for most things in this day and age,
changes are appearing in an effort to keep up with the pace of a
mechanized, modern lifestyle.

When I was a little girl I spent hours upon hours at my grandmother's home in the suburbs of Dallas, Texas. She taught me many
things during those hours with a patience that has to be compared to
Job's. At the age of five she began teaching me to do needlework—all kinds of needlework such as crocheting, knitting, tatting,
embroidery, needlepoint, hairpin lace, and quilting. I completed my
first quilt at the age of five. It measured one and one-half feet square
and kept many a doll warm and snug.

A quilt, broadly speaking, is anything made of two pieces of
material with padding between and held together by stitches. However, common usage has restricted the term to refer to a bed covering. The three layers of the quilt are referred to as the top, or the
pieced portion, the padding, or the filling, and the backing material.
A quilter is one who makes the patchwork or applique tops, or who
stitches the three layers of a quilt together. The two kinds of

needlework used by the quilter are patchwork and quilting. Patch-work is the piecing together of fabrics in the quilt top. Quilting is the method of fastening together the three layers of the quilt.

The technique of joining three layers of fabric with tiny stitched designs was first developed in the Middle East. It became a necessary craft of pioneer homemaking in America and then a product of the desire for home beauty. Quilts were made for efficiency's sake, using up scraps of material from old clothing or old quilts. There were times when two solid sheets of material were used, one for the top and one for the backing, in order that the beautiful stitched designs used to quilt the layers together might be admired. The essence of the most beautiful quilts was in the selection of the color, the fabric and its texture, and the pattern used to compose each square in the patchwork top. Each quilt top was painstakingly pieced by hand with patches from baby's first nightshirt, mother's bridal gown, brother's military uniform, and other cloths that carried their own history or significance. Then the tops were attached to a large frame and were quilted by hand by the neighborhood women at the quilting bee, a social occasion which also offered food, music, and conversation. The quilts were padded with wool that was carded by hand or with cotton batting. Each finished quilt was a masterpiece, a diary written by needle. But things are changing. Artisans today still carry out the process of making quilts as Grandmother made them, with possibly the only exception being in the kind of padding used. Housewives, however, those who still know much about needlework, may be let-ting the machine age take over.

In researching the hypothesis in the preceding statement I ques-tioned approximately seventy-five people about quilting before find-ing ten informants who answered "yes" to my question, "Do you know how to make a patchwork quilt?" The seventy-five people ranged in age from twenty-two years to eighty-three years old and live in Texas or New Mexico at the present. I began by noting what I was taught as a girl by my grandmother. Then I questioned members of my family and acquaintances, then neighbors, and finally people off of the street wherever I happened to be. The ten who responded "yes," all women, were captured to answer my other questions as follows: "Where did you learn to make quilts? What do you use for raw material? What do you pad your quilts with? Do you sew your quilt tops by hand or by machine? What patterns or designs have you used for your patchwork tops? Do you do embroidery work on your quilts? Do you quilt or stitch the layers of your quilt together by hand or by machine? Do you do 'fancy' quilting or use some other method of fastening the three layers together? What are the sizes of the quilts you've made? Briefly give me the steps you went through in con-structing your quilts from beginning to end. Could you tell me a little about yourself?"

The answers to the first question did not surprise me. I had ex-pected to discover that others had learned quilting from a family member as I had from my grandmother. Six out of the ten informants learned to quilt from their mothers. Referring to the list of informants, they were informants A, B, C, F, I, and H. One informant, D, learned to quilt at her church. She belongs to the Mormon religion and explained that it is quite common for needlework classes to be incorporated into the church's women's organization. Informants E and C, informant E being myself, learned to make quilts from their grandmothers. Informant C had also learned much from her mother. Informant G learned to quilt at the Y.W.C.A. in San Jose, New Mexico. Informant J, my grandmother, could not recall where she had learned to make quilts. She said, "I just picked it up like I did my crochet."

In answer to the question on the raw materials used, eight out of the ten used scraps from sewing, informants A, B, C, E, F, G, H, I, and J. Informants D and H, both members of the Mormon church, do not piece the tops of their quilts, as a general rule. Their quilts are made as a joint effort, usually cooperating with other women in their church. Someone else does the patchwork tops and informants D and H make elaborate designs in stitching the layers of the quilts together. Out of the eight women who pieced their quilt tops using scraps of material from their sewing, informants I and C have also bought material at times to use in making their quilt tops. My grandmother used old clothes that her children had outgrown. Once she used a part of my baby blanket in a crazy quilt top, which my sister owns today.

The answers obtained from "What do you pad your quilts with?" were interesting. Traditionally carded wool or cotton batting was used. Only informant I, seventy-five years old, can remember using carded wool as a young girl growing up in Mexico. Only informants A and J, my grandmother, use cotton batting today. Informant B had once used cotton batting, but now she and informants C, D, I, and H use the new 100% polyester dacron fiber fill. Informants F and G use old blankets when available. I was informed that some quilters do not pad their quilts here in the Southwest due to the mild climate. I myself, informant E, have not had the opportunity to pad a large quilt and cannot remember what I padded my doll's quilt with when I was five, although it was probably cotton batting. Since that time I have only stitched quilt tops or made infant quilts which I did not pad. It is necessary to have a large area in which to pad and stitch the three layers of a quilt together due to the size of the quilting frame.

The answers to the question, "Did you sew your quilt tops by hand or by machine?" lent some support to my hypothesis that the machine has crept into the craft of quilt making. Eight of the informants, B, C, D, E, F, H, I, and J, do some or all of their patchwork piecing by machine now, although they once made quilts entirely by hand. Only informants A and G still piece their patchwork by hand. My grandmother, informant J, began to piece by machine in 1930 when Grandfather bought her a treadle sewing machine.

I obtained a good list of patterns or designs used by the informants on their patchwork tops. They are as follows: "mosaic," "Yankee pride," "fish tails," "flock of birds," "Dutch windmill," "Dolly Madison star," "mill wheel," "double Irish chain," "tree of Paradise," "glittering star," "lady of the lake," "double wedding ring," "endless stairs," "nine patch," "bow tie," "bear's claw," "rocky road to Dublin" or "drunkard's path" when the color arrangement is varied, "fan," "brick work," "Dutch doll" or "Dutch girl and boy" (applique), "Log cabin," "block patch," "Texas star," "Joseph's coat," "crazy quilt," "clown quilt" (liquid embroidery), "Southern Bell" (applique), "old fashioned garden" or "Grandmother's flower garden," "overall boy fishing" (applique), "farm life" (embroidery), and "five patch" patterns. Refer to diagrams in appendix.

Some pieced tops are occasionally decorated with embroidery work. In answer to the question, "Do you do embroidery work on your quilts?" four informants, B, C, E, and I have done some kind of embroidery work on quilts. Informant C, however, does not use needle and thread anymore to do her embroidery work. She uses a new creation called liquid embroidery, which is a tube of paint that writes like a ball-point pen. These can be bought in several colors and produce the same effect as painting by brush except that greater detail can be achieved by the amateur artist.

There is one step in quilt making in which the machine has not taken over as yet. This step is in fastening the layers of the quilt together. In answer to the question, "Do you quilt or stitch the layers of your quilt by hand or machine?" eight informants, A, B, C, D, E, H, I, and J replied that they fastened the layers by hand. Only informant J, Grandmother, used a machine and that was just after Grandfather bought her a treadle machine around 1930. Two informants, F and G, tack their quilts at various intervals by hand rather than stitch the three layers together. Informants D and E also use tacking as an alternative to quilting or stitching, most often when they need to finish a quilt in a short time. When the quilts were fastened with stitching only two informants, B and E, used stitches other than a straight running stitch. Informant B used the fan, square, or feather stitches and informant E used embroidery stitches. Refer to diagrams in appendix.

Only informants H, I, and J did what could be termed fancy quilting work. With a straight running stitch these three informants made designs in chain, star, bird, rabbit, and diagonal patterns. Informant J, who was the only one to ever quilt by machine, did so by making straight diagonal lines across the entire quilt. She also sewed many quilts by hand.

The steps in construction were basically the same for all of the informants except in the use of a quilting frame. Informants G and F, who only tacked their quilts at various intervals, opted to use the floor. But all of the informants did follow the same sequence of steps, first stitching the quilt top in a chosen pattern, and then padding the quilt and fastening the three layers together either on a frame or on the floor. The quilts ranged in sizes from crib size to 90″ by 180″, all of the informants having done one or the other size, or both.

So in summing up, what are the changes that have come about in quilt making, and has the machine begun to take over? From the results of this research, first, not every woman can make a quilt, at least not in the younger generation, as can be seen by the number of people questioned before ten were found that have done so. The ages of those same ten support the statement also, due to the fact that the two youngest were twenty-two and thirty-three years old. Second, new materials are being used for piecing and filling. Scraps are not all that is pieced; "boughten" material is used also. And cotton batting or carded wool have been replaced by another marvel of invention, 100% polyester dacron fiber fill. I suppose that is because, as informant C said, "It makes the quilts warmer, and also when you wash them they don't go together and bunch up." Third, in quilting the layers of the quilts together, if simple tacking is not done, it appears that less elaborate designs are being used now than once were by most quilters. It's as if there is a short cut for everything now. And fourth, embroidery can now be done with a ball-point. That's not to say that painting as opposed to stitching doesn't have its own intricacies. Fifth and foremost, but probably not the last change that will occur, the sewing machine has begun to replace the nimble fingers. Eight of the informants, including my grandmother, do some or all of their patchwork by machine now. "No, we don't piece by hand anymore. It's too time consuming. We sew it by machine," said informant I. Also as *Redbook Magazine* states, "Pieced designs of geometrical shapes are easy to assemble because often they have straight seams, which may be sewed on a sewing machine."[2] And then there are the ads for quilt kits in *Family Circle:* "You can make it entirely by machine. You cut the small geometric shapes out [the shapes are already printed on the fabric] of printed cotton and stitch them together by machine."[3] Later: "This luxurious quilt is stitched together by machine then quilted by hand."[4]

What happened to the days when women gathered together to piece patches and quilt up a storm? Perhaps the song at the beginning of this paper should be rendered anew:

Grannie sits in her sewing machine chair.
The heater blows her dyed brown hair.
The silent children around her sit,
Glued to the T.V. like idiots.
She tells them the story of London Town;
They say, "Grannie, could you keep it down!"
Each part of her quilt is a printed page,
Where T.V. serials changed 'twixt youth and age.

Notes

1. Origin unknown, verse is quoted by Rose G. Kretsinger and Carrie A. Hall in their book, *The Romance of the Patchwork Quilt in America* (New York, n.d.), section by Rose Kretsinger.

2. "The Redbook Handicrafter," *Redbook Magazine* (March, 1973), p. 54.

3. "Patchwork: Upbeat Decorating Theme," *The Family Circle* (February, 1976), p. 112.

4. "The Rich Velveteen Quilt, Updated and Easy," *The Family Circle* (October, 1976), p. 150.

Informants

A. Betty Wagoner, eighty-one years old, 1300 West Madero, sp. 3, Las Cruces, New Mexico 88201. Born in Hope, New Mexico, the daughter of a cow rancher of Scotch-Irish and Indian descent. Walked six miles to school and completed sixth grade. Married at the age of fifteen, had four daughters and one boy. Worked hoeing cotton, milking cows, and waiting on tables. After the death of her first husband she married again in 1963. Lives alone now in a small mobile home that her second husband left to her after his death. Pieces and quilts her quilts entirely by hand using old scraps and cotton batting, with a simple running stitch. Has used all the patterns diagrammed in this paper, with the exception of the clown pattern, and others she can't remember. She said, "Momma done quilt'in all my life and I was used to it. I was a good hand at sewin'."

B. Maggie Hethcox, sixty-two years old, lives in a mobile home in the pine forest of the Gila Wilderness area, Mimbres Valley Rt. 15, Box 550, Hanover, New Mexico 88041. Worked at a shirt factory, a cannery, a tire factory, and a factory making shells for the Navy. Picked cotton, milked cows, worked as a janitor. Born in La Mesa, New Mexico. Completed the ninth grade. Enjoys camping, fishing, deer hunting, dominoes, and sewing. Learned to quilt from her mother, Mrs. Wagoner, and makes several quilts a year for gifts. Sews patches by machine now, but once pieced by hand. Uses scraps from sewing or old clothes and polyester fiber fill. Quilts her layers by hand using fan, square, or feather stitches. She has done "nine patch," "farm life quilt," "Dutch doll," "brick lay," "Texas star," "drunkard's path," "rocky road to Dublin," "fan," "Dutch windmill," "bowtie," "improved nine patch," "block," "log cabin," "flower garden," "bear claw."

C. Ruthie Hethcox, forty years old, born in Carazozo, New Mexico, now lives next door to her mother-in-law, Maggie Hethcox, same address. Raised in a rural area, her parents of French, English, Irish, and Welsh descent. Married in the eleventh year of school and has four children. Learned to quilt from her mother, Maggie Hethcox, and Betty Wagoner. Pieces her quilts by hand if the pattern is intricate, by machine if blocks. Quilts by hand using a straight running stitch. Pieces scraps and some bought material, and uses polyester fiber fill. Has made five quilts: "block." "Joseph's coat," "crazy quilt," "clown quilt," "Southern Bell." "I'd sit down in the evening and I just had Robby here, and I'd sew on my quilt until bedtime. I just make 'em to use because they're nice and it saves on buying covers."

D. Margaret Macdonald, fifty-three years old, 117 Isabella, El Paso, Texas 79912. Born in Indiana, Anglo-Saxon descent. Was a registered nurse, now a housewife. Says she is not a domestic person. Makes quilts at her church, Mormon, and does the quilting of the layers by hand with a simple running stitch. Tacks quilts by hand also. Pieces patches by machine when she helps with a quilt top. Uses acrylic or polyester fiber fill. Used "block" and "Dutch doll" patterns. Learned to quilt at church. "All the ladies at the church wanted to make a quilt and got together at a house. And I felt so stupid everyone sitting there patching. And I got off in a corner by myself and I learned."

E. The author of paper, twenty-two years old, 8633 Saratoga, El Paso, Texas 79912. Born in Dallas of Irish, English, Dutch, Welsh, and Cherokee Indian descent. Attending college at night, owns and operates an infant care center in the day. Enjoys all needlework, cooking, writing short stories, playing guitar, camping. Pieces patches by hand or machine and quilts by hand or tacks. Never padded a quilt. Uses scraps from sewing. Has made "crazy quilt," "block," and "Dutch doll" tops. Uses running or embroidery stitches.

F. Zelda Chavez, forty-four years old, 5256 Marietta, El Paso, Texas 79932. Housewife, born in Oklahoma of Indian, Irish, and English descent. She dropped out of her junior year of high school to marry and has seven children. Worked in school cafeterias and enjoys sewing and embroidery. Sews her pattern patches by hand and her block patches by machine. Only tacks her quilts by hand. Uses scraps from her sewing and old blankets for filling. Can't remember the patterns she used. "Learned to patch from my mother. Some I did in patterns . . . I used them for the children's beds. It was kind of a necessary work."

G. Ruth Ann Burkman, thirty-three years old, 2133 Woodfin, El Paso, Texas 79925. Born in Belen, New Mexico, of Spanish, Irish, and Swedish descent. Attended one year of college, and is studying for real estate license. She sews, enjoys ceramics, tennis, golf, bowling, and reading. Sews her patches by hand and tacks her quilts, using scraps for piecing and old blankets for filling. Uses the "block" design. "I went to quilting class at the Y in San Jose. I made a lot of pillow tops and one large quilt . . . to take on picnics."

H. Janice Stone, thirty-four years old, 302 Limonite, El Paso, Texas. Born in Douglas, Arizona, of Swiss descent. Attended business college, keeps books for her husband. Enjoys cooking, sewing, music, and reading. Has three boys. Attends the Mormon church. Only does quilting; other women of the church do the tops. She quilts by hand making chain or star patterns with a running stitch. Learned quilting from her mother.

I. Levinia Jackson, seventy-five years old, 120 Lindberg, El Paso, Texas. Born in Colonia Juarez, Chihuahua, Mexico, of English and Danish descent. Parents came to Mexico from Denmark. Attended high school in Mexico and one year of college at B.Y.U. in Utah. Member of Mormon church, enjoys cooking, sewing, quilting, and embroidery. Does her piecing by machine but her quilting and applique work by hand. Uses dacron batting now but wool when she was younger, and scraps from sewing. Uses a straight running stitch in patterns to quilt. Made "sun bonnet girls," "Southern Bell," "double ring," "nine patch," "five patch," "overall boy fishing."

J. Vera E. Jones Yeatts, eighty-three years old, 7345 Dillon, Houston, Texas 77017, born in Melisse, Texas, 1895. Went to teacher's college, taught school nine years, was married and had four children, thirteen grandchildren, six great-grandchildren. She is informant, E's grandmother. Pieces and quilts by hand or machine, running stitch, cotton batting, scraps.

Chronological & Bibliographical Listings of Texas Folklore Society Publications/*Herbert C. Arbuckle, III*

Chronological and Bibliographical Listings of Texas Folklore Society Publications

Herbert C. Arbuckle, III

Herbert C. Arbuckle, III, is a bibliophile and a Dobie scholar, a re-
corder of Mexican folklore, and a long-time contributor to the
Masonic Lodge journal. He also knows more about the history of the
Texas Folklore Society publications than anybody else I've come
across and has all of the Society's published or sponsored works in
his private library. As a result, he was the logical member to compile
the bibliography of the Society's publications. That sort of work is
tedious and eye-wracking, and the Society is deeply in debt to Herb
for his labors. This bibliographical record of publications will be a
boon to scholars long after we are gone.
Editor.

ORDER OF ENTRY

The Chronological Listing
Regular Series of Numbered Publications
Books Issued in lieu of Numbered Publications
Pamphlets
The Range Life Series
Paisano Books Series
El Paisano Newsletter
Special Reference Publications

KEY TO ABBREVIATIONS

*PTFS-1*r   Denotes a numbered, annual volume, usually subtitled
Publications of the Texas Folklore Society and given a number in
Roman numerals. The *1* means Publication Number 1, while the *r*
means a reprint edition.

ExB-1   Denotes an extra book given out by the Society in lieu of a numbered annual publication. The *ExB* stands for *Extra Book,* while the *1* means the first extra book given out. These books are found in the section titled "Books Issued in lieu of Numbered Publications."

P-1r   Denotes a pamphlet printed by the Society. The *1* means the first pamphlet issued by the Society, while the *r* means a reprint of the same.

RLS-4r   Denotes a book in the Range Life Series. The *4* means the fourth book in the series and the *r* means a reprint edition.

PBS-1r   Denotes a book in the Paisano Books Series. The *1* means the first Paisano Book, while the *r* means a reprint edition.

EPNL-1   Denotes an issue of the *El Paisano* newsletter that was issued by the Society in 1948, 1949, and 1950. The *1* refers to the number of the issue.

SRP-1   Denotes the one book which I could not classify anywhere else, and decided to call Special Reference Publications.

THE CHRONOLOGICAL LISTING

Whole #	*Cross Ref. #*	*Year*	*Title*
1	P-1	1912	*Some Current Folk-Songs of the Negro*
2	PTFS-1	1916	*Round the Levee*
3	PTFS-2	1923	*Coffee in the Gourd*
4	PTFS-3	1924	*Legends of Texas*
5	PTFS-4	1925	*Happy Hunting Ground*
6	PTFS-5	1926	*Rainbow in the Morning*
7	PTFS-6	1927	*Texas and Southwestern Lore*
8	PTFS-7	1928	*Follow de Drinkin' Gou'd*
9	ExB-1	1930	*Coronado's Children*
10	PTFS-8	1930	*Man, Bird, and Beast*
11	PTFS-9	1931	*Southwestern Lore*
12	PTFS-10	1932	*Tone the Bell Easy*
13	PTFS-11	1933	*Spur-of-the-Cock*
14	ExB-2	1934	*Tall Tales from Texas*
15	PTFS-12	1935	*Puro Mexicano*
16	ExB-3	1936	*Swing and Turn: Texas Play-Party Games*
17	PTFS-13	1937	*Straight Texas*
18	PTFS-14	1938	*Coyote Wisdom*
19	PTFS-15	1939	*In the Shadow of History*
20	PTFS-16	1940	*Mustangs and Cow Horses*
21	PTFS-17	1941	*Texian Stomping Grounds*

22	RLS-1 & ExB-4	1942	*My Rambles as East Texas Cowboy Hunter, Fisherman, Tie-Cutter*
23	RLS-2	1943	*Ed Nichols Rode a Horse*
24	RLS-3	1943	*A Tenderfoot Kid on Gyp Water*
25	RLS-4	1943	*A Stove-Up Cowboy's Story*
26	PTFS-18	1943	*Backwoods to Border*
27	PTFS-19	1944	*From Hell to Breakfast*
28	RLS-5	1945	*The Prairie Dog Lawyer*
29	PTFS-20	1945	*Gib Morgan, Minstrel of the Oil Fields*
30	P-2	1946	*When the Woods Were Burnt*
31	PTFS-21	1946	*Mexican Border Ballads and Other Lore*
32	ExB-5	1947	*Adventures with a Texas Naturalist*
33	EPNL-1	1948	*El Paisano, I-1*
34	PTFS-22	1949	*The Sky is my Tipi*
35	EPNL-2	1949	*El Paisano, I-2*
36	EPNL-3	1949	*El Paisano, I-3*
37	EPNL-4	1949	*El Paisano, I-4*
38	EPNL-5	1949	*El Paisano, I-5*
39	ExB-6	1949	*Folk Laughter on the American Frontier*
40	EPNL-6	1950	*El Paisano, I-6*
41	EPNL-7	1950	*El Paisano, I-7*
42	PTFS-23	1950	*Texas Folk Songs*
43	RSNP-24	1951	*The Healer of Los Olmos and Other Mexican Lore*
44	ExB-7	1952	*The Typical Texan, Biography of an American Myth*
45	PTFS-25	1953	*Folk Travelers, Ballads, Tales, and Talk*
46	PTFS-26	1954	*Texas Folk and Folklore*
47	ExB-8	1955	*Tales of Old-Time Texas*
48	PTFS-27	1957	*Mesquite and Willow*
49	PTFS-28	1958	*Madstones and Twisters*
50	ExB-9	1958	*"With His Pistol in His Hand," A Border Ballad and Its Hero*
51	PTFS-29	1959	*and horns on the toads*
52	PTFS-30	1961	*Singers and Storytellers*
53	PTFS-31	1962	*The Golden Log*
54	ExB-10	1963	*Folklore of the Oil Industry*
55	PTFS-32	1964	*A Good Tale and a Bonnie Tune*
56	P-3	1964	*Folksong and Folksong Scholarship*
57	ExB-11	1964	*Friends of Thunder, Folktales of the Oklahoma Cherokees*
58	P-4	1965	*Mody Boatright, Secretary and Editor, 1943-1964*
59	PBS-1	1966	*Mirrors, Mice, & Mustaches*
60	PTFS-33	1966	*The Sunny Slopes of Long Ago*
61	ExB-12	1966	*Tales from the Big Thicket*
62	P-5	1967	*Eyes on Texas, Fifty Years of Folklore in the Southwest*

63	PTFS-34	1968	*Tire Shrinker to Dragster*
64	PBS-2	1967	*Pecos Tales*
65	PBS-3	1969	*Aunt Puss & Others, Old Days in the Piney Woods*
66	PBS-4 & ExB-13	1969	*Deep Like the Rivers, Stories of my Negro Friends*
67	PBS-5	1970	*Texas Folk Medicine, 1,333 Cures, Remedies, Preventives, & Health Practices*
68	PTFS-35	1971	*Hunters & Healers: Folklore Types & Topics*
69	ExB-14	1971	*There Was a King in Ireland...Five Tales from Oral Tradition*
70	PTFS-36	1972	*Diamond Bessie & The Shepherds*
71	PTFS-37	1972	*Observations & Reflections on Texas Folklore*
72	SRP-1	1973	*Analytical Index to Publications of the Texas Folklore Society, Volumes 1-36*
73	ExB-15	1973	*Mody Boatright, Folklorist, A Collection of Essays*
74	PTFS-38	1974	*The Folklore of Texan Cultures*
75	PTFS-39	1975	*Some Still Do: Essays on Texas Customs*
76	PTFS-40	1976	*What's Going On? (In Modern Texas Folklore)*
77	ExB-16	1977	*Myths & Folktales of the Alabama-Coushatta Indians of Texas*
78	PTFS-41	1978	*Paisanos: A Folklore Miscellany*
79	PTFS-42	1979	*Built in Texas*
80	ExB-17	1980	*Mexican Folktales from the Borderland*
81	PTFS-43	1981	*Legendary Ladies of Texas*
82	PTFS-44	1982	*T for Texas: A State Full of Folklore*

REGULAR SERIES OF NUMBERED PUBLICATIONS

PTFS-1   Thompson, Stith, ed., *Publications of the Folk-Lore Society of Texas, Number I.* Austin: The Folk-Lore Society of Texas, 1916. Paperback. First edition, first issue. 111 p.

PTFS-Ir   Thompson, Stith, ed., *Round the Levee, Publications of the Texas Folk-Lore Society, Number I, 1916.* Austin: Texas Folk-Lore Society, 1935. Hardback. Reprint edition of 1935, with "Upon This Rock:—A Reprint Notice," by J. Frank Dobie. 111 p.

N.B.: It is interesting to note that only in PTFS-1 is the Society called "The Folk-lore Society of Texas"; in all others, it is "The Texas Folk-Lore Society" or "The Texas Folklore Society." *Cf.* P-1

	and subsequent pamphlets, p. 12, for a similar situation *re* the name of the Society.
PTFS-2	Dobie, J. Frank, ed., *Publications of the Texas Folk-Lore Society, Number II.* Austin: The Texas Folk-Lore Society, 1923. Paperback. First edition, first issue. 110 p.
PTFS-2r	Dobie, J. Frank, ed., *Coffee in the Gourd, Publications of the Texas Folk-Lore Society, Number II, 1923.* Austin: Texas Folk-Lore Society, 1935. Hardback. Reprint edition, 1935, with "Rebaptized in Ink," by J. Frank Dobie. 111 p.
	N.B.: PTFS-1 and PTFS-2 were issued originally in paper covers only. It is generally held by authorities that any hardbacked first editions are simply rebindings of the first edition, first issues.
PTFS-3a	Dobie, J. Frank, ed., *Legends of Texas, Publications of the Texas Folk-Lore Society, Number III.* Austin: The Texas Folk-Lore Society, 1924. Paperback. First edition, first issue. With an "Editor's Preface" by J. Frank Dobie. 279 p. + x.
PTFS-3b	Dobie, J. Frank, ed., *Legends of Texas, Publications of the Texas Folklore Society, Number III.* Austin: The Texas Folk-Lore Society, 1924. Hardback, bound in blue cloth. First edition, first issue. With an "Editor's Preface" by J. Frank Dobie. 279 p. + x.
PTFS-3r	Dobie, J. Frank, ed., *Legends of Texas, Publications of the Texas Folk-Lore Society, Number III.* Austin: The Texas Folk-Lore Society, 1924. Paperback. Second edition. With an "Editor's Preface" by J. Frank Dobie. 282 p. + x.
PTFS-3r	Dobie, J. Frank, ed., *Legends of Texas, Publications of the Texas Folk-Lore Society, Number III.* Austin: The Texas Folk-Lore Society, 1924. Hardback, bound in blue cloth. Second edition. With an "Editor's Preface" by J. Frank Dobie. 282 p. + x.
PTFS-3r	Dobie, J. Frank, ed., *Legends of Texas, Publications of the Texas Folklore Society, Number III.* Hatboro, Pennsylvania: Folklore Associates, Inc., 1964. Hardback. Reprint edition. With a "Preface to the Reprint Edition" by Wilson M. Hudson and an "Editor's Preface" by J. Frank Dobie. 279 p. + x.
PTFS-3r	Dobie, J. Frank, ed., *Legends of Texas, Volume I, Lost Mines and Buried Treasure.* Gretna, Louisiana: Pelican Publishing Company, 1975. Paper-

back. With an "Editor's Preface" by J. Frank
Dobie. 132 p.

PTFS-3r   Dobie, J. Frank, ed., *Legends of Texas, Volume II,
            Pirates' Gold and Other Tales.* Gretna, Louisiana:
            Pelican Publishing Company, 1975. Paperback.
            With an "Editor's Preface" by J. Frank Dobie.
            144 p.

PTFS-4   Dobie, J. Frank, ed., *Publications of the Texas Folk-Lore
            Society, Number IV.* Austin: The Texas Folk-Lore
            Society, 1925. Paperback. First edition, first
            issue. With "A Preface with a Proposal" by L. W.
            Payne, Jr., and "Forward Remarks by the Editor"
            by J. Frank Dobie. 133 p.

PTFS-4   Dobie, J. Frank, ed., *Publications of the Texas Folk-Lore
            Society, Number IV.* Austin: The Texas Folk-Lore
            Society, 1925. Hardback. First edition, first
            issue. With "A Preface with a Proposal" by L. W.
            Payne, Jr., and "Forward Remarks by the Editor"
            by J. Frank Dobie. 133 p.

PTFS-4r   Dobie, J. Frank, ed., *Happy Hunting Ground, Publica-
            tions of the Texas Folklore Society, Number IV.*
            Hatboro, Pennsylvania: Folklore Associates, Inc.,
            1964. Hardback. Reprint edition. With a "Preface
            to the Reprint Edition" by Wilson M. Hudson, "A
            Preface with a Proposal" by L. W. Payne, Jr., and
            "Forward Remarks by the Editor" by J. Frank
            Dobie. Also printed in this book (in the back) is
            *When the Woods Were Burnt, Published in
            Memory of Leonidas Warren Payne, Jr.* (q.v., P-2),
            and a facsimile of the "First Published Pamphlet
            of the Texas Folklore Society." 133 p. + 26 p.

PTFS-5   Dobie, J. Frank, ed., *Publications of the Texas Folk-Lore
            Society, Number V.* Austin: The Texas Folk-Lore
            Society, 1926. Paperback. First edition, first
            issue. With "Remarks Necessary and Un-
            necessary" by J. Frank Dobie. 190 p.

PTFS-5   Dobie, J. Frank, ed., *Publications of the Texas Folk-Lore
            Society, Number V.* Austin: The Texas Folk-Lore
            Society, 1926. Hardback. First edition, first
            issue. With "Remarks Necessary and Un-
            necessary" by J. Frank Dobie. 190 p.

PTFS-5r   Dobie, J. Frank, ed., *Rainbow in the Morning, Publica-
            tions of the Texas Folklore Society, Number V.*
            Hatboro, Pennsylvania: Folklore Associates, Inc.,
            1965. Hardback. Reprint edition. With a "Preface
            to the Reprint Edition" by Wilson M. Hudson and
            "Remarks Necessary and Unnecessary" by J.
            Frank Dobie. Also printed in this book (in the

PTF5-6 · Dobie, J. Frank, ed., *Texas and Southwestern Lore, Publications of the Texas Folk-Lore Society, Number VI.* Austin: The Texas Folk-Lore Society, 1927. Paperback. First edition, first issue. With "The Editor's Prerogative" by J. Frank Dobie. 259 p.

PTF5-6 · Dobie, J. Frank, ed., *Texas and Southwestern Lore, Publications of the Texas Folk-Lore Society, Number VI.* Austin: The Texas Folk-Lore Society, 1927. Hardback. First edition, first issue. With "The Editor's Prerogative" by J. Frank Dobie. 259 p.

PTFS-6r · Dobie, J. Frank, ed., *Texas and Southwestern Lore, Publications of the Texas Folk-Lore Society, Number VI.* Austin: The Texas Folk-Lore Society, 1934. Hardback. Second printing, July, 1934. With "The Editor's Prerogative" by J. Frank Dobie. 259 p.

PTFS-6r · Dobie, J. Frank, ed., *Texas and Southwestern Lore.* (Publications of the Texas Folklore Society, Number VI.) Dallas: Southern Methodist University Press, 1967. Hardback. Facsimile edition. With "The Editor's Prerogative" by J. Frank Dobie. 259 p.

PTFS-7 · Dobie, J. Frank, ed., *Follow de Drinkin' Gou'd, Publications of the Texas Folk-Lore Society, Number VII.* Austin: The Texas Folk-Lore Society, 1928. Paperback. First edition, first issue. With "Report, Sir" by J. Frank Dobie. 201 p.

PTFS-7 · Dobie, J. Frank, ed., *Follow de Drinkin' Gou'd, Publications of the Texas Folk-Lore Society, Number VII.* Austin: The Texas Folk-Lore Society, 1928. Hardback. First edition, first issue. With "Report, Sir" by J. Frank Dobie. 201 p.

PTFS-7r · Dobie, J. Frank, ed., *Follow de Drinkin' Gou'd.* (Texas Folklore Society Publication Number VII.) Dallas: Southern Methodist University Press, 1965. Hardback. Facsimile edition, 1965. With "Report, Sir" by J. Frank Dobie. 201 p.

N.B.: In the first edition, paperback (PTFS-7), the title given on the paper cover is *Foller de Drinkin' Gou'd,* while the title given on the title page is *Follow de Drinkin' Gou'd.* This seems to be the only instance of a title changing from cover to title page in the entire run of forty of the Society's numbered publications.

PTFS-8 · Dobie, J. Frank, ed., *Man, Bird, and Beast, Publications of the Texas Folk-Lore Society, Volume VIII, 1930.*

	Austin: The Texas Folk-Lore Society, 1930. Paperback. First edition, first issue. With "Just a Word" by J. Frank Dobie. 185 p.
PTFS-8	Dobie, J. Frank, ed., *Man, Bird, and Beast, Publications of the Texas Folk-Lore Society, Volume VIII, 1930.* Austin: The Texas Folk-Lore Society, 1930. Hardback. First edition, first issue. With "Just a Word" by J. Frank Dobie. 185 p.
PTFS-8r	Dobie, J. Frank, ed., *Man, Bird and Beast.* (Texas Folk-lore Society Publication Number VIII.) Dallas: Southern Methodist University Press, 1965. Hardback. Facsimile edition, 1965. With "Just a Word" by J. Frank Dobie. 185 p.
	N.B.: The title given of PTFS-8 is the only one in which the word *Volume* is used; the entire rest of the forty-volume run use the word *Number* followed by a Roman numeral to denote place in the series. It is interesting to note that this uniformity of notation was used when SMU Press reprinted this book (PTFS-8r) in 1965: there is old *Number,* in place of *Volume,* right where the others in the series have it.
PTFS-9	Dobie, J. Frank, ed., *Southwestern Lore, Publications of the Texas Folk-Lore Society, Number IX, 1931.* Austin and Dallas: The Texas Folk-Lore Society and The Southwest Press, 1931. Paperback. First edition, first issue. With "Saludas!" by J. Frank Dobie, 199 p. + v.
PTFS-9	Dobie, J. Frank, ed., *Southwestern Lore, Publications of the Texas Folk-Lore Society, Number IX, 1931.* Austin and Dallas: The Texas Folk-Lore Society and The Southwest Press, 1931. Hardback. First edition, first issue. With "Saludas!" by J. Frank Dobie. 199 p. + v.
PTFS-9r	Dobie, J. Frank, ed., *Southwestern Lore.* (Texas Folk-lore Society Publication Number IX.) Dallas: Southern Methodist University Press, 1965. Hardback. Facsimile edition, 1965. With "Saludas!" by J. Frank Dobie. 198 p. + v.
PTFS-9r	Dobie, J. Frank, ed., *Southwestern Lore, Publications of the Texas Folklore Society, Number IX.* Hatboro, Pennsylvania: Folklore Associates, Inc., 1965. ' Hardback. Reprint edition. With a "Preface to the Reprint Edition" by Wilson M. Hudson and "Saludas!" by J. Frank Dobie. 198 p. + v.
PTFS-10	Dobie, J. Frank, ed., *Tone the Bell Easy, Publications of the Texas Folk-Lore Society, Number X, 1932.* Austin: The Texas Folk-Lore Society, 1932.

	Paperback. First edition, first issue. With "Muchas Gracias" by J. Frank Dobie. 200 p.
PTFS-10	Dobie, J. Frank, ed., *Tone the Bell Easy, Publications of the Texas Folk-Lore Society, Number X, 1932.* Austin: The Texas Folk-Lore Society, 1932. Hardback. First edition, first issue. With "Muchas Gracias" by J. Frank Dobie. 200 p.
PTFS-10r	Dobie, J. Frank, ed., *Tone the Bell Easy.* (Texas Folk-lore Society Publication Number X.) Dallas: Southern Methodist University Press, 1965. Hardback. Facsimile edition, 1965. With "Muchas Gracias" by J. Frank Dobie. 200 p.
PTFS-11	Dobie, J. Frank, ed., *Spur-of-the-Cock, Publications of the Texas Folk-Lore Society, Number XI, 1933.* Austin: The Texas Folk-Lore Society, 1933. Paperback. First edition, first issue. 113 p.
PTFS-11	Dobie, J. Frank, ed., *Spur-of-the-Cock, Publications of the Texas Folk-Lore Society, Number XI, 1933.* Austin: The Texas Folk-Lore Society, 1933. Hardback. First edition, first issue. 113 p.
PTFS-11r	Dobie, J. Frank, ed., *Spur-of-the-Cock.* (Texas Folklore Society Publication Number XI.) Dallas: Southern Methodist University Press, 1965. Hardback. Facsimile edition, 1965. 113 p.
PTFS-12	Dobie, J. Frank, ed., *Puro Mexicano, Texas Folk-Lore Society Publications-Number XII.* Austin: Texas Folk-Lore Society, 1935. Paperback. First edition, first issue. With "Prefatory Wisdom" by J. Frank Dobie. 261 p. + x.
PTFS-12	Dobie, J. Frank, ed., *Puro Mexicano, Publications of the Texas Folk-Lore Society, Number XII.* Austin: Texas Folk-Lore Society, 1935. Hardback. First edition, second issue. With "Prefatory Wisdom" by J. Frank Dobie. 261 p. + x.
PTFS-12r	Dobie, J. Frank, ed., *Puro Mexicano.* (Texas Folklore Society Publication Number XII.) Dallas: Southern Methodist University Press, n.d. Hardback. With "Prefatory Wisdom" by J. Frank Dobie. 261 p. + x.
PTFS-12r	Dobie, J. Frank, ed., *Puro Mexicano.* (Texas Folklore Society Publication Number XII.) Dallas: Southern Methodist University Press, 1969. Hardback. Facsimile edition, 1969. With "Prefatory Wisdom" by J. Frank Dobie. 261 p. + x.
N.B.:	It is generally believed that PTFS-12 is the last of the Society's numbered publications to be issued in paperback. It is also very difficult to describe the first edition, hardback, copies of the

Society's numbered publications for they seem to have been issued in several different states of binding, as well as have been sold unbound and then of course the buyer could bind them as he wished. Hence, a first edition of the Society's numbered publications does indeed back up the old truism, "You can't tell a book by its cover."

PTFS-13   Dobie, J. Frank, and Mody Boatright, eds., *Straight Texas, A Texas Folk-Lore Society Book.* Austin: The Steck Company, Publishers, 1937. First edition, first issue, of the Society's Publication Number XIII. With "Taking It Straight" by J. Frank Dobie. 348 p.

PTFS-13r   Dobie, J. Frank, ed., and Mody C. Boatright, assoc. ed., *Straight Texas, Publications of the Texas Folk-Lore Society, Number XIII.* Hatboro, Pennsylvania: Folklore Associates, Inc., 1966. With a "Preface to the Reprint Edition" by Wilson M. Hudson and "Taking It Straight" by J. Frank Dobie. 348 p.

PTFS-14   Dobie, J. Frank, Mody C. Boatright, and Harry H. Ransom, eds., *Coyote Wisdom.* (Texas Folk-Lore Society Publications, Number XIV.) Austin: Texas Folk-Lore Society, 1938. First edition. With "Pertinences and Patrons" by The Editor. 300 p.

PTFS-14r   Dobie, J. Frank, Mody C. Boatright, and Harry H. Ransom, eds., *Coyote Wisdom.* (Texas Folklore Society Publication Number XIV.) Dallas: Southern Methodist University Press, 1965. Facsimile edition, 1965. With "Pertinences and Patrons" by The Editor. 300 p.

N.B.:   Although the "Pertinences and Patrons" in PTFS-14 is not signed, it was written by J. Frank Dobie. In an inscription examined in one copy of PTFS-14, Bertha McKee Dobie wrote "In most of the Publications of the Texas Folk-Lore Society some pages were written by Frank, but this volume contains only his editor's foreword."

PTFS-15   Dobie, J. Frank, Mody C. Boatright, and Harry H. Ransom, eds., *In the Shadow of History, Texas Folk-Lore Society Publications, Number XV.* Austin: Texas Folk-Lore Society, 1939. First edition. 187 p. + iv.

PTFS-15r   Dobie, J. Frank, Mody C. Boatright, and Harry H. Ransom, eds., *In the Shadow of History, Texas Folk-Lore Society Publications, Number XV.* Hatboro, Pennsylvania: Folklore Associates Inc., 1966. With a "Preface to the Reprint Edition" by

	Wilson M. Hudson. 186 p. + iv.
PTFS-16	Dobie, J. Frank, Mody C. Boatright, and Harry H. Ransom, eds., *Mustangs and Cow Horses*. (Publications Number XVI of the Texas Folk-Lore Society.) Austin: Texas Folk-Lore Society, 1940. First edition. Illustrated. With an introduction. 429 p. + xi.
PTFS-16r	Dobie, J. Frank, Mody C. Boatright, and Harry H. Ransom, eds., *Mustangs and Cow Horses*. (Texas Folklore Society Publication Number XVI.) Dallas: Southern Methodist University Press, 1965. Second edition, 1965. Illustrated. With an introduction. 429 p. + xi.
PTFS-17	Dobie, J. Frank, Mody C. Boatright, and Harry H. Ransom, eds. *Texian Stomping Grounds, Texas Folk-Lore Society Publications Number XVII*. Austin: Texas Folk-Lore Society, 1941. First edition. With "A Man Deserves a Heath" by Harry H. Ransom. 162 p.
PTFS-18	Dobie, J. Frank, gen. ed., and Mody C. Boatright and Donald Day, eds., *Backwoods to Border, Texas Folk-Lore Society Publications, Number XVIII*. Austin and Dallas: Texas Folk-Lore Society and University Press in Dallas, Southern Methodist University, 1943. First edition. With "Twenty Years an Editor" by J. Frank Dobie. 235 p. + xv.
PTFS-18r	Boatright, Mody C., and Donald Day, eds., *Backwoods to Border*. (Publications of the Texas Folklore Society, Number XVIII.) Dallas: Southern Methodist University Press, 1967. Facsimile edition, 1967. With "Twenty Years an Editor" by J. Frank Dobie. 235 p. + xii.
PTFS-19	Dobie, J. Frank, gen. ed., and Mody C. Boatright and Donald Day, eds., *From Hell to Breakfast, Texas Folk-Lore Society Publications, Number XIX*. Austin and Dallas: Texas Folk-Lore Society and University Press in Dallas, Southern Methodist Universty, 1944. First edition. With "How Far Is It From Hell To Breakfast?" by Mody C. Boatright and Donald Day. 215 p. + x.
PTFS-19r	Boatright, Mody C., and Donald Day, eds., *From Hell to Breakfast*. (Publications of the Texas Folklore Society, Number XIX.) Dallas: Southern Methodist University Press, 1967. Facsimile edition, 1967. With "How Far Is It From Hell To Breakfast?" by Mody C. Boatright and Donald Day. 214 p. + viii.

PTFS-20   Boatright, Mody C., *Gib Morgan, Minstrel of the Oil Fields*. (Texas Folk-Lore Society Publication, Number XX.) El Paso: Texas Folk-Lore Society, 1945. First edition. Illustrated by Betty Boatright. Designed and printed by Carl Hertzog of El Paso. With a "Preface" by Mody C. Boatright. 104 p. + xi.

PTFS-20r   Boatright, Mody C., *Gib Morgan, Minstrel of the Oil Fields*. (Texas Folklore Society Publication, Number XX.) Dallas: Southern Methodist University Press, 1965. Second printing, 1965. Illustrated by Betty Boatright. Designed by Carl Hertzog of El Paso. With a "Preface" by Mody C. Boatright. 104 p. + xi.

PTFS-21   Boatright, Mody C., ed., *Mexican Border Ballads and Other Lore. Publication of the Texas Folklore Society, XXI.* Austin: The Texas Folk-Lore Society, 1946. First edition. With "The War and After" by Mody C. Boatright. 140 v. + vii.

PTFS-21r   Boatright, Mody C., ed., *Mexican Border Ballads and Other Lore.* (Publications of the Texas Folklore Society, Number XXI.) Dallas: Southern Methodist University Press, 1967. Facsimile edition, 1967. 143 p. + v.

             N.B.:   It is easy to tell the difference between PTFS-21 and PTFS-21r. On pp. v-vii of PTFS-21, one will find the "Index" and no "Table of Contents," and on p. iii, one finds Boatright's "The War and After." In PTFS-21r, Boatright's preface is left out, there is a page marked "Contents," and the "Index" is where it should be, bound in at the back.

PTFS-22   Boatright, Mody C., ed., *The Sky is my Tipi.* (Publication of the Texas Folklore Society, Number XXII.) Austin and Dallas: The Texas Folklore Society and University Press in Dallas, 1949. First edition. 243 p. + ix.

PTFS-22r   Boatright, Mody C., ed., *The Sky is my Tipi.* (Publications of the Texas Folklore Society, Number XXII.) Dallas: Southern Methodist University Press, 1966. Facsimile edition, 1966. 243 p. + ix.

             N.B.:   Although not given on the title page of either edition, there is a subtitle given on the dust jacket on the first edition of PTFS-22. The subtitle is *Kiowa-Apache Tales and Lore.*

PTFS-23   Owens, William A., *Texas Folk Songs.* (Publications of the Texas Folklore Society, Number XXIII.) Austln and Dallas: The Texas Folklore Society and University Press in Dallas, 1950. First edition. Musical arrangements by Willa Mae Kelly Koehn. With a "Preface" by William A. Owens, 302 p.

PTFS-23r   Owens, William A., *Texas Folk Songs, Texas Folklore Society Publication XXIII*. Dallas: SMU Press, 1976. Second edition, revised and enlarged. Musical transcriptions by Jessie Ann Owens. 190 p. + xx. With a "Preface" and "Introduction" by William A. Owens and "Notes on Musical Transcriptions" by Jessie Ann Owens.

PTFS-24   Hudson, Wilson M., ed., *The Healer of Los Olmos and Other Mexican Lore.* (Publication of the Texas Folklore Society, Number XXIV.) Austin and Dallas: The Texas Folklore Society and Southern Methodist University Press, 1951. First edition. Illustrated by Jose Cisneros. With "How This Book Took Shape" by Wilson M. Hudson and "Charm in Mexican Folktales" by J. Frank Dobie. 139 p. + ix.

PTFS-25   Boatright, Mody C., Wilson M. Hudson, and Allen Maxwell, eds., *Folk Travelers, Ballads, Tales, and Talk.* (Publication of the Texas Folklore Society, Number XXV.) Austin and Dallas: The Texas Folklore Society and Southern Methodist University Press, 1953. First edition. 261 p.

PTFS-26   Boatright, Mody C., Wilson M. Hudson, and Allen Maxwell, eds., *Texas Folk and Folklore.* (Publications of the Texas Folklore Society, Number XXVI.) Dallas: Southern Methodist University Press, 1954. First edition. Drawings by Jose Cisneros. With a "Preface" by Mody C. Boatright, Wilson M. Hudson, and Allen Maxwell. 356 p. + xv.

PTFS-26r   Boatright, Mody C., Wilson M. Hudson, and Allen Maxwell, eds., *Texas Folk and Folklore.* (Publications of the Texas Folklore Society, Number XXVI.) Dallas: Southern Methodist University Press, 1955. Second printing, 1955. Drawings by Jose Cisneros. With a "Preface" by Mody C. Boatright, Wilson M. Hudson, and Allen Maxwell. 356 p. + xv.

PTFS-27   Boatright, Mody C., Wilson M. Hudson, and Allen Maxwell, eds. *Mesquite and Willow.* (Publications of the Texas Folklore Society, Number XXVII.) Dallas: Southern Methodist University Press, 1957. First edition. With a "Preface" by Mody C. Boatright, Wilson M. Hudson, and Allen Maxwell. 203 p. + viii.

PTFS-28   Boatright, Mody C., Wilson M. Hudson, and Allen Max-
           well, eds., *Madstones and Twisters.* (Publications
           of the Texas Folklore Society, Number XXVIII.)
           Dallas: Southern Methodist University Press,
           1958. First edition. With a "Preface" by Mody C.
           Boatright, Wilson M. Hudson, and Allen Maxwell.
           169 p. + x.

PTFS-29   Boatright, Mody C., Wilson M. Hudson, and Allen Max-
           well, eds., *and horns on the toads.* (Publications
           of the Texas Folklore Society, Number XXIX.)
           Dallas: Southern Methodist University Press,
           1959. First edition. With a "Preface" by Mody C.
           Boatright, Wilson M. Hudson, and Allen Maxwell.
           237 p. + x.

PTFS-30   Boatright, Mody C., Wilson M. Hudson, and Allen Max-
           well, eds., *Singers and Storytellers.* (Publications
           of the Texas Folklore Society, Number XXX.)
           Dallas: Southern Methodist University Press,
           1961. First edition. 298 p. + vi.

PTFS-31   Boatright, Mody C., Wilson M. Hudson, and Allen Max-
           well, eds., *The Golden Log.* (Publications of the
           Texas Folklore Society, Number XXXI.) Dallas:
           Southern Methodist University Press, 1962. First
           edition. 168 p. + vi.

PTFS-32   Boatright, Mody C., Wilson M. Hudson, and Allen Max-
           well, eds., *A Good Tale and a Bonnie Tune.* (Pub-
           lications of the Texas Folklore Society, Number
           XXXII.) Dallas: Southern Methodist University
           Press, 1964. First edition. 274 p. + vi.

PTFS-33   Hudson, Wilson M., and Allen Maxwell, eds., *The Sunny
           Slopes of Long Ago.* (Publications of the Texas
           Folklore Society, Number XXXIII.) Dallas: South-
           ern Methodist University Press, 1966. First edi-
           tion. With a "Preface" by Wilson M. Hudson and
           Allen Maxwell. 204 p. + viii.

PTFS-34   Hudson, Wilson M., ed., *Tire Shrinker to Dragster.*
           (Publications of the Texas Folklore Society Num-
           ber XXXIV.) Austin: The Encino Press, 1968.
           First edition. Designed by William D. Wittliff.
           With a "Preface" by Wilson M. Hudson. 248 p.
           + viii.

PTFS-35   Hudson, Wilson M., ed., *Hunters & Healers: Folklore
           Types and Topics.* (Publications of the Texas
           Folklore Society Number XXXV.) Austin: The
           Encino Press, 1971. First edition. Designed by
           William D. Wittliff. With a "Preface" by Wilson
           M. Hudson. 171 p. + xii.

PTFS-36   Hudson, Wilson M., ed., *Diamond Bessie & The*

Shepherds. (Publications of the Texas Folklore Society Number XXXVI.) Austin: The Encino Press, 1972. First edition. Designed by William D. Wittliff. With a "Foreword" by Wilson M. Hudson. 158 p. + x.

PTFS-37 Abernethy, Francis Edward, ed., *Observations & Reflections on Texas Folklore.* (Publications of the Texas Folklore Society Number XXXVII.) First edition. Illustrated, with photographs by Francis Edward Abernethy and line drawings by James R. Snyder. Designed by William D. Wittliff. Austin: The Encino Press, 1972. With "A Preface (In which the editor presents his credentials, among other things)" by Francis Edward Abernethy. 151 p. + x.

PTFS-38 Abernethy, Francis Edward, ed., and Dan Beaty, music ed., *The Folklore of Texan Cultures.* (Publications of the Texas Folklore Society, Number XXXVIII.) Austin: The Encino Press, 1974. First edition. In Commemoration, The American Bicentennial, 1776-1976. Illustrated throughout with photographs and drawings. With a "Preface" by Francis Edward Abernethy and "The Cultures of Texas" by R. Henderson Shuffler." Designed by William D. Wittliff. 366 p. + xxxi.

PTFS-39 Abernethy, Francis Edward, ed., *Some Still Do: Essays on Texas Customs.* (Publications of the Texas Folklore Society Number XXXIX.) Austin: The Encino Press, 1975. First edition. Designed by William D. Wittliff. With "Amateur and Professional Folklorists" by Wilson M. Hudson and "Some Still Do, An Essay on Customs" by Francis Edward Abernethy. 153 p. + xx.

PTFS-40 Abernethy, Francis Edward, ed., *What's Going On? (In Modern Texas Folklore).* (Publications of the Texas Folklore Society Number XL.) Austin: The Encino Press, 1976. First edition. Designed by William D. Wittliff. Illustrated throughout with photographs. With "Preface: 'Ga'nt as a gutted snowbird' or a rose by any other name would-or at least should. . . ." by Francis Edward Abernethy. 309 p. + xiii.

PTFS-41 Abernethy, Francis Edward, ed., *Paisanos: A Folklore Miscellany.* (Publications of the Texas Folklore Society Number XLI.) Austin: Encino Press, 1978. First edition. Designed by William D. Wittliff. Line drawings by Linda Miller Roach. With "Preface: In which the editor apologizes to those readers who thought they were buying a bird book about roadrunners" by Francis Edward Abernethy. 180 p. + xii.

PTFS-42   Abernethy, Francis Edward, ed., *Built in Texas.* (Publications of the Texas Folklore Society Number XLII.) Waco: E-Heart Press, 1979. First edition. Line drawings by Reese Kennedy. Photographs by editor. With "Preface (In which the editor reflects upon his perambulations and peregrinations)" by Francis Edward Abernethy. 276 p. + xi.

PTFS-43   Abernethy, Francis Edward, ed., *Legendary Ladies of Texas.* (Publications of the Texas Folklore Society Number XLIII.) Dallas: E-Heart Press, 1981. First edition. Illustrated. With "Preface: In which the editor searches his soul, encounters the need for an agonizing reappraisal, and finally realizes that he is living in sin—and likes it" by Francis Edward Abernethy. Paper and hardback. 224 p. + xii.

PTFS-44   Abernethy, Francis Edward, ed., *T For Texas: A State Full of Folklore.* (Publications of the Texas Folklore Society Number XLIV.) Dallas: E-Heart Press, 1982. First edition. Illustrated. With "Preface: In which the editor celebrates his tenth anniversary" by Francis Edward Abernethy.

BOOKS ISSUED IN LIEU OF NUMBERED PUBLICATIONS

ExB-1   Dobie, J. Frank, *Coronado's Children, Tales of Lost Mines and Buried Treasures of the Southwest.* Dallas: The Southwest Press, 1930. Illustrated by Ben Carlton Mead. First edition, first issue, with the word *clean* omitted from the dedication page. Issued in lieu of a numbered publication for 1930. 367 p. + xvi.

ExB-2   Boatright, Mody C., *Tall Tales from Texas.* Dallas: The Southwest Press, 1935. Illustrated by Elizabeth E. Keefer. Foreword "A Preface on Authentic Liars," and "Special Edition for the Texas Folk-Lore Society" printed notation (on front free endpaper, both by J. Frank Dobie. Issued in lieu of a numbered publication for 1934. 100 p. + xxiv.

N.B.: The title page of ExB-2 gives its title as *Tall Tales from* Texas, while both Dobie's "Special Edition for the Texas Folk-Lore Society" and the pasted-on label on the front board call the book *Tall Tales from Texas Cow Camps,* and the spine simply says *Tall Tales.* There seem to be no available records to resolve the title.

ExB-3 Owens, William A., *Swing and Turn: Texas Play-Party Games.* Dallas: Tardy Publishing Company, 1936. With a printed notation on the front free endpaper, "Special Edition for the Texas Folk-Lore Society," by J. Frank Dobie. Issued in lieu of a numbered publication for 1936. 117 p. +xxxiii.

ExB-4 Wright, Solomon Alexander, *My Rambles as East Texas Cowboy Hunter, Fisherman, Tie-Cutter.* Austin: Texas Folklore Society, 1942. Arranged, with an introduction, by J. Frank Dobie. Illustrated by B. E. Lewis. Range Life Series Book Number One, under the general editorship of J. Frank Dobie. Designed by Carl Hertzog of El Paso. Issued in lieu of a numbered publication for 1942. 159 p. + xiii.

ExB-5 Bedichek, Roy, *Adventures with a Texas Naturalist.* Garden City, N.Y.: Doubleday & Co., Inc., 1947. Illustrated by Ward Lockwood. Issued in lieu of a numbered publication for 1947. 293 p. + xx.

ExB-6 Boatright, Mody C., *Folk Laughter on the American Frontier.* New York: The Macmillan Company, 1949. Issued in lieu of a numbered publication for 1949. 182 p. + viii.

ExB-7 Leach, Joseph, *The Typical Texan, Biography of an American Myth.* Dallas: Southern Methodist University Press, 1952. Illustrated, with a frontispiece by Jose Cisneros. Designed by Carl Hertzog of El Paso. Issued in lieu of a numbered publication for 1952. 178 p. + xiii.

ExB-8 Dobie, J. Frank, *Tales of Old-Time Texas.* Boston: Little, Brown and Company, 1955. Illustrated by Barbara Latham. "First Edition" on copyright page. Issued in lieu of a numbered publication for 1955. 336 p. + xvi.

ExB-9 Paredos, Americo, *"With His Pistol in His Hand," A Border Ballad and Its Hero.* Austin: University of Texas Press, 1958. Illustrated by Jo Alys Downs. Issued in lieu of a numbered publication for 1958. 262 p. + xii.

ExB-10 Boatright, Mody C., *Folklore of the Oil Industry.* Dallas: Southern Methodist University Press, 1963. Illustrated by William D. Wittliff. Issued in lieu of a numbered publication for 1962. 220 p. + vii.

ExB-11 Kilpatrick, Jack F., and Anna G. Kilpatrick, *Friends of Thunder, Folktales of the Oklahoma Cherokees.*

Dallas: Southern Methodist University Press, 1964. Issued in lieu of a numbered publication for 1964. 197 p. + xviii.

ExB-12   Abernethy, Francis E., ed., *Tales from the Big Thicket.* Austin and London: University of Texas Press, 1966. Illustrated with photographs. Issued in lieu of a numbered publication for 1966. 244 p. + xii.

ExB-13   Emmons, Martha, *Deep Like the Rivers, Stories of my Negro Friends.* Austin: The Encino Press, 1969. Paisano Book Number Four, under the general editorship of Wilson M. Hudson. Illustrated with woodcuts. Designed by William D. Wittliff. Issued in lieu of a numbered publication for 1968. 109 p. + ix.

ExB-14   Dillon, Myles, collector and translator, *There Was A King in Ireland . . . Five Tales from Oral Tradition.* Austin and London: The University of Texas Press for the Texas Folklore Society, 1971. Illustrated by Jose Cisneros. Issued in lieu of a numbered publication for 1970. 114 p.

ExB-15   Speck, Ernest B., ed., *Mody Boatright, Folklorist, A Collection of Essays.* Austin and London: The University of Texas Press for the Texas Folklore Society, 1973. With an introduction by Ernest B. Speck, a biographical essay by Harry H. Ransom, and a foreword by Wayland D. Hand. Issued in lieu of a numbered publication for 1973. 198 p. + xxvi.

ExB-16   Martin, Howard D., *Myths & Folktales of the Alabama Coushatta Indians of Texas.* Austin: The Encino Press, 1977. Illustrated title page. With a foreword by Francis Edward Abernethy. Issued in lieu of a numbered publication for 1977. 114 p. + xxxvii.

ExB-17   Aiken, Riley, *Mexican Folktales from the Borderland.* Dallas: Southern Methodist University Press, 1980. Foreword by Francis Edward Abernethy, drawings by Dennis Zamora. Issued in lieu of a numbered publication for 1980. 159 p. + xv.

PAMPHLETS

P-1   Thomas, W. H., *Some Current Folk-Songs of the Negro.* Austin: The Folk-lore Society of Texas, 1912. 13 p.

P-1r   Thomas, Will H., *Some Current Folk-Songs of the Negro.* Austin: Texas Folk-Lore Society, 1936. Reprint of P-1, with an explanation entitled "Will Thomas and the Texas Folklore Society," by

J. Frank Dobie added.

N.B.: It is interesting to note that the title, given on p. 3 of both P-1 and P-1r is *Some Current Folk-Songs of the Negro and their Economic Interpretation.*

P-2   Boatright, Mody C., ed., *When the Woods Were Burnt, Published in Memory of Leonidas Warren Payne, Jr.* Austin: The Texas Folk-Lore Society, 1946. Designed by Carl Hertzog of El Paso, Texas. 26 p.

P-3   Coffin, Tristram P., John Greenway, W. Edson Richmond, D. K. Wilgus, George Foss, *Folksong and Folksong Scholarship: Changing Approaches and Attitudes.* With introductory remarks by Roger D. Abrahams. Illustration by William D. Wittliff. Reprinted from *A Good Tale and A Bonnie Tune,* Texas Folklore Society Publication XXXII. Dallas: Southern Methodist University Press, 1964. Paperback, 74 p.

P-4   Hudson, Wilson M., Ed., *Mody Boatright, Secretary and Editor, 1943-1964.* Austin: The Texas Folklore Society, 1965. 29 p.

P-5   Hand, Wayland D., *Eyes on Texas, Fifty Years of Folklore in the Southwest.* Austin: The Texas Folklore Society, 1967. Design and production by William D. Wittliff of the Encino Press. 28 p.

THE RANGE LIFE SERIES

RLS-1   Wright, Solomon Alexander, *My Rambles as East Texas Cowboy Hunter, Fisherman, Tie-Cutter.* Austin: Texas Folklore Society, 1942. Arranged, with an introduction, by J. Frank Dobie. Illustrated by B. E. Lewis. Designed by Carl Hertzog of El Paso. 159 p. + xiii.

RLS-2   Cutbirth, Ruby Nichols, *Ed. Nichols Rode a Horse,* Dallas: Texas Folklore Society and University Press in Dallas. 1943. Frontispiece by Jerry Bywaters. 134 p. +

RLS-3   Benedict, Carl Peters, *A Tenderfoot Kid on Gyp Water.* Austin and Dallas: Texas Folklore Society and University Press in Dallas, 1943. With an introduction by J. Frank Dobie. Illustrated with three photographs and with four sketches by Carl Peters Benedict. Limited to 550 copies. Designed by Carl Hertzog of El Paso. 115 p. + xviii.

RLS-4   McCauley, James Emmit, *A Stove-Up Cowboy's Story.*

Austin and Dallas: The Texas Folklore Society and the University Press in Dallas, 1943. With an introduction by John A. Lomax. Illustrated by Tom Lea. Limited to 700 copies. Designed by Carl Hertzog of El Paso. 73 p. + xxii.

RLS-4r   McCauley, James Emmit, *A Stove-Up Cowboy's Story.* Dallas: Southern Methodist University Press, 1965. With an introduction by John A. Lomax and an afterword by Carl Hertzog. Illustrated by Tom Lea. Designed by Carl Hertzog of El Paso. 76 p. + xxii.

RLS-5   Coombos, Charles E., *The Prairie Dog Lawyer.* Austin and Dallas: Texas Folklore Society and University Press in Dallas, 1945. With a foreword by Amon Carter. 287 p. + xv.

PAISANO BOOKS SERIES

PBS-1   Hendricks, George D., *Mirrors, Mice, & Mustaches, A Sampling of Superstitions & Popular Beliefs in Texas.* Austin: The Texas Folklore Society, 1966. Paisano Books Number One, Wilson M. Hudson, Editor. Paperback. 110 p. + xiv.

PBS-1r   Hendricks, George D., *Mirrors, Mice, & Mustaches, A Sampling of Superstitions & Popular Beliefs in Texas.* Austin: The Texas Folklore Society, 19. Paisano Books Number One, Wilson M. Hudson, Editor. Paperback. Reprint of the first edition, PBS-1. 110 p + xiv.

N.B.:   The only way to tell the two above books apart is to look for the table of contents page. If the table of contents is printed facing p. 1, it is a first edition; if on the other hand the table of contents is printed facing p. xiv, it is the reprint.

PBS-2   Patterson, Paul, *Pecos Tales.* Austin: The Encino Press for the Texas Folklore Society, 1967. Paisano Books Number Two, Wilson M. Hudson, Editor; Paisano Advisory Board, John Q. Anderson, Edwin W. Gaston, Jr., and Norman L. McNeil. Designed by William D. Wittliff. 101 p. + x.

PBS-3   Emery, Emma Wilson, *Aunt Puss & Others, Old Days in the Piney Woods.* Austin: The Encino Press, 1969. Paisano Books Number Three, Wilson M. Hudson, Editor; Paisano Advisory Board, John Q. Anderson, Edwin W. Gaston, Jr., and Norman L. McNeil. Designed by William D. Wittliff. 101 p. + x.

PBS-4   Emmons, Martha, *Deep Like the Rivers, Stories of my

Negro Friends. Austin: The Encino Press, 1969. Paisano Books Number Four, Wilson M. Hudson, Editor; Paisano Advisory Board, John Q. Anderson, Edwin W. Gaston, Jr., and Norman L. McNeil. Designed by William D. Wittliff. 109 p. + ix.

PBS-5   Anderson, John Q., compiler and ed., *Texas Folk Medicine, 1,333 Cures, Remedies, Preventives, & Health Practices.* Austin: The Encino Press, 1970. Paisano Books Number Five, Wilson M. Hudson, Editor; Paisano Advisory Board, John Q. Anderson, Edwin W. Gaston, Jr., and Norman L. McNeil. Illustrated with woodcuts by Barbara Matthews Whitehead. Designed by William D. Wittliff. 91 p. + xix.

"EL PAISANO" NEWSLETTER

EPNL-1   Boatright, Mody C., ed., *El Paisano,* I-1 (December, 1948). One sheet, 8½ by 11 in., light blue, printed on both sides.

EPNL-2   Boatright, Mody C., ed., *El Paisano,* I-2 (March, 1949). One sheet, 8½ by 11 in., yellow, printed on both sides.

EPNL-3   Boatright, Mody C., ed., *El Paisano,* I-3 (June, 1949). One sheet, 8½ by 11 in., pink, printed on both sides.

EPNL-4   Boatright, Mody C., ed., *El Paisano,* I-4 (September, 1949). One sheet, 8½ by 11 in., light blue, printed on both sides.

EPNL-5   Boatright, Mody C., ed., *El Paisano,* I-5 (December, 1949). One sheet, 8½ by 11 in., light blue, printed on both sides.

EPNL-6   Boatright, Mody C., ed., *El Paisano,* I-6 (March, 1950). Three sheets, 8½ by 11 in., white, each sheet printed on one side only, by mimeograph.

EPNL-7   Boatright, Mody C., ed., *El Paisano,* I-7 (June, 1950). One sheet, 8½ by 11 in., light pink, printed on both sides.

SPECIAL REFERENCE PUBLICATIONS

SRP-1   Bratcher, James T., *Analytical Index to Publications of The Texas Folklore Society, Volumes 1-36.* Dallas: Southern Methodist University Press, 1973. With a foreword by Wilson M. Hudson, a preface by James T. Bratcher, and a "Historical Note on the Texas Folklore Society" by Francis

Edward Abernethy. Illustrated with photographs
and drawings. Typographical adviser, Carl Hertzog of El Paso. 322 p. + xxi.

Contributors

FRANCIS EDWARD ABERNETHY is professor of English at Stephen F. Austin State University and for ten years has been Secretary-Editor of the Texas Folklore Society.

MRS. JOHN Q. ANDERSON has been a school teacher, newspaper editor and journalist, and index editor and now resides in Ruston, Louisiana. She has attended and has actively participated in the Society's meetings since 1952.

HERBERT C. ARBUCKLE, III—piercing blue eyes, wavy brown hair, ruggedly handsome—is the Society's official bibliographer. He writes for the Masonic magazine and teaches math at Fay H. Moody High School in Corpus Christi.

LAWRENCE CLAYTON is Dean of the College of Arts and Sciences at Hardin-Simmons University, past president of the Society, and scholar in American literature and modern folklore.

R. L. COWSER, JR., is chairman of the Department of Modern Languages at Wharton County Junior College. He has contributed to the Society's programs as well as publishing in other scholarly folklore and pop culture journals.

JAMES M. DAY, professor of English at the University of Texas at El Paso and Director of the El Paso Centennial Museum, is past president and one of the most active and productive members of the Society.

WAYNE ECHOLS is a traveling cowboy who has worked on ranches in five states. He always returns to Dickens, Texas, to restore his soul.

MARTHA EMMONS taught Methusaleh when he was in grade school and finished her career in the English Department of Baylor University. She is the ranking member of the Society, the *grande dame* who presented her first paper before the Society in 1924.

JIM HARRIS teaches English at New Mexico Junior College in Hobbs, is Fiction and Folklore Editor of *Southwest Heritage,* and was one-time editor of *Southwestern American Literature.* He is a poet and the owner of The Hawk Press.

DOLORES L. LATORRE is a linguist and anthropologist and has lived a remarkable life in North and Latin America. She has published *The Mexican Kickapoo Indians, Cooking and Curing with Mexican Herbs,* and "A Mexican Folk Interpretation of Schizophrenia and Their Attempts to Cure It." She lives in an ante-bellum rock house in Austin.

JAMES WARD LEE, past president of the Society, is professor of English at North Texas State University, past editor of *Southwestern American Literature, Studies in the Novel,* the Southwest Writers Series, and editor of the bibliography of Southwestern literature.

GLEN E. LICH teaches English and German at Schreiner College in Kerrville. He is a three-quarters-German native of the Hill Country who occasionally renews his *Deutschtum* in the Old Country.

CHARLES E. LINCK, JR., is professor of English at East Texas State University, past president of the Texas College English Association, Associate Editor of the *Evelyn Waugh Newsletter* and *Evelyn Waugh, A Checklist.*

GAIL Y. LITTON is a senior majoring in creative writing and journalism at the University of Texas at El Paso. She also writes poetry and short stories for children and works for the *El Paso Times.*

LYNN and CAMPBELL LOUGHMILLER of Whitehouse have shared forty-eight years of vocational and avocational life. Both are dedicated travelers and investigators and perceptive students of the human and natural condition. They are the authors of *Big Thicket Legacy.*

AL LOWMAN is a research associate at the Institute of Texan Cultures in San Antonio. His long-time interest in history, folklore, and art has produced *Printing Arts in Texas* and *Printer at the Pass: The Work of Carl Hertzog* and numerous other articles.

NANCY PATRICK of Big Spring is a school teacher and a recent masters graduate of Hardin-Simmons University with a major in English.

She has published two articles on Jesse Stuart in the *Jack London Newsletter.*

PAUL PATTERSON of Crane is the Society's resident cowboy. He also taught in the Pecos for forty years, careful to stay within the bounds of his beloved ranch country where he could keep on the lookout for good stories, "be they fact, fiction, fancy, or folklore." All of which produced *Sam McGoo and Texas Too, Pecos Tales,* and *Crazy Women in the Rafters.*

PATT ROACH of Abilene teaches business and English at Trent I.S.D.

LOU RODENBERGER teaches English at Blinn College (Bryan Branch), has published articles on the South and Southwest, is presently at work on a book on the rural school teacher, 1920-1950, and is editing a collection of short fiction by Texas women.

ERNESTINE P. SEWELL is professor of English at the University of Texas at Arlington, a scholar and a prolific writer, editor of *English in Texas,* and past president of the Society.

WILLIAM N. STOKES, JR. is the society's counselor and a doctor of jurisprudence from Yale. He has taught in a university, was an officer in the Navy in World War II, has presided over banks, and has authored two books. He is amply qualified for his position.

LESLIE M. THOMPSON, an athlete of known repute, is Dean of the Graduate School, Director of Research Services, and Professor of English at Georgia Southern College in Statesboro.

MARTHA ANNE TURNER is a retired professor of English at Sam Houston State University, where she taught creative writing and literature of the Southwest. She is a prolific writer and author of numerous books.

JUNE R. WELCH is a lawyer who teaches history and is the Academic Dean of the University of Dallas. In his spare time he has written thirteen books.